Indians of the Rio Grande Delta

TEXAS ARCHAEOLOGY AND ETHNOHISTORY SERIES

THOMAS R. HESTER, EDITOR
THOMAS N. CAMPBELL, VOLUME EDITOR

INDIANS OF THE RIO GRANDE DELTA

Their Role in the History of Southern Texas and Northeastern Mexico

By Martín Salinas

UNIVERSITY OF TEXAS PRESS
AUSTIN

Requests for permission to reproduce material from this work should be sent to Permissions, University of Texas Press, Box 7819, Austin, Texas 78713-7819.

⊗ The paper used in this publication meets the minimum requirements of American National Standard for Information Sciences—Permanence of Paper for Printed Library Materials, ANSI Z39.48-1984.

Library of Congress Cataloging-in-Publication Data

Salinas, Martin, 1956–
   Indians of the Rio Grande delta: their role in the history of southern Texas and northeastern Mexico / by Martin Salinas. — 1st ed.
      p.   cm. — (Texas archaeology and ethnohistory series)
   Includes bibliographical references.
   ISBN 0-292-73047-0 (alk. paper). — ISBN 0-292-73055-1 (pbk. : alk. paper)
      1. Indians of North America—Texas—Antiquities.   2. Indians of North America—Texas—History.   3. Indians of Mexico—Antiquities.   4. Indians of Mexico—History.   5. Rio Grand Valley—Antiquities.   I. Title.   II. Series.
   E78.T4S25   1990
   976.4'01—dc20   89-16737
                                                           CIP

To My Parents

Contents

Foreword

This volume, authored by Martín Salinas, represents the first detailed archival study of the American Indian populations of the early historic period in the Lower Rio Grande Valley of Texas and Mexico. This region, often referred to as the Rio Grande delta, is distinctive both physiographically and environmentally. Archaeological research in the area has been spotty. The major set of data on Rio Grande delta archaeology remains the A. E. Anderson collection, housed at the Texas Archeological Research Laboratory, University of Texas at Austin. Anderson was a civil engineer who recorded sites with precision and amassed a carefully labeled collection often used by researchers. More recent archaeological research, by the University of Texas at Austin, the Texas Historical Commission, Prewitt and Associates (consulting archaeologists in Austin), and others has yet to provide a detailed synthesis of the region's prehistory.

Martín Salinas has, on the other hand, meticulously examined the myriad of documents left behind by the Spanish and has extracted from these the scattered bits of information on Indian groups who lived on both sides of the Rio Grande. At the time of historic contact, the Indian peoples of that region were in turmoil, many displaced from original territories and seeking alliances with other groups. This aspect of the Indian cultural patterns in the early historic era has often been overlooked. The anthropologist is not dealing with pristine aboriginal groups, but rather with peoples whose lifeways had already been disrupted. The causes of disruption are carefully detailed by Salinas.

With the publication of Salinas' work, combined with the earlier publications of T. N. Campbell that deal with the Indians of other parts of southern Texas and northeastern Mexico, anthropologists and archaeologists, as well as historians and others interested in European-American Indian interaction at the time of contact, now have a solid body of data with which to work. Many erroneous views of these Indian groups will now be dispelled.

As series editor, I would like to thank Martín Salinas for his hard work in bringing this manuscript to publication stage. Additionally, both Salinas and I owe much to Professor T. N. Campbell for his continuing input and encouragement.

Thomas R. Hester

Acknowledgments

Several people merit my special thanks for their interest, valuable assistance, and continuous encouragement during the preparation of this book. Among these are Dr. Jeremiah F. Epstein, professor of anthropology at the University of Texas, Austin, and Dr. Dee Ann Story, former director of the Texas Archeological Research Laboratory and professor of anthropology at the University of Texas, Austin, who stressed the need for detailed ethnohistoric studies of Indian populations who formerly lived along the lower Rio Grande. I am greatly in debt to Dr. T. N. Campbell, professor of anthropology emeritus at the University of Texas, Austin, who generously provided guidance and continuous support throughout the study. Dr. Thomas R. Hester, director of the Texas Archeological Research Laboratory and professor of anthropology at the University of Texas, Austin, is due acknowledgment for making the publication of this book possible.

Staff members of the following institutions have my sincere appreciation for their assistance and orientation: Barker Texas History Center and Benson Latin American Library, University of Texas, Austin; General Land Office of Texas, Spanish Document Section, Austin; Municipal Archives of Reynosa, Reynosa, Mexico; Nuestra Señora del Refugio de los Esteros, Matamoros, Mexico; Parish Church of San Fernando, San Fernando, Mexico; and Texas Catholic Archives of Austin, Austin. I wish to express my thanks to Thomas Brayshaw of the Gilcrease Museum, Tulsa, Oklahoma, for providing a copy of Jean Louis Berlandier's Carrizo Indian illustration. I also thank Cynthia Banks, whose photographic skills put in my hands López de la Cámara Alta's 1758 map, one of the key sources of information for the area.

Special thanks are extended to my sister M. T. Salinas for contributing some of her valuable time, assisting in typing the work. Last but not least, the support provided by my parents greatly contributed to the completion of this work.

Martín Salinas

Indians of the Rio Grande Delta

CHAPTER I

Introduction

THIS STUDY began with one general objective: to retrieve from primary documents the maximum amount of recorded information about historic Indian groups native to a definable physiographic unit, the delta of a large river, the Rio Grande, and to determine if these Indian groups in any way differed from Indian groups native to surrounding areas. The Rio Grande delta of northern Tamaulipas and southern Texas is included in an extensive coastal plain whose Indians, for the most part, subsisted by hunting and gathering. As the delta was better watered and richer in food resources than adjacent areas, it should have been occupied by a larger number of Indian populations whose cultures had at least some distinctive features.

The approach to achieving this objective was to find documents that refer by name to Indian groups linked with the delta and to segregate all the information recorded for each ethnic unit. It soon became apparent that, because of European confusion concerning the names of these units, as well as various documentary inadequacies, the matter of ethnic unit identification was critical, so critical that it became the prime concern of the study whose results are presented here. As documents that refer by name to Indian groups of the Rio Grande delta and vicinity date mainly after 1746, clear ethnic identities were needed in order to determine which groups were native to the area and which had been displaced into the area by Spanish colonization in adjacent areas, particularly Nuevo León, where permanent Spanish colonization began about 1596, or some 150 years before formal colonization of lands along the lower Rio Grande.

Recognition of this need enlarged the scope of documentary research. In order to demonstrate that a particular Indian group seen somewhere along the lower Rio Grande was an immigrant group from another area, it was necessary to find documents indicating that this group had lived elsewhere at an earlier date. In this effort to distinguish between native and immigrant groups, it soon became evident that previous scholars, in trying to categorize the Indian groups of Nuevo León and Tamaulipas, had never collected and analyzed all the recorded information about each group. Pioneer studies that refer to the area have created ahistorical and unrealistic scenarios by lumping data found only in published sources (see Ruecking 1953, 1954a, 1954b, 1955a, 1955b). In other words, they had not seriously grappled with the basic problem of Indian group identification in the context of a long period of displacement by colonizing Europeans. This study has not cleared up all the confusion, but it may be claimed that some progress has been made in that direction.

Intermittently, over a period of four years, primary Spanish documents were searched for information on the historic Indian groups of a large area in northeastern Mexico and southern Texas. Facsimile copies of innumerable documents from the official archives of Spain and Mexico were available at the University of Texas at Austin, principally in the Benson Latin American Library and in the Barker Texas History Center. Some documents in these collections have been published, but most of them have not. A few useful documents not included in the University of Texas collections were found in the Texas Catholic Archives of Austin and in the Spanish document section of the General Land Office of Texas, also in Austin. In the lower Rio Grande area and vicinity local archives were examined, including the municipal archives of Reynosa and various early parish churches, such as those of Matamoros and San Fernando. Some use was also made of the microfilm services of the Genealogical Society of Utah, Salt Lake City, which has copied the registers of numerous missions and early churches of Mexico.

Many documents pertaining to specific Indian groups were found by making use of various archival guides, especially that of Bolton (1965), and by noting bibliographic citations in various historical studies. But some of the most informative sources were discovered simply by reading or closely scanning miscellaneous documents in the collections available.

The documents, which cover a period of more than 250 years, were written by numerous individuals, mostly Spaniards who were submitting reports to higher officials of both church and state. There is no indication that any of these individuals were instructed to collect detailed information on the territorial range and culture of any specific Indian group. This kind of information was only now and then casually recorded, and it is upon these bits and pieces of information that this study has been largely based.

The information retrieved from all documents was excerpted in full, and each excerpt was keyed to all Indian groups named. A separate file was maintained for each Indian group, and in each file all the excerpted information was arranged in chronological order. Generalized information presented without allusion to named Indian groups was filed separately for comparison with the more specific information. Careful chronological ordering of information led, in many instances, to recognition of immigrant groups who had joined groups native to various sections of the lower Rio Grande area.

The documents used in this study refer to Indians in two ways. Some documents, especially the earliest ones, refer to unnamed Indian groups seen by Europeans in areas that can be identified. Other documents refer to Indians by names of either native or Spanish origin, and these named groups are usually identified with specific localities or limited areas. Both kinds of documents have value because they contain descriptive information about Indians, but the later documents that refer to Indians by group names usually contain much more descriptive information. Unfortunately, this descriptive information was often linked with two or more associated Indian groups: some, native to the identified area; others, migrants displaced by Spanish colonists elsewhere. The most informative documents used are identified below in chronological order and presented under four headings that reflect increasing Spanish dominance in northeastern Mexico and a corresponding decline in Indian populations.

Period 1. Early Exploration and Travel, 1519–1600. Documents for this period are few in number and are linked with a short span of time, 1519–1535. Documents written between 1535 and 1600 were found to contain no useful information on Indian populations. The period began, during the years 1519–1523, when Francisco Garay, the governor of Jamaica, sponsored exploration along the coast of the Gulf of Mexico and attempted to establish a Spanish settlement near the mouth of the Rio Grande. Various documents that refer to Garay's activities do not mention Indian groups by name, but nevertheless contain bits of information about Indians who were undoubtedly native to the Rio Grande delta (Fernández de Navarrete 1955, 3:98–102; Herrera 1945, 3:372–373, 4:265; Díaz del Castillo 1955, 1:421, 2:105–106; Cervantes de Salazar 1971, 2:111, 284; Mártir de Anglería 1944, 570–573; López de Gómara 1954, 2:282).

Some twelve years later, in 1535, Alvar Núñez Cabeza de Vaca, after escaping from his Indian captors in southern Texas, appears to have crossed the Rio Grande not very far west of the delta area and traveled across parts of northern Tamaulipas and Nuevo León on his way westward to the Pacific Ocean. Two documents (Cabeza de Vaca 1542; Oviedo y Valdés 1959, 4:287–318) describe specific Indian encampments visited in northeastern Mexico. Cabeza de Vaca gave names for Indian groups of southern Texas, but after crossing the Rio Grande, he recorded no names for the groups that he encountered while traveling, probably because he lacked writing materials and the groups encountered were too numerous for him to recall their names when his account was written a few years later. Although names of Indian groups are missing, the descriptive details recorded about each encampment visited are valuable because of the early date and because later documents covering the same area are much less informative about Indian behavior.

Period 2. Spanish Settlement of Nuevo León and Displacement of Indian Groups from the Monterrey-Cadereyta-Cerralvo Area, 1600–1747. The first permanent settlement of Nuevo León began shortly before 1600. For the seventeenth century the most outstanding document is a history of early Nuevo León that was begun by Alonso de León (León, Chapa, and Sánchez de Zamora 1961) of Cadereyta. In 1648 León wrote the first part of this volume, which contains descriptive information on specific Indian groups and also a generalized description of Indian cultures in the area. León's work was continued by Juan Bautista Chapa, who recorded the native names of approximately 350 Indian groups of Nuevo León. He obtained the names from lists compiled by a former governor of Nuevo León, Martín Zavala. Chapa also added to the volume a copy of the diary kept during the expedition to the Rio Grande delta led by Alonso de León, Jr., in 1686.

After 1700 various documents refer to remnants of displaced Indian groups who were living in eastern Nuevo León and who made periodic attacks on Spanish settlements. These identify numerous Indian groups by name but say little about their cultures. One special folio of documents connected with the Spanish mission known as Divina Pastora de Santillana is fairly informative (Velasco 1715–1753, 285–338; Bueno de la Borbolla 1749, 206–210; Garza 1750, 218–219, 222–230, or 268–269, 272–280; Escandón 1749a, 195–199, or 245–250; 1749b, 441; 1749c, 190–194). For this period a few maps were compiled showing locations of certain Indian groups (Alvarez Barreiro 1729, map, 1730, 108–118; Wheat 1957, 82–84, map 115c). In 1735 Fernández de Jáuregui Urrutia (1963) recorded the names of fifty-four Indian groups who had attacked Spanish settlements in Nuevo León. Each Spanish settlement was described, and the names of all Indian groups who had attacked it were listed. The main value of all these Nuevo León sources lies in the fact that they permit identification of Indian groups who later migrated to the lower courses of the Rio Grande and the Río San Fernando.

Period 3. Colonization of Tamaulipas, 1747–1757. The area now known as Tamaulipas was extensively colonized by José de Escandón in 1747 and shortly afterward. Certain documents connected with this colonization program present, for the first time, information on Indian groups associated with the Rio Grande delta and its immediate vicinity. The historian Gabriel Saldívar has collected and published many documents connected with Escandón's exploration of the area and plans for foundation of fourteen Spanish towns, including two towns on the lower Río San Fernando and the lower Rio Grande (Escandón 1946; Saldívar 1943). After the Spanish communities had been established, various officials made inspection trips to evaluate progress, and their reports contain much information on Indian populations (Escandón 1751; Organización de las Misiones 1946, 77–89; Tienda de Cuervo 1929, 1930; López de la Cámara Alta 1946, 1758, map).

Period 4. Decline of Indian Populations and Loss of Ethnic Identities, 1757–1886. Documents of this period are numerous, but few of them contain substantial amounts of information on the surviving Indian populations. One document of 1767 has special value because it refers to Indian groups of the poorly known area along the Gulf coast north of the Rio Grande delta (Ortíz Parrilla 1767, 1–36) and is associated with a detailed map of that area (Cartografía de Ultramar 1953, map 112). Other documents, mainly written between 1770 and 1780, refer to Indians still living at missions and indicate how difficult it was for missionaries to obtain new recruits to replace declining mission Indian populations (Gómez 1942; Estado de las Misiones 1946, 48–73; Riperdá 1772, 392–438; Cabello 1780a). Still later documents, written principally between 1790 and 1800, yield further information on declining Indian populations (Barragán 1793a, 1793b; Noticias de los Conventos 1790–1814). The last important information on Indian groups living along the lower Rio Grande was obtained by A. S. Gatchet in 1886, when he recorded two Indian languages still spoken by a few surviving Indians (Swanton 1940, 55–121).

In the documents used for this study, it was found that the majority of Indian groups were known only by descriptive names of Spanish origin. Others were known by names of native origin. The documents rarely correlated a Spanish name with a name of native origin. This situation led to formulation of a theory that might explain this confusion in ethnic group identification. According to the theory, northeastern Mexico was originally occupied almost entirely by hunting and gathering Indian populations. Hunters and gatherers could effectively exploit their natural environments only by dispersing themselves. Thus over a fairly large area, there would be hundreds of foraging units, each having a distinctive name. Initially, the Spanish colonists found it burdensome to keep track of all these native names and began to coin new names of Spanish origin for sets of Indian groups associated with restricted areas. Later, after many Indian groups had been displaced by Spaniards, remnant groups collected in various localities, and again Spanish names were applied. Thus, through time, Spanish names replaced more and more native names. Some native names, however, were never replaced and continued in use. The theory explains the confusion of names, but it does not lead to correlation of specific native names with specific Spanish names.

CHAPTER 2

The Environmental Setting

THE VARIOUS Indian groups under consideration here were associated with one major physiographic unit, a plain adjacent to the Gulf of Mexico usually referred to as either the Gulf Coastal Plain or the Gulf Coastal Lowlands (West 1964, 57–61). These Indians were more specifically associated with a segment of the coastal plain lying between the Río San Fernando of northern Tamaulipas and the Nueces River of southern Texas. The distance between the mouths of the two rivers is approximately 200 miles. The Rio Grande and its delta are roughly midway between the lower courses of the Río San Fernando (75 miles) and the Nueces River (125 miles). As will be noted again later, the three rivers are the only perennial streams that traverse this segment of the coastal plain and discharge water into the Gulf of Mexico. Streams in the intervening areas are small and intermittent.

In northeastern Mexico, notably between Ciudad Victoria, Tamaulipas, and Monterrey, Nuevo León, which are separated by a distance of approximately 150 miles, the inland boundary of the coastal plain is formed by frontal ranges of a chain of mountains known as the Sierra Madre Oriental. Between these high mountains and the Gulf coast to the east, a few more or less isolated mountain masses, lower in elevation, are irregularly distributed, the principal ones being Sierra de Tamaulipas, Sierra de San Carlos, Sierra de Pamoranes, Sierra Papagayos, and Sierra de Picachos. North of the Rio Grande, there are no mountain ranges, and the margin of the coastal plain is marked by the Balcones Escarpment of the Edwards Plateau of central Texas.

All the major streams of northeastern Mexico begin in the Sierra Madre Oriental or in the mountains of Coahuila farther to the northwest, and they flow either eastward into the Gulf of Mexico or generally northeastward or

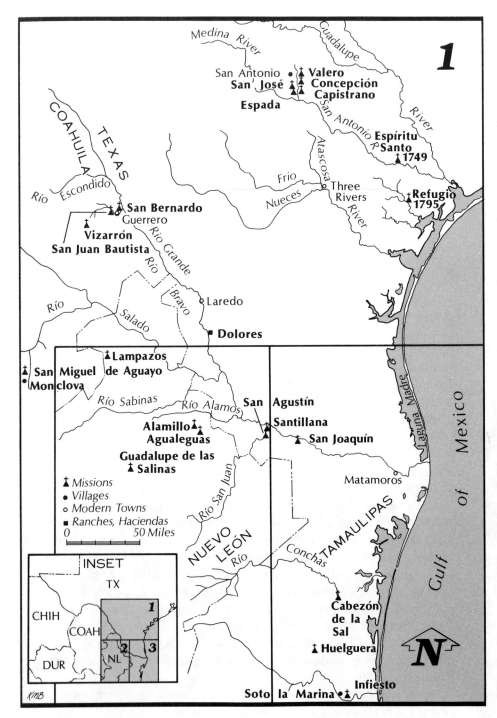

Map 1. Rio Grande delta and vicinity

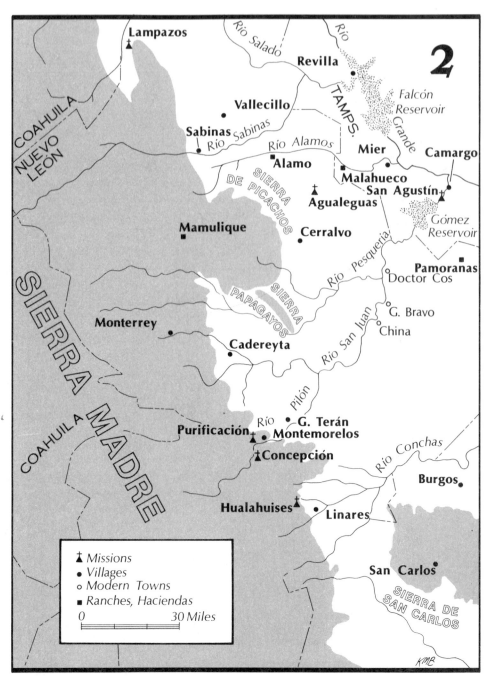

Map 2. Western section of the study area

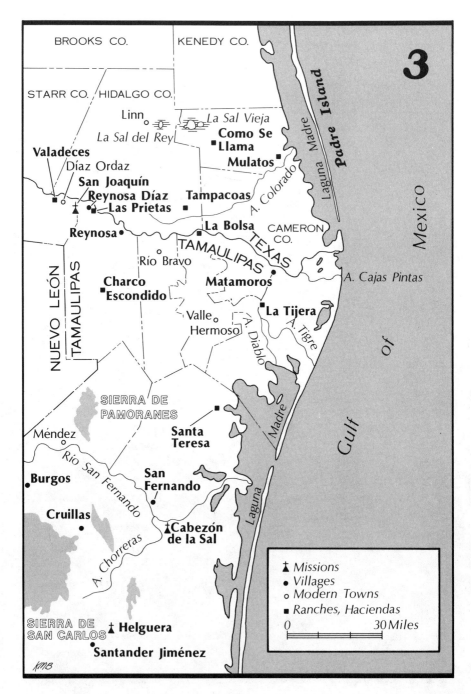

Map 3. Eastern section of the study area

eastward to enter the Rio Grande. It was along the constantly flowing sections of these streams that Indian populations were most consistently reported by early European observers. The Río San Fernando is the northernmost stream that flows into Laguna Madre of Tamaulipas, which is divided from the Gulf of Mexico by a sand barrier. Between this river and the Rio Grande below Camargo, there are no perennial streams. To the west, however, several constantly flowing streams enter the Rio Grande in that section of the river lying between Camargo and Laredo, the principal ones being the Río San Juan, the Río Alamos, and the Río Salado. Here a notable concentration of Indian groups was recorded between the Rio Grande and the Sierra de Picachos to the south, the Cerralvo area of northern Nuevo León. Another notable concentration was in the delta of the Rio Grande, the prime concern of this study. North of the Rio Grande very few Indian groups were recorded in the poorly watered area lying between that river and the Nueces.

The Rio Grande Delta

The Rio Grande is one of the major rivers of the North American continent. It originates in southwestern Colorado and flows some 1,885 miles to reach the Gulf of Mexico near Brownsville and Matamoros. It is the only river entering the Gulf of Mexico west of the Mississippi that is large enough to have developed a delta of classic proportions (Trowbridge 1923, 102; Cook 1958, 52; Lohse 1958, 55–56; Brown et al. 1980, 20). This delta begins about 14 miles upstream from Reynosa, or about 85 miles above the mouth of the river, and fans out symmetrically to include approximately 100 miles of the Gulf coast. It disrupts the western Gulf pattern of offshore bar islands and coastal lagoons, separating the Laguna Madre of southern Texas from the Laguna Madre of northern Tamaulipas. The delta distributaries and their floodplains are mainly in Cameron, Willacy, and Hidalgo counties of Texas, and in the municipalities of Matamoros, Valle Hermoso, Río Bravo, and Reynosa of Tamaulipas.

Today it is difficult to visualize the Rio Grande delta as it was prior to 1900. During the present century, most of the area has been cleared of vegetation and leveled for use in irrigation agriculture, and the flow of the river has been greatly reduced by upstream dams and reservoirs on the Rio Grande and its major tributaries. Only by documentary research and the study of small relict areas is it possible to gain impressions of what the delta area as a whole was really like when inhabited only by American Indians.

In the delta area, fresh water in quantity was always available. In times of local drought, the main channel of the Rio Grande continued to flow. When the river was in flood, water from the main channel and the distributary channels overflowed, and the adjacent depressions contained ponded water for long periods. When heavy local rainfall coincided with heavy upriver flooding, the delta had a superabundance of water. It is doubtful that the entire surface of the delta was ever covered by water. Scattered here and there, mainly along the divides between distributaries, were small elevations that rose above the highest flood levels. These were the best places for human campsites.

Rainfall in the delta area comes mainly in early fall (August–October) and occasionally in late spring and early summer (May–June). Based on a thirty-year observation period, Carr (1967, 5, Table 1; see also Carta de Climas 1970, map) calculates the average annual rainfall of the delta as 24.27 inches. Rainfall noticeably decreases with greater distance from the Gulf shoreline. The Rio Grande delta is known for its mild winters (Carr gives the average annual temperature as 74° F.), and only occasionally in winter does temperature fall to the freezing point, lasting only a few days. For nine months of the year (March–November), southeasterly winds predominate (Brown et al. 1980, 26–31). Heavy rains and strong winds caused by tropical storms occur mainly during the month of September.

Modern studies of Rio Grande delta vegetation indicate that formerly much of that area was covered by dense woody vegetation (Blair 1950, 102–103; Johnston 1955, 47–124; Brown et al. 1980, 105–107, map), and this is to some extent confirmed by observations recorded in early historical documents. Along the main channel of the Rio Grande, as well as along some of the major distributaries, was a dense fluvial woodland consisting of trees, shrubs, and vines, including groves of palms. Elsewhere there were dense thickets of thorny brush. Near the coast, however, woody vegetation was replaced by saline grasses. Up the Rio Grande, beyond the delta, the floodplain vegetation was dominated by thorny brush. The greater variety and wider distribution of woody vegetation on the delta added to the food potential for aboriginal populations.

The Rio Grande delta is included in W. Frank Blair's (1950, 103–105) Tamaulipan biotic province, which covers a large area in southern Texas and northeastern Mexico. No special study seems to have been made of animal forms connected with the delta as a physiographic unit. Blair does recognize the delta by referring to it as the Matamoran district. Nearly all of the land animal species of this Matamoran district occur elsewhere in the Tamaulipan biotic province, only 14 of 154 species being restricted to the delta. Blair's survey did not include birds, but Edward A. Kutac (1982, 79–83) indicates that 320 species of birds have been recorded in the Santa Ana National Wildlife Refuge, which is located within the delta. No tallies of freshwater and marine fish species have been found, but the number must be impressive. Such information as is available indicates a notable faunal richness in the Rio Grande delta. Because of the abundance of water and the heavy vegetative cover, many species are probably present in greater numbers than elsewhere in the Tamaulipan biotic province.

Two inland areas adjacent to the Rio Grande delta have considerable importance, mainly for negative reasons. In both areas the terrain is flat to slightly rolling; there are no mountains nearby; and they lack perennial streams. As will be shown later, in these areas European observers rarely noted Indian encampments, and they never referred to these areas as occupied by numerous specifically named Indian groups. It seems evident that, because of limited resources, they were not continuously occupied. This conclusion should be of interest to scholars who have tried to trace Cabeza de Vaca's route across southern Texas and northeastern Mexico.

The first of these two areas lies south of the Rio Grande and between the lower Río San Juan and the Gulf coast, mainly in the Mexican municipalities of China and General Bravo in Nuevo León and in the municipalities of Reynosa (southern section), Méndez, and San Fernando (northern sections) in Tamaulipas. Streams originating in the Sierra Madre Oriental bypass this area, the Río San Juan passing northward to the Rio Grande, and the Río San Fernando eastward to the Gulf of Mexico. The second area is also an area bypassed by all perennial streams, and it is covered by a sheet of eolian sand, now largely anchored by vegetation. This sandy plain lies mainly in parts of several Texas counties, including Willacy, Kenedy, Brooks, Hidalgo, and Jim Hogg.

CHAPTER 3

Historical Background

AS MOST of the information about the Indian groups under consideration here is derived from documents written by Spanish colonists of northeastern Mexico, particularly those of Nuevo León, this information cannot be properly interpreted without some knowledge of two major historical developments. One of these was the expansion of the settlement frontier of Nuevo León eastward toward the Gulf of Mexico, and the other was the massive colonization of Tamaulipas by José de Escandón in the middle eighteenth century. Indian troubles on the eastern frontier of Nuevo León were the prime reason for formal colonization of Tamaulipas.

Eastward Expansion of the Spanish Settlement Frontier in Nuevo León, 1596–1746

In any attempt to identify the Indian populations of the Rio Grande delta area, it is essential to distinguish, when possible, between Indian groups native to that area and Indian groups displaced into it by the expansion of Spanish settlements elsewhere in northeastern Mexico. As the earliest permanent Spanish settlements were along the mountain front of Nuevo León, the first Indians to be displaced from their traditional territories were those of that state. Primary documents, as well as detailed studies made by historians of the area, make it clear that some of the Indians of Nuevo León eventually moved eastward and northeastward to the coast of northern Tamaulipas and the lower part of the Rio Grande valley. In the first half of the eighteenth century, a large number of Indian population fragments occupied what is now eastern Nuevo León. These were frequently hostile and attacked small settlements on the Spanish frontier. A rather prolonged period of Indian troubles in eastern Nuevo León eventually led to a large-scale colonization program for that part of northeastern Mexico now known as Tamaulipas.

The earliest efforts to colonize Nuevo León had begun by 1577, but these efforts resulted only in a temporary occupation. Relatively small groups of Spaniards came to the Monterrey and Cerralvo areas from provinces that had been established earlier, Nueva Vizcaya to the west and Pánuco to the southeast. Among these were Spaniards who were especially interested in profiting from the slave trade. They attacked various Indian encampments of the Nuevo León area and took captives who were chained and sold for work in mines near Zacatecas, Sombrerete, Mazapil, and elsewhere farther south in New Spain. As these Spaniards did not have enough manpower to withstand repeated attacks by angry Indians, they were driven from the Nuevo León area by an Indian revolt that culminated in 1587 (León, Chapa, and Sánchez de Zamora, 1961, 44, 54–56, 58; Hoyo 1972, 1:81–83, 113–120, 123–136, 166–170).

By 1596 some of the Spanish settlers who had been driven out by Indians in 1587 returned to the Monterrey area, and thereafter other settlers began to arrive. This time the Spanish occupation of Nuevo León was permanent. The lands most preferred by Spaniards were along the valleys of streams flowing northeastward out of the Sierra Madre Oriental and out of outlying mountain ranges north of Monterrey (Pérez-Maldonado 1947, 14–19; Hoyo 1972, 1:149–153, 295–298, 2:303–311, 324–325).

From the Indian point of view, the most important development in Nuevo León early in the seventeenth century was the introduction of the *encomienda* system. In its Nuevo León setting, the *encomienda* was a legal title to possession of an Indian group bestowed by the governor of Nuevo León upon a large landowner. As described by Eugenio del Hoyo (1972, 2:316), when a landowner informed the governor of an Indian ranchería without an owner, the governor presented him with an *encomienda* title. After this legal sanction had been formalized, the landowner, or *encomendero,* went to the Indian ranchería with an armed force, usually surprising it by appearing at dawn. Captured Indians were put in chains and taken to the *encomendero's* lands, where they were carefully watched by a superintendent and armed guards. When a work period ended, the Indians were released so that they would not have to be fed. Some women and children, however, were kept for work as servants and also to serve as hostages. Each time the Indians were needed for work, armed men were sent to bring them back. Although this system had been prohibited as early as 1542, laws were not easy to enforce on distant frontiers. As the province of Nuevo León grew, landowners had to go farther out on the frontier to find unclaimed Indians.

In time local judges in various Spanish settlements of Nuevo León were authorized to give permits for *encomienda* raids on Indian encampments. There are numerous legal documents showing that *encomienda* Indians were sold, rented, shared, bartered, inherited, mortgaged, and given as dowry. It is undoubtedly this aspect of the Spanish occupation of Nuevo León that caused so much Indian resentment and led to numerous attacks on Spanish frontier settlements during the second half of the seventeenth century (Hoyo 1972, 2:357, 398–402, 434–438, 442, 446). The slave raids also continued, but in a legalized way. Indians convicted of serious crimes, such as revolting against Spaniards, were sentenced to be sold to labor contractors, who took them to other parts of New Spain.

The Indians of Nuevo León had been able to cope with their earlier enslavement problem by driving the small Spanish population from the area, but coping with the *encomienda* system was much more difficult for them. Too many Spaniards had entered their area, and expulsion was no longer possible. The Indians lacked European firearms, horses, and especially techniques for assembling men from their numerous, widely dispersed territories and marshaling these forces effectively in attacks on Spanish settlements. Many Indian groups had been much reduced in size by slave raids and especially by epidemics of diseases introduced by Spaniards. Evidently survivors of some groups accepted their fate and worked for Spaniards. Others, however, who had survived in larger numbers, withdrew to areas some distance from Spanish settlements, particularly in what is now eastern Nuevo León. From this area they continued their resistance to Spaniards by harassment of the smaller, outlying Spanish settlements.

In an effort to end abuses of Indians, about the year 1698 the *encomienda* system was abolished in Nuevo León and a system of *congregas* was inaugurated. Indians were no longer to be captured and attached to *encomiendas*. Instead, the Indian groups were to be brought together at *congregas* (towns) near Spanish missions. These congregated Indian groups were to elect their own governing officials, but each *congrega* was to be supervised by a missionary and "protected" by a Spanish *capitán*. But the *encomienda* system did not disappear immediately; the *encomienda* was merely disguised under the name *congrega*. The old *encomendero* became the Indian protector only in name. It was not until 1715 that Francisco Barbadillo y Victoria, sent by the viceroy of New Spain, enforced the abolition of the *encomienda* system that had become known as the *congrega* system. Then he established new missions and rejuvenated old missions. By 1716 numerous remnants of various Indian groups were represented in these missions, but by 1723 the Indians began to desert them after Barbadillo y Victoria left the province. In 1728 Pedro de Rivera reported that of the several thousand Indians who had been in missions, only about seven hundred remained. The Indians had returned to their lands, mainly on the eastern frontier of Nuevo León, and had resumed their attacks on Spanish settlements. In 1735 the governor of Nuevo León, José Antonio Fernández de Jáuregui Urrutia, listed the names of forty-five Indian groups that had caused trouble at Spanish settlements since 1715. Many of these were living on the eastern frontier between Monterrey and the Gulf coast. Thus the eastern frontier of Nuevo León was no better off than it had been before the mission system had been established, and it was this problem that eventually led, in 1747, to the rapid and massive colonization of Tamaulipas (Velasco 1715–1753, 329–338; Barbadillo y Victoria 1715, 65; Cavazos Garza 1963, 375–385; Copia de las Actas 1753, 1–24; Lozada 1732, 80–102; Fernández de Jáuregui Urrutia 1963, xi–xii, 12–23; Rivera y Villalón 1945, 129, 131–132).

There is a complex identity problem connected with the Indian groups recorded as living in eastern Nuevo León and vicinity during the first half of the eighteenth century, some of whom eventually moved farther eastward and northward to the lower Río San Fernando and Rio Grande valleys. Their names, as recorded in contemporary documents, are often not native names, but descriptive names applied to them by Spaniards. It is only rarely that documents record Indian group names of Spanish origin along with their native names. Few of the native names can be equated with the names of numerous groups recorded previously in the seventeenth century. Hence, it is not possible to establish continuities for many specific ethnic units because of these alterations in group names. It seems reasonable to suppose that the Spanish names were most often applied to associated remnants of Indian groups whose native names were too numerous for Spaniards to cope with.

Escandón's Colonization of Tamaulipas, 1746–1752

Prior to 1746 most of what is now known as Tamaulipas had no Spanish settlements. The coastal plain from the Río Pánuco northward to the San Antonio River of Texas was commonly referred to as El Seno Mexicano. After colonization by José de Escandón, it became known as the Province of Nuevo Santander. This new province was organized for various reasons, but principally because of fear that Europeans other than Spaniards might occupy the area and because some of its Indian groups repeatedly attacked Spanish communities in eastern Nuevo León.

Escandón's settlement program was unusual for the time because of its magnitude. Several thousand Spanish families from various areas of Mexico were escorted by soldiers to thirteen localities in which towns were established. The summary presented here will be concerned only with settlements in what is now northern Tamaulipas. Information is drawn from primary documents (Escandón 1751, 1753, 1946; Organización de las Misiones 1946; Saldívar 1943; Yerro 1749). These contain valuable information on terrain and Indian populations. It is in these documents that the names of numerous Indian groups were recorded for the first time.

Escandón's carefully planned project was achieved in two stages: (1) exploration of the area and selection of sites for settlement and (2) movement of settlers to the various sites and formal foundation of towns. After the towns had been established, Escandón and other officials made inspection trips and submitted reports on their progress.

The exploration phase involved the use of some eight hundred soldiers drawn from various military establishments of northeastern Mexico and Texas. These soldiers from diverse areas assembled at seven rendezvous points and traveled toward the mouth of the Rio Grande, where they were to join Escandón and his own party of two hundred soldiers. Escandón's route started in the region known as Sierra Gorda, the Sierra Madre Oriental of present southwestern Tamaulipas and the adjoining part of San Luis Potosí.

Descending the Sierra near present Jaumabe, Escandón reached the lowlands west of Sierra de Tamaulipas, and moved in a northeasterly direction along the Gulf coast. His base camp on the Rio Grande seems to have been near the present city of Matamoros. With the various military parties converging toward the mouth of the Rio Grande were numerous servants and laborers, a few missionaries, and small groups of mission Indians from Nuevo León and Coahuila.

Documents recording the travel of these military parties are very informative, for some traversed areas about which little was known. One of the parties that traveled southward from the lower San Antonio River of Texas was astonished to find that the Nueces River flowed into the Gulf of Mexico near present Corpus Christi. It had long been believed, and this is shown by maps of that time, that the Nueces River flowed southward to join the Rio Grande. According to these documents, there were extensive areas both north and south of the Rio Grande delta that were poor in water resources and were not continuously occupied by Indians. Indians were numerous only along the Rio Grande and along the lower Río San Fernando some eighty miles south of the Rio Grande. At least thirty-one separately named Indian groups were recorded for the Rio Grande delta alone. The documents also seem to indicate that between these two rivers, inland from the coast, was an unoccupied area that served as a linguistic and cultural boundary zone.

As the Spanish settlements were to be based on irrigation agriculture, town sites selected by Escandón and his associates were confined to the two rivers. No sites were chosen within the delta of the Rio Grande. All Rio Grande sites were on the south bank of the river upstream from modern Reynosa, well above the distributary channels of the delta. Diversion of water for irrigation purposes is easier when water is confined to a single channel in a wide floodplain. Placement of towns along the south bank of the Rio Grande was determined mainly by the fact that all supply centers and markets were southward. Escandón's management of the exploration phase, completed in 1747, impressed the viceroy of Mexico, who granted Escandón the title of Count of Sierra Gorda and also presented him with the award known as Caballero de Santiago.

The settlement phase began in 1748, when Escandón advertised his colonization plan in various parts of Mexico, particularly Querétaro, San Luis Potosí, Charcas, Huasteca, Nuevo León, and Coahuila. For each Spanish family he offered free land, ten years of tax exemption, up to two hundred pesos for moving costs, and other opportunities to improve its economic position. Escandón also arranged for a mission to be established near each Spanish settlement.

In December 1748 Escandón led some three thousand Spaniards out of Querétaro and took a northeastward route across the Sierra Madre Oriental. The colonists brought furniture and farming equipment, as well as droves of horses, cattle, sheep, and goats. These colonists settled in the southern part of present-day Tamaulipas. Most of the colonists who settled in northern Tamaulipas came from various parts of Nuevo León. These undoubtedly knew something about the lands they were to settle, for some ranchers of northern Nuevo León had grazed cattle along the south bank of the Rio Grande as early as 1734.

When he reached the Río San Fernando in 1749, Escandón found settlers from Nuevo León waiting for him to establish the village of San Fernando, but he postponed official settlement of this village until he had returned from the Rio Grande. In traveling from the Río San Fernando to establish the first Rio Grande settlement at Camargo, Escandón did not follow a direct route across the intervening area, which was deficient in water. Instead, he proceeded westward up the Río San Fernando and then turned northwestward to strike the Río San Juan, following it downstream to its junction with the Rio Grande. On the Rio Grande only two towns were founded in 1749, Camargo and Reynosa, but by 1752 both Mier and Revilla had been organized.

In 1750 Escandón made an inspection tour of the first three settlements he had established in northern Tamaulipas and recorded the following population figures: San Fernando, 294; Camargo, 456; and Reynosa, 223. At all three places, irrigation systems were under construction; various Indian groups were said to be living nearby and showing interest in living at missions. For Camargo, obviously the most flourishing settlement, Escandón also recorded a livestock census: 5,272 horses and mules, 932 cattle, and 27,935 goats. Later documents connected with these five Spanish population centers contain much information on Indian populations of northern Tamaulipas and southern Texas.

CHAPTER 4

The Rio Grande Delta

IN THIS chapter data on the Indians of the Rio Grande delta are presented in two sections. The first section summarizes early European observations of Indians who were not identified by group names. These observations come from a few documents of the sixteenth and seventeenth centuries, all written prior to Escandón's colonization of Tamaulipas in the middle eighteenth century. The lengthy second section presents information on Indian populations whose names were recorded in numerous documents. As some are known only from documents of 1747 and 1757, and little is known about them other than their names, these are covered together in a special subsection. After this the better-known groups are treated individually and presented in the alphabetic order of their names.

One aspect of this chapter requires special comment. The names of a few Indian groups associated with the delta are descriptive names coined by Spaniards, and these names were also applied to other Indian groups in adjacent or more distant areas. For example, Indians referred to as Come-crudos were recorded as living in the delta area and also on the lower Río San Fernando to the south: Documentary evidence indicates that these two geographically separated groups did not speak the same language or even know about each other. Spaniards had applied the same descriptive name to both groups and had failed to record their native names. Why they did so was not explained. In such cases, in this as well as in subsequent chapters, all groups given the same Spanish name are presented as a unit, but with clear indication of the geographic separations involved. Cross-references will tie each of these unitary presentations to other areas.

Early Spanish Contact: Unnamed Indian Groups

Garay and the Rio Grande Delta, 1519–1523

Between 1519 and 1521 the governor of Jamaica, Francisco Garay, sent out small fleets to explore and colonize the Gulf coast between the Florida of Ponce de León and the territory farther west that had been explored by captains sent out by the governor of Cuba, Diego Velásquez. During this period five expeditions landed at the mouth of a river referred to in the record of the last expedition as Río de las Palmas. Eugenio del Hoyo (1972, 1:5–23) has convincingly argued that the Río de las Palmas of these early expeditions was the Rio Grande. Apparently the confusion among historians about the identity of Río de las Palmas results from the fact that four different rivers flowing into the Gulf of Mexico were, at one time or another, referred to as Río de las Palmas.

While exploring the Gulf of Mexico littoral between Veracruz and Florida, a four-ship fleet commanded by Alonso Alvarez de Pineda arrived at the mouth of a river later known as Río de las Palmas, the Rio Grande. This was on a northbound voyage late in the summer of 1519. The fleet stopped there for forty days in order to careen the vessels. Forty Indian rancherías were seen on both sides of the river by an exploring party that went up the river for a distance of six leagues (about sixteen miles). The Indians treated the Spaniards in a friendly manner, and Pineda's men bartered with them (1521 Real Cédula, in Fernández de Navarrete 1955, 3:98–102; Hoyo 1972, 1:5–6).

After hearing Alvarez de Pineda's report, Garay sent 150 men, seven horses, and some artillery, in three ships, commanded by Diego de Camargo, to occupy the land along the river that had been visited by Alvarez de Pineda. These ships also carried lime, bricks, and several brick masons for the construction of a fort. Late in the summer of 1520, they seem to have arrived at the same locality previously visited by Alvarez de Pineda. This time the Spaniards went up the river in boats for a distance of eleven leagues and landed near some Indian encampments. For several days the Indians tolerated Camargo's men, but this did not last very long. A large number of Indians joined together and threatened Camargo, who decided to attack. While on the way to burn one of the Indian camps, Camargo's little army was broken up by the Indians. The soldiers tried to escape: some, by land; others, by water. The Spanish boats were driven from the river by a large number of Indian canoes. The Indians killed at least eighteen Spanish soldiers and all seven of the horses. The Spanish fleet then sailed southward toward Veracruz. During the unexpected retreat, the Spaniards had no time to secure enough food for travel by ship, and Camargo had to let his healthiest men travel southward by land along the coast (Herrera 1945, 3:372–373; Hoyo 1972, 1:6–7).

In the meantime, Garay, who had received no news from Camargo, sent a reinforcement ship with more than fifty soldiers and seven horses. The ship was commanded by Miguel Díaz de Aux, who did not find any trace of Camargo. After fighting with hostile natives, apparently on the same river, Díaz de Aux landed at Veracruz one month after Camargo had arrived there (Díaz del Castillo 1955, 1:421, 2:105). Later, Garay sent a second ship, with forty soldiers and ten horses, which also ended up at Veracruz (Cervantes de Salazar 1971, 2:111, 284).

Legal rights to colonize the territory explored by Alvarez de Pineda and Camargo were given to Garay in 1521 (Fernández de Navarrete 1955, 3:98–102). On July 27, 1523, Garay personally took command of a sixteen-ship fleet that departed from Jamaica with 600 men, 150 horses, 200 harquebuses, 30 crossbows, and some artillery. On July 25 Garay's fleet anchored at the mouth of the Río de las Palmas, or Rio Grande. Gonzalo de Ocampo was ordered to explore the river in a small vessel, and he ascended it for about fifteen leagues to a locality where several tributary streams joined the river. Three days later Ocampo returned, declaring that upriver the land was undesirable and uninhabited. Although this was not the case, Garay believed him.

Garay then landed four hundred men and all the horses and ordered that the vessels continue along the coast toward the Pánuco while he and his army followed by land. The first three days of travel southward were across the southern part of the Rio Grande delta, which was described as a dreadful land because of the marshy conditions. An account of the remainder of the journey southward need not be given here, since it was beyond the limits of the Rio Grande delta.

The various documents pertaining to Garay's attempt to colonize the Rio Grande delta contain no names for Indian groups, but they do indicate a remarkable population density for hunting and gathering groups. If we take the reports at face value, at least forty separate Indian encampments were seen by a single Spanish exploring party while traveling eighteen miles upstream. One encampment was near the mouth of the Rio Grande. The Indians were initially friendly, but soon became hostile for reasons not recorded. It is clear that the Indian groups along the river had an abundance of canoes, which unfortunately were not described. As will be seen later, the same notable population density was again reported over two hundred years later, when José de Escandón listed the names of over thirty Indian groups for the Rio Grande delta.

Spanish Shipwrecks, 1554

In April 1554 ships of the fleet of New Spain were blown off course, and three of them were wrecked on the shore of Padre Island in the latitude of present-day Port Mansfield. This historical episode has received considerable attention because the wrecked ships have been found and materials have been salvaged from them by underwater archaeology (see Arnold and Weddle 1978). The shipwreck survivors, numbering about twenty-six, walked southward along the coast in the direction of Pánuco, near modern Tampico. Only one individual reached Pánuco alive, Marcos Mena, a Dominican friar. Mena's recollection of the experience was written down by Dávila Padilla (1955, 273–290), but the description of Indians encountered is not very informative. Mena made no distinctions among the various Indian groups encountered; in fact, he made it appear that one hundred warriors from the same Indian group had pursued the Spaniards all the way from the Port Mansfield area to Pánuco, a distance of some three hundred miles. This is not believable. In the account it is possible to identify the Rio Grande, which was crossed on rafts, and some distance south of the river, the Spaniards were attacked by Indians who had bows and arrows and seemed to be interested in the clothing worn by some of the Spaniards. In all encounters Indians merely followed the Spaniards, killing one of them now and then.

Spanish Expeditions to the Rio Grande Delta, 1686–1688

Between the years 1686 and 1688, in an effort to find La Salle's Fort St. Louis, three Spanish expeditions, two going by land and one by sea, entered the Rio Grande delta area, which was believed to be where the French fort was located. Although Indian populations were encountered by these expeditions, no group names were recorded for the delta. The Indians were either wary or hostile. Although a few captives were taken, lack of interpreters made it impossible for the Spaniards to communicate with them.

The first expedition, recorded in a diary, was led by Alonso de León in June and July of 1686 (León, Chapa, and Sánchez de Zamora 1961, 194–202; route interpreted by Reyes 1944, 159–180; see also Weddle 1973, 54–65). He set out from Cadereyta, Nuevo León, proceeded down the Río

San Juan, and eventually reached the Rio Grande at a locality below the later site of Camargo. The route to the sea coast was along the south bank of the Rio Grande. The first Indian encampment on the Rio Grande was seen somewhere in the present municipal district of Díaz Ordaz, possibly near Valadeces. When the Indians saw León's advance scouting party, they abandoned their ranchería and swam across to the north bank of the Rio Grande. León tried to make a peaceful contact, but one of the Indians began shooting arrows across the narrowest part of the channel. Shortly after passing on down the river, the Spaniards came to a wooded area almost three miles wide and noted that Indians of that area had cleared footpaths through the woods. This appears to have been in the neighborhood of present-day Reynosa Díaz, which is at the western end of the Rio Grande delta.

Farther down the river a Spanish scouting party camped near a hill, probably La Mesa in the municipal district of Valle Hermoso. In this locality forty Indians were encountered, and these fled as soon as the Spaniards were seen. León and his men returned to their main camp, leaving a piece of white cloth, biscuits, tobacco, and other items as a sign of peaceful intent. The next day León and twenty men set out to visit these Indians, from whom they hoped to obtain a guide. The gifts left near the hill had been left untouched, but shortly thereafter fifty Indians came out of a nearby wooded area. León tried in vain to persuade the Indians to approach. He left some cloth and a knife in a tree. Only after the Spaniards had moved some distance away did the Indians approach the gifts, which they took, leaving a bundle of feathers. The Indians then waved some sort of feathered banner to signal the Spaniards to come forward and take the return gift of feathers. For a time afterward, the Indians followed the Spaniards at a distance, remaining close to the edge of a wooded area.

After two more days of travel, thirty Indians appeared on the north bank of the Rio Grande, apparently at a point near the present boundary line between Cameron and Hildago counties, Texas. They made hostile gestures while two men played on flutes. Later the same day, sixty Indians followed the Spaniards at a distance. It was in this locality, described as a plain, that León observed massed footprints indicating that an estimated three hundred Indians had participated in some sort of ceremony. This dancing ground was seen after passing a lake, probably Vaso del Culebrón in the present municipal district of Valle Hermoso.

Three days afterward the Spaniards set up camp near present El Gomeño, where today the distributary known as Arroyo Cajas Pintas leaves the main channel of the Rio Grande. At this place they found the site of an Indian encampment judged to have been abandoned some two weeks earlier. A barrel stave was noted in the camp debris.

Later the same day, another Indian ranchería was seen, from which the Indians fled. León managed to capture three women, and from them he obtained two words of unknown meaning, *zaguili* and *taguili*. At this encampment several artifacts of European manufacture were noted: part of a broken pipe, a damaged ship's bolt, a chain link, and a piece of glass. These probably came from European ships wrecked on the coast, for next day the Gulf shoreline was reached.

Afterward León and some of his men traveled at least twenty-one miles southward along the coast. At various localities near the beach, abandoned Indian encampments were noted. In some of these, "sticks" were observed still standing, which León interpreted as remains of houses. While traveling along the Gulf shoreline, the Spaniards noted things that had washed ashore: three damaged canoes, planks from ships, and in one place green cornstalks. In the expedition diary, nothing is said about corn being grown by Indians of the delta area.

On the return trip up the Rio Grande, at a point said to be twenty-nine miles from the coast, or about fifteen miles east of modern Reynosa, Indian footprints were seen leading to a crossing of the Rio Grande. Eventually the Spaniards arrived at the first Indian encampment that they had previously seen, and this time they decided to capture some of the Indians. In a skirmish two Indians were killed, and two boys were captured.

The following year, in February 1687, León was again sent to the Rio Grande delta to continue the search for La Salle's French fort. This second expedition went northward from Cerralvo, Nuevo León, to reach the Rio Grande and traveled downstream along the north bank of the river. As no diary of this second expedition has been found, all that is known is that many encampments of hostile Indians were seen (León, Chapa, and Sánchez de Zamora 1961, 201–203).

The third expedition to the Rio Grande delta was made in 1688 by Manuel Rivas and Andrés de Pez, each in command of a ship, who had been ordered to search the coast northward from Tampico (Rivas 1688, 7–17). These ships anchored at the mouth of the Rio Grande. An exploring party in small boats saw Indians who made signs for them to land. These Indians were given bread, honey, and tobacco, which they contemptuously tossed to the ground. Later two boatloads of armed men were sent up the river, and during the second day of travel, many Indians were seen on both banks of the Rio Grande. Some Indians shot arrows at the

Spanish boats, and when a gun was fired, they all fled. Later, three days after the two ships had left the mouth of the Rio Grande, a boat was sent ashore on what is now southern Padre Island and met Indians who were friendly enough to offer the Spaniards fish to eat.

The records of these three expeditions to the Rio Grande delta, as do earlier and later accounts, show that the area was well populated with Indian groups who lived by hunting and gathering. The negative attitude toward Europeans was essentially the same as that recorded by accounts of the Garay expeditions over 150 years earlier. When Escandón visited the delta area some 60 years later, the attitude toward Europeans had changed: all groups were friendly and eager to please. Although no group names were recorded by these three expeditions of 1686–1688, the documents contain observations on Indian behavior rarely mentioned in other documents.

Named Indian Groups

Indian Groups Recorded Only in Documents of 1747 and 1757

Here, in order to avoid repetition of the same minimal information for each Indian group, consideration will be given collectively to a rather large number of Indian units whose native names were listed for the Rio Grande delta area and its immediate vicinity in documents of 1747 and 1757 and thereafter were never again mentioned in primary documents. This amounts to segregated treatment of those Indian groups about which little is known beyond the recorded native name. Despite the dearth of information for each group, mere knowledge of the names has considerable value, for it reflects the fact that the Rio Grande delta was relatively rich in food resources and could support numerous local groups whose livelihood was based on hunting, fishing, and plant-food collecting. This agrees with information recorded over two hundred years earlier, during 1519–1523, when Garay attempted to establish Spanish settlements along the Rio Grande near the coast. The Garay records contain no ethnic group names, but they do indicate that the Spaniards may have seen as many as forty Indian rancherías.

Groups Recorded in 1747.
This section is restricted to information contained in Escandón's report of his reconnaissance of 1747 (Escandón 1946, 65, 67, 94), supplemented by information in an anonymous, undated document that is obviously based on Escandón's report (Saldívar 1943, 32–33). Information from both documents is presented in Table 1, which alphabetically lists groups according to their location with respect to the Rio

Table 1
Rio Grande Delta Groups in 1747

South of Rio Grande Escandón	Anonymous Document
(13) Apemapem or Apernapem	Apen napen
(7) Aretpeguem	Aretpeguem
(5) Atanguipacanes or Atanaguispacanes	Atanaguaypacam
(8) Calexpaquet	Alacalerpaguet
(12) Cospacam	Coospascan
(15) Guajopoctiyo or Guajepocotiyo	Guajopoco ayo
(14) Humalayapem or Humalaiapem	Vmalayapem
(11) Igiguipacam	Not included
(4) Inyopacanes	Not included
(9) Sagutmapacam	Not included
(10) Sicalasyampaquet	Si. Cajayn paguet
(16) Sumacualapem	Sanacualapem
(6) Zaulapaquet or Saulapaquet	Saulapaguet

North of Rio Grande Escandón	Anonymous Document
(6) Cootajam	Cootajanam
(10) Coucuguyapem	Concuguyapem
(13) Hueplapiaguilam	Lugplapiaguilam
(1) Hunpuzliegut	Vnpuncliegut
(14) Imasacuajulam	Masa cuajulam
(8) Parammatugu	Paranpa matuju
(9) Perpepug	Perpepug
(5) Peumepuem	Peupuetem
(12) Pexpacux	Perpacug
(4) Segujulapem	Segujulapem
(7) Sepinpacam	Sepin pacam
(11) Tlanchugin	Clancluiguygu
(2) Tunlepem	Tugum lepem

Note: Numbers in parentheses indicate order in which groups are listed in the two documents.

See text for Ayapaguemes, Comecrudos, Mayapemes, Saulapaguemes, and Tanaquiapemes.

Grande between the coast and the junction of this river and the Río San Juan. As Escandón's report seems to have listed the Indian groups in rough geographic order from east to west, his listing order is shown by numbers given in parentheses. The total number of ethnic units listed in Table 1 is twenty-six, with thirteen Indian groups located north of the river and thirteen south of it. It must be remembered that these are not the only Indian groups recorded for the delta area in 1747. They are merely the most poorly known groups. Other groups, all recorded in later documents, are given separate treatment elsewhere.

In his report Escandón recorded a few descriptive details that referred primarily to Indian groups living south of the Rio Grande (his base camp was somewhere near modern Matamoros). He estimated that some twenty-five hundred families lived south of the river and said that among these groups the Comecrudos had the largest population. He noted that there were no "apostates" in the area, which probably means that remnants of Indian populations displaced by Spaniards from other areas had not yet arrived. He further noted that the Indians hunted (deer and birds mentioned) and fished; that bows and arrows were used; that men wore no clothing and women wore only skirts made of animal skins or grass; and that smoke signals were used for distant communication.

For some unknown reason, the author of the anonymous, undated document gave Spanish meanings for the native names of eight Indian groups listed as living north of the Rio Grande. No meanings were given for native names of any groups listed as living south of the Rio Grande. The eight names, in alphabetical order, are given below, accompanied by Spanish meanings and comments on the most appropriate English translations of the Spanish meanings.

Lugplapiaguilam: *chiles mochos.* Both words in this Spanish phrase have multiple connotations. *Chile* here probably means "penis," not "pepper," and the phrase may refer to some slight surgical modification of male genitalia.

Masa cuajulam: *los que andan solos,* or "those who travel about alone." The Spanish phrasing suggests that there may be some connection between the Masacuajulames and a remnant Indian group known as Anda el Camino ("wanderers"), first recorded in 1790. Like the Masacuajulames, the Anda el Camino were linked with the north side of the Rio Grande.

Paranpa matuju: *bermejos los hombres,* literally "red the men," which
may refer to skin color or, perhaps more likely, to male use of red
pigment for body painting on special occasions.

Perpacug: *los que se amarran sus partes con una bolsita,* or "those who
tie up their genitalia in a small bag." This obviously refers to males
only.

Perpepug: *cabezas blancas,* or "white heads." This may refer to the
forehead.

Peupuetem: *los que hablan diferente,* or "those who speak differently."

Segujulapem: *los que viven en los Guiachs,* apparently meaning "those
who live in huisache thickets."

Sepin pacam: *los salineros.* This could mean those who mine or "make"
salt, or salters, that is, those who apply salt to something, or simply
those who live near the salt lakes. It is possible that this name is in
some way connected with the saline lakes north of the Rio Grande
delta, at least one of which was a Spanish source of salt in the second
half of the eighteenth century.

As Escandón seems to have obtained the names for delta Indian groups
from a Comecrudo leader, it is possible that many of the names are recorded in the Comecrudo language, or at least have Comecrudo prefixes
and suffixes attached to names from another language. Linguists have had
little success in interpreting these names. The only clear-cut case of a
Comecrudo name is Sepinpacam, which can be equated with words in
A. S. Gatschet's Comecrudo vocabulary collected in 1886, nearly 140
years after Escandón began recording names for Rio Grande delta groups.

Groups Recorded in 1757.   During an inspection tour of 1757, ten years
after Escandón's reconnaissance of 1747, Agustín López de la Cámara
Alta recorded the names of fourteen ethnic units for the Rio Grande delta
area and immediate vicinity. One of the groups was not Indian, but black
(Negro). The names of all fourteen groups were entered on a map, but
only nine of the names were listed in the official report (López de la Cámara Alta 1946, 16, 1758, map). Four names that appear in both documents are unique in that they do not appear in any other Spanish documents. Presumably these refer to Indian groups that Escandón did not hear
about in 1747, perhaps because they lived north of the Rio Grande and
some distance away from the river. The names, along with variant spell-
ings and map interpretations, are given below:

Catanamepaque: southeast of a lake that appears to be the salt lake now
  known as La Sal del Rey, in northeastern Hidalgo County.
Comesecapemes: near the present boundary between Cameron and
  Willacy counties.
Gumesecapom (or Gumescapem): south of another lake, apparently the
  one now known as La Sal Vieja, of northwestern Willacy County.
Uscapemes (or Usapemes): in present Cameron County, just north of the
  modern city of Brownsville.

In his report, after identifying these four groups, along with four additional Indian groups, López de la Cámara Alta made a few observations.
All these Indians, he said, were tattooed, men on the face only, women on
both face and body. He noted that the tattoo patterns did not seem to reflect ethnic group differences. His somewhat vague remarks about their
speech seem to indicate that they spoke dialects of the same language. The
only clue to identification of this presumed language lies in the fact that
López de la Cámara Alta's delta groups included the Tanaquiapemes, from
whom Joseph Antonio Ladrón de Guevara (1738, 63) obtained three
words in 1738. The three words can be recognized in the Comecrudo vocabulary collected by Gatschet in 1886 (Swanton 1940, 55–118). This bit
of evidence is suggestive, but cannot be regarded as proof of a Comecrudo
connection.

Aguichacas

The Aguichacas were first recorded in 1780 as one of eight Indian groups
said to be living near the Gulf coast just south of the Rio Grande (Cabello
1780a, 35–39), and in 1793 they were again listed as one of fifteen groups
from the same area (Barragán 1793a, 39–42). There is no clear record of
any Aguichacas entering Spanish missions anywhere. Various missionary
reports merely list them as among the Indian groups living at or near Reynosa and Mier between the years 1790 and 1814 (Noticias de los Conventos 1790–1814, 1, 3, 5, 13, 135–136, 221, 237, 239).
  As all Indian groups listed with the Aguichacas can be linked with the
Rio Grande delta and its immediate vicinity, it appears very likely that the
Aguichacas were native to that area. In documents dating from 1747 to
1757, which pertain to Escandón's exploration and settlement of northern
Tamaulipas, no name even remotely resembling Aguichacas was recorded
for the Rio Grande delta or elsewhere. It is possible that the Aguichacas
were present but were overlooked, or they may have been a subdivision of
some Indian group recorded under a different native name.

Anda el Camino

The name Anda el Camino (Spanish for "wanderers") was first recorded in 1790, and it has not been found in documents written after 1818. Between 1790 and 1793, a series of missionary reports referred to Anda el Camino as being one among various Indian groups who lived in the general vicinity of Reynosa and who sometimes visited that town as well as the surrounding Spanish ranches (Noticias de los Conventos 1790–1814, 1, 3, 5; Barragán 1793a, 39–42). The only document that refers to a native-style encampment of Anda el Camino is a report by the Conde de Sierra Gorda (1798, 1–5), which placed it on a Spanish land grant known as Potrero del Espíritu Santo. The lands of this grant extended northward from the Rio Grande to Arroyo Colorado and covered a large part of present-day Cameron County, Texas. At this encampment there were said to be eighty-two individuals (thirty-six men, twenty-six women, eleven boys, and nine girls). It was noted that the Anda el Camino and other Indian groups in the vicinity frequently visited the small Spanish ranching settlements of the Rio Grande delta area.

Between 1793 and 1818, Anda el Camino were recorded in documents pertaining to various missions and churches of San Antonio, Mier, Reynosa, and Matamoros. Several Indian groups from the lower Rio Grande entered missions at San Antonio, but only one Anda el Camino individual was actually recorded, a woman identified in 1793 at Mission San José y San Miguel de Aguayo (Pedrajo 1793, 121, 131). Some of the Anda el Camino were said to be living in the vicinity of Mier between 1809 and 1818 (Noticias de los Conventos 1790–1814, 13, 219, 221, 237, 239; Bedoya 1816, table; Numana 1817, table; Antillán 1818, table). At Reynosa, Anda el Camino were noted in documents written between 1797 and 1816 (Noticias de los Conventos 1790–1814, 136; Bolton 1965, 446–451), and at least one source refers to them as still living in the delta area east of Reynosa. The parish church registers of Nuestra Señora del Refugio de los Esteros of Matamoros identify thirteen Anda el Camino individuals between 1804 and 1814 (Matamoros Registers MS).

Such information as is available today indicates that the Anda el Camino originally lived in the Rio Grande delta area. It seems reasonable to believe that this Spanish name was applied to remnants of one or more Indian groups whose native names were recorded by Escandón in 1747. Their identity as Anda el Camino was lost in the early nineteenth century at various localities along the Rio Grande between Mier and Matamoros.

Ayapaguemes

This name is known from only two primary documents, both written in the middle eighteenth century. The first is an anonymous, undated document believed to have been written about 1748 (Saldívar 1943, 36). Circumstantial evidence indicates that this document could not have been written prior to 1747. In it there is a brief reference to Indians living along the lower Rio Grande, and an Indian man, known as Santiago, is identified as the leader of both Comecrudos and Ayapaguemes. From this it may be inferred that the two groups were closely related and probably sometimes shared encampment localities south of the Rio Grande.

The second document, written in 1757, is a description of the new Spanish colony of Nuevo Santander (later Tamaulipas) by López de la Cámara Alta (1758, map; 1946, 116), in which the Ayapaguemes are listed as one of nine Indian groups of the lower Rio Grande. At that time they lived on the northern side of the river. A map of 1758 places the Ayapaguemes in an area that appears to lie within what is now western Cameron County, Texas. López de la Cámara Alta stated that the nine groups had seventeen hundred "warriors." He observed that all were tattooed, fished by use of the bow and arrow, and apparently spoke the same language. The close association of Comecrudos and Ayapaguemes indicated in the anonymous document suggests that the Ayapaguemes may have spoken the Comecrudo language recorded by Gatschet near Reynosa Díaz in 1886 (Swanton 1940, 35–118).

Some modern maps that show the distribution of Indian groups in northeastern Mexico have mistakenly placed the Ayapaguemes on the lower Río San Fernando instead of the lower Rio Grande (Saldívar 1943, map; Jiménez Moreno 1943, map). Isabel Eguilaz de Prado (1965, 46, 69, map 2) seems to have misinterpreted López de la Cámara Alta's document, placing this group just south of modern Reynosa. It is apparent that the Ayapaguemes, who were not recorded after 1757, either declined in numbers and lost their identity by merging with the Comecrudos or were later recorded under another name.

The Borrados and Carrizos are discussed in chapter 6.

Casas Chiquitas

The Casas Chiquitas (Spanish for "little houses") were first recorded in 1777 during the official survey of a large land grant known as Llano Grande. This grant extended northward from the Rio Grande in the vicinity of present-day Mercedes, Texas, and included land on both sides of the boundary between Cameron and Hidalgo counties. The survey record indicates that an unspecified number of Casas Chiquitas were encamped in a thickly wooded area (Copia Certificada 1790, 28; Davenport and Wells 1918–1919, 219–221). Three years later, in 1780, the Casas Chiquitas were listed as one of nine Indian groups then living somewhere north of the Rio Grande (Cabello 1780a, 37).

Thereafter, mainly between the years 1790 and 1800, the Casas Chiquitas were several times mentioned as one of the Indian groups who lived in the general vicinity of Reynosa, the most easterly of the Spanish settlements along the lower Rio Grande (Noticias de los Conventos 1790–1814, 1, 3, 5; Barragán 1793a, 39–42), and at least some of them were congregated at Mission San Joaquín del Monte of Reynosa (Bolton 1965, 449). It is clear, however, that other Casas Chiquitas remained in the delta area at least until the end of the eighteenth century. In 1798 the Conde de Sierra Gorda (1798, 1–5) reported that forty-eight Casas Chiquitas were living on lands of the Llano Grande grant, where they were first reported in 1777. This population of forty-eight included twenty-three men, thirteen women, six boys, and six girls. In the same year another document referred to Casas Chiquitas as living in the coastal territory east of Reynosa (Noticias de los Conventos 1790–1814, 136). The Conde de Sierra Gorda said that the Casas Chiquitas and other Indians frequently visited the small ranching settlements of the Rio Grande delta area.

A few Casas Chiquitas, along with other Indians from the lower Rio Grande, entered Spanish missions at San Antonio. In 1793 two Casas Chiquitas women and the young daughter of one of them were identified as living at Mission San José y San Miguel de Aguayo (Pedrajo 1793, 121), and in 1796 the same three individuals were identified, not as Casas Chiquitas, but as Borrados (Huisar 1796, 162). The remainder of the Casas Chiquitas seem to have lost their ethnic identity at or near Reynosa during the nineteenth century. The last clear records date from 1814 (Noticias de los Conventos 1790–1814, 22) and 1831 (Guerra Cabasos 1831, 7). A few Casas Chiquitas may have survived as late as 1886 at Charco Escondido, Tamaulipas, some twenty miles south of Reynosa, where remnants of several Indian groups were collectively referred to as Carrizos (Hodge 1971, 1:209, 211; Branda 1976, 146).

As the Casas Chiquitas were seen living under native conditions only in the Rio Grande delta area, it appears likely that a Spanish name was applied to one or more remnants of Indian groups whose native names were recorded by Escandón in 1747. Their identity as Casas Chiquitas was lost among the few Indians who survived the mission period at Reynosa and San Antonio.

Comecrudos

Comecrudos is a Spanish phrase that is perhaps best translated as "those who eat raw foods." After 1741 this superficially descriptive name was used by Spaniards in referring to at least three sets of Indians who were encountered near the Gulf coast of modern Tamaulipas, one in extreme southern Tamaulipas, a second near the mouth of the Río San Fernando, and a third on the delta of the Rio Grande. Such information as is now available suggests that these three sets of Indians were unrelated and knew little or nothing about each other. This has led to considerable confusion among scholars, who have often assumed that the name Comecrudos was applied by Spaniards to scattered portions of the same population unit. The Comecrudos of southern Tamaulipas will not be discussed here, since they are known only from a single document of 1777 that names them as one of three Indian groups said to be represented at Mission San Juan Capistrano de Suances, near Altamira, northwest of Tampico. The two other groups of this mission were identified by local native names, Panguayes and Pasitas, and there is no information that permits linkage of these Comecrudos of southern Tamaulipas with the two better known sets of Comecrudos much farther to the north (González de Santianés 1773, 373; see also Saldívar 1943, map).

Comecrudos of the Río San Fernando. These Comecrudos were first mentioned in documents of 1741 as being one of five Indian groups represented by the Pinto Indian Capitán Marcos Villanueva, who participated in a peace treaty with the government of Nuevo León (Fundación de Presidios 1741, 20–21). The Indian groups led by this Indian, probably including the Comecrudos, had attacked the Spanish frontier of Nuevo León. Although other groups associated with the Río San Fernando led by Capitán Villanueva had fled from missions of Nuevo León, the Comecrudos do not seem to have entered any of the missions of that province as supposed by authors of documents written in 1741.

Escandón's account indicates that the Comecrudos lived in one or more rancherías near the mouth of the Río San Fernando. The ranchería he visited contained about 150 families. Although these people were hunters and gatherers, Escandón made it clear that fishing in coastal lagoons and nearby saline lakes was an important source of food. They gave Escandón and his men both raw and cooked fish, which indicates that these Comecrudos did not eat all their foods raw. Some of the fish taken were identified as *besugo* (seabream). Escandón mentioned that these Indians kept fish alive in netted enclosures, but this may refer to use of netted fish weirs instead of keeping live fish taken by other methods (Escandón 1946, 34–35, 43, 47, 58, 59).

In 1747 Escandón learned from the Comecrudos that two years earlier, apparently in 1745, a French vessel had been wrecked on the nearby Gulf coast. The Comecrudos had attacked the survivors and had killed all except two children. Some of the sailors were eaten, apparently in some sort of ceremonial setting. The two children, however, went southward and reached Tampico with help from the leader of a southern group identified as Capitán Morales. The Comecrudos salvaged from the French ship things that interested them. Escandón was given a few items they still had, including several European hats and five coins minted in the years 1739 and 1740. The Indians had taken a boat from the ship, apparently rowing it up the Río San Fernando, and by use of log rollers had moved it overland to one of the inland lakes, where it was used in fishing. This does not necessarily imply that the Comecrudos had no dugout canoes of their own manufacture. They probably recognized the value of the boat's large size and greater stability (Escandón 1749b, 420; 1946, 34–35, 43, 58–59; Vedoia 1749, 154).

An undated, anonymous document, probably written about 1748, confirmed Escandón's information on the location of the Comecrudos, and it also noted that some of the Tanaquiapemes were living close to the Comecrudos, their combined populations being given as two hundred families (Saldívar 1943, 34).

In 1749 Mission Cabezón de la Sal was established near present-day San Fernando, and the Comecrudos helped dig its irrigation canal. Apparently none of the Comecrudos actually lived at the mission, for there was never enough food (Escandón 1751, 105; Valcarcel 1756, 102; Villaseñor E. 1967, 1187). A mission inspection report of 1752 (Organización de las Misiones 1946, 85) noted that the missionary tried to congregate the Comecrudos and Tanaquiapemes at Mission Cabezón de la Sal, but this was foiled by a flood that damaged the mission, its irrigation canal, and its fields.

Later, in 1757, the Comecrudos were again said not to be at the mission, but living in a ranchería near the salt lakes referred to as Salinas de la Barra, near the mouth of Río San Fernando. Nearby was another ranchería occupied by Quedejeños. Both groups were said to have visited the mission from time to time (Tienda de Cuervo 1929, 349–350, 352). López de la Cámara Alta (1758, map, 1946, 109, 112) stated that the Comecrudos had 160 warriors, and he noted that, on one occasion, he had been confronted by 350 Comecrudos. His map of the area placed the name Comecrudos in two localities: one east of the Arroyo Chorreras and south of the Río San Fernando; the other north of the Río San Fernando near its mouth. This suggests that the Comecrudos were numerous enough to live in two encampments.

As late as 1770 the Comecrudos had not yet formally entered Mission Cabezón de la Sal, but they were evidently living near it (Gómez 1942, 63; Estado de las Misiones 1946, 68). Later missionaries, however, appear to have regarded the Comecrudos as part of the mission Indian population (Vidal de Lorca 1788, 33). By 1793, after Mission Cabezón de la Sal was abandoned by its missionaries, some of the Comecrudos, 129 in number, moved with other Indians to Mission Helguera, about eight miles from Santander Jiménez (Serie de Documentos 1783–1800, 38–40; Barragán 1793a, 39–42, 1793b, 344; Sierra Gorda 1794, 356; Ocaranza 1955, 449). None of the Indians who moved to Mission Helguera remained there very long, apparently returning to the lower Río San Fernando. These, along with the Comecrudos, were recorded there as late as 1818 (Bedoya 1816, table; Numana 1817, table; Antillán 1818, table).

In 1747 Escandón recorded certain details that seem to show that the Comecrudos of the Río San Fernando were unrelated to the Comecrudos of the Rio Grande. On the Río San Fernando, none of the Indians could tell him how far it was to the Rio Grande or even suggest a good route to follow. Several Río San Fernando Indians, however, accompanied Escandón to the Rio Grande, where they were unable to serve as interpreters. Apparently the two sets of Comecrudos knew nothing about each other.

Comecrudos of the Rio Grande. Although the evidence is not very clear, the Comecrudos of the Rio Grande may have been first referred to, as early as 1730, in connection with certain Indian groups associated with the Río San Juan (Velasco 1715–1753, 303; Garza 1750, 274). The first unquestionable reference to the Comecrudos of the Rio Grande is in Escandón's account of his reconnaissance of 1747 (Escandón 1946, 61; Vedoia 1749, 155–156; Saldívar 1943, 34–35). Escandón's main source of information on Indians of the Rio Grande delta came from a Comecrudo leader, Capitán Santiago, who was clearly the acknowledged leader of other Indian groups of the area. Capitán Santiago summoned other Indians by use of smoke signals, and some two hundred Indian families came to the locality of Escandón's camp, which seems to have been somewhere near modern Matamoros. Escandón obtained from Capitán Santiago the native names of thirty Indian groups said to be living along the lower Rio Grande, sixteen groups south of the river and fourteen north of it. The Comecrudos were apparently more numerous than other Indian groups of the delta area and seem to have lived very near the Gulf coast south of the river.

In 1749 Mission San Joaquín del Monte was established at Reynosa, and the next year Escandón (1751, 49; Valcarcel 1756, 106) reported the Comecrudos as one of six Indian groups that had come to live at or near the mission. He gave the Comecrudo population as 149 (47 men, 102 women and children), and he further stated that these Comecrudos had been born and reared on the south bank of the Rio Grande. In 1753 Escandón again visited Reynosa and noted the continued presence of Comecrudos (Ladrón de Guevara 1753c, 325). Four years later, in 1757, López de la Cámara Alta inspected Spanish settlements along the Rio Grande and noted the presence of ninety-five Comecrudos (thirty-three families) at Reynosa (Tienda de Cuervo 1929, 373, 376, 381, 1930, 108, 302). Most of these reports refer to shortage of food at the mission, forcing the Indians frequently to go out and search for food.

After 1770 various documents continued to report the presence of Comecrudos at Mission San Joaquín del Monte, or near Reynosa, or living in the area east of Reynosa (Gómez 1942, 61–62; Estado de las Misiones 1946, 68; Cabello 1780a, 36–37; Ballí and Hinojosa 1785, 1–3; Vidal de Lorca 1788, 33; Revillagigedo 1966, 86; Noticias de los Conventos 1790–1814, 130, 135–136; Bolton 1965, 449). In 1802 Reynosa was moved downstream to its present location, but apparently most of the Comecrudos remained at the old mission site at present Reynosa Díaz (Translación de Reinosa 1956; Ballí 1809, 1–5). The Comecrudos were still reported in the Reynosa area as late as 1834 (Guerra Cabasos 1831, 1–7; Berlandier 1980, 2:590).

At least twenty-five Comecrudos were still living in the Reynosa area in 1886, when Gatschet collected an extensive Comecrudo vocabulary from two elderly men (see chap. 9). It is quite clear that the Comecrudo language known to modern linguists was the language spoken by Comecrudos of the Rio Grande (Gatschet 1891, 38; Swanton 1940, 5, 55; Goddard 1979, 363, 380). There is no indication that any of the Comecrudos of the Reynosa area had come there from the low Río San Fernando.

Como se Llaman

The Indians known as Como se Llaman (Spanish for "What is their name?") were first recorded in 1772 as living in what is now northern Willacy County, Texas, some thirty-five miles north of the Rio Grande (Riperdá 1772, 401–402, 422). They were encamped between a Spanish ranch known as Carricitos and a salt lake known as Purificación (now called La Sal del Rey). Two Spaniards from the Reynosa area bought two girls, aged two and three, from the Como se Llaman. For the older girl, her parents received a horse, four goats, two sheep, a cloak, a white cloth, a knife, and a small bag of food; for the younger girl an unspecified amount of jewelry was given. The same source indicates that missionaries from San Antonio had been recruiting neophytes from Indian groups of this area, including the Como se Llaman.

Documents pertaining to Reynosa for the period 1790–1793 refer to Como se Llaman as being among the Indian groups who visited Reynosa and various surrounding ranches (Noticias de los Conventos 1790–1814, 1, 3, 5; Barragán 1793a, 39–42). Then in 1794 the Como se Llaman were said to be living on lands of a Spanish grant known as Las Mesteñas y Petitas y La Abra, which was in the area where Cameron, Hidalgo, and Willacy counties join. The land survey record refers to a well that was being used by the Como se Llaman (Davenport and Wells 1918–1919, 220–221). Four years later, in 1798, the Conde de Sierra Gorda (1798, 1–5) said that the Como se Llaman were living at a place known as Las Norias, possibly referring to the well mentioned in the land survey record of 1794. In this Las Norias encampment, fifty-three Como se Llaman individuals were living (twenty-three men, seventeen women, four boys, and nine girls).

Thereafter, the Como se Llaman were said to have visited Reynosa on occasion, and some of them actually entered its mission, San Joaquín del Monte. An unspecified number of Como se Llaman had also entered Mission San Agustín de Laredo of Camargo sometime between 1764 and 1809 (Noticias de los Conventos 1790–1814, 136; Bolton 1965, 446–451). Two Como se Llaman individuals were identified in the registers of the parish church at Matamoros, known as Nuestra Señora del Refugio de los Esteros (Matamoros Registers MS, entries for 1802 and 1813). The last reference to Como se Llaman is a brief statement made by Jean Louis Berlandier (1980, 2:590) in 1824. He reported Como se Llaman and other Indians living in small huts near Reynosa. In summer they roamed the countryside in search of food.

The evidence seems clear enough that the Como se Llaman originally lived on or near the northern portion of the Rio Grande delta. They probably represented one or more Indian groups whose native names were recorded by José de Escandón as living in the delta area in 1747. Como se Llama survived as the name of a modern ranch in western Willacy County (Sal del Rey MS; Davenport and Wells 1918–1919, 220–221).

Cotonames

Largely because two samples of the Cotoname language were collected in the nineteenth century, the Cotonames have been of considerable interest to linguists. Ethnohistorians, however, have not made full use of the documentary record in determining just where the Cotonames were living when first seen by Europeans. These Indians have usually been thought of as native to northern Tamaulipas. The earliest documents consistently place them on the opposite side of the Rio Grande in what is now extreme southern Texas.

The first clear record of the Cotonames was made in 1757 in connection with an official inspection of the new frontier settlements along the lower Rio Grande (López de la Cámara Alta 1946, 119, 125; Tienda de Cuervo 1929, 432). Cotonames and other Indian groups were seen at Camargo and Revilla (near present Ciudad Guerrero). These Indians were said to live north of the Rio Grande, and in one source they were linked with salt lakes said to be about 60 leagues (156 miles) from Revilla. The distance figure may be in error, since the lakes referred to were probably La Sal Vieja and La Sal del Rey of Hidalgo and Willacy counties, which are only some 70 miles from Revilla. A map, drawn by López de la Cámara Alta (1758, map) during this visit, shows Cotonames east of Revilla and just east of a salt lake that apparently represented La Sal del Rey. Although this map is inaccurate in many respects, it gives some impression of the location of Cotonames at the time. It seems more reasonable to conclude that the Cotonames known in 1757 probably ranged over an area now covered by Hidalgo and Starr counties of Texas.

A document of 1770 (Gómez 1942, 62), in referring to the Spanish town of Reynosa, mentioned that several Indian groups, including the Cotonames, were then living about fifteen miles north of the Rio Grande. This would place them somewhere in present Hidalgo County.

The next year, 1771, the Cotonames were again recorded as living in the same area, and reference was made to a locality about twenty-one miles north of the Rio Grande. Here the Cotonames were said to be working for Spaniards in the production of salt at a saline lake, apparently the one known as Purificación, or La Sal del Rey, which is in eastern Hidalgo County. In that year soldiers were sent from San Antonio to collect Indians for one of the San Antonio missions (Cantú 1771, 128; Riperdá 1772, 415–432). The soldiers surrounded the Cotonames and tied up many of the Indians, but were halted by the arrival of Spanish guards from the salt works at the saline lake. The San Antonio soldiers were persuaded to release the Cotonames, who were said to have claimed a connection with Mission San Joaquín del Monte of Reynosa. The main point at issue was that the Cotonames were outside the jurisdiction of the San Antonio missions, and it was illegal for a mission to recruit Indians from another jurisdiction. This episode reflects the difficulties that San Antonio missions were having in obtaining Indians to stabilize their declining mission Indian populations.

In 1780 Domingo Cabello (1780a, 37) listed Cotonames among the Indian groups then living near the Gulf coast on both sides of the Rio Grande. Various mission reports between the years 1790 and 1793 refer to Cotonames as one of the Indian groups who went to Reynosa and camped near that town or at various small ranching settlements in the vicinity (Noticias de los Conventos 1790–1814, 1, 3, 5; Barragán 1793a, 39–42). In 1794 Juan José Ballí received a large land grant north of the Rio Grande known as Salvador del Tule. The survey proceedings, which include a map, indicate that some of the Cotonames annually visited a portion of that grant, which was located in or near the northeastern part of present Hidalgo County (Sal del Rey MS; Davenport and Wells 1918–1919, 221–222).

In a report of 1797–1798, Zacatecan missionaries named the Cotonames as one of ten Indian groups living east of Reynosa. These missionaries considered the Cotonames to be living within the jurisdiction of Mission San Joaquín del Monte of Reynosa (Noticias de los Conventos 1790–1814, 136). In 1798 the Conde de Sierra Gorda (1798, 1–5) compiled a table that enumerated Indian groups then living along the lower Rio Grande east of Reynosa. He linked the Cotonames with a place known as Las Salinas, some fifty-six miles from Reynosa. Las Salinas probably refers to the salt lake known as Purificación, or La Sal del Rey. The Cotonames said to be connected with this locality numbered thirty-two (fifteen men, nine women, five boys, and three girls). The Conde de Sierra Gorda noted that various Indian groups of the area frequently camped near small Spanish ranching settlements along the lower Rio Grande.

Bolton (1965, 446–451), who examined the registers of missions at

Reynosa and Camargo, noted an unspecified number of Cotonames recorded at Mission San Joaquín del Monte (Reynosa) and Mission San
Agustín de Laredo (Camargo). The San Joaquín registers covered the
years 1790–1816, and those of San Agustín, the years 1764–1810. One
woman was recorded for the year 1802 in the marriage register of the parish church at Matamoros (Nuestra Señora del Refugio de los Esteros).
This woman was married to a mulatto man from Cerralvo, Nuevo León
(Matamoros Registers MS; Bolton 1965, 447).

Various documents dating from 1808 to 1831 indicate that Cotonames
were still living near towns along the south bank of the Rio Grande, particularly Reynosa and Mier (Noticias de los Conventos 1790–1814, 221,
237). A report of 1831 (Guerra Cabasos 1831, 6–7) refers to nine Cotonames at Reynosa. It is clear that the Cotonames continued to decline in
numbers during the nineteenth century and that they eventually lost their
ethnic identity through absorption by the Spanish-speaking population of
the lower Rio Grande area.

The last Cotonames seem to have been recorded in 1886 by the linguist,
A. S. Gatschet. In that year he recorded 125 Cotoname words obtained
from a few individuals then living at Las Prietas on the south bank of the
Rio Grande in Tamaulipas. The name Las Prietas referred to a river crossing, or ford, near Old Reynosa, now known as Reynosa Díaz. The collected words came mainly from three individuals, two of whom may have
been classified as Cotonames. As Gatschet was able to elicit so few Cotoname words, it is evident that his informants, who spoke Spanish well,
had not spoken the Cotoname language in everyday life since they were
small children (Powell 1891, 68; Swanton 1940, 5, 55, 118–121). While
at Las Prietas, Gatschet also learned that a few Cotonames were still living
north of the Rio Grande at a locality known as Las Norias, which may be
the same as Norias Cardeña recorded in early land grant documents. If the
two place names are synonymous, then in 1886 some of the Cotonames
were living somewhere east of the modern community of Linn, which is
about eighteen miles north of Edinburg in Hidalgo County.

Since Gatschet's time it has been learned that, in 1828, Berlandier
(1980, 2:430–431) collected a vocabulary of 104 words from a small
group of Indians who were visiting Camargo. This group was known to
citizens of Camargo as Carrizos, but other Indians with whom they were
associated called them Yué. This Carrizo-Yué vocabulary has been studied by Ives Goddard (1979, 370), who reports that the language is the
same as that recorded by Gatschet at Las Prietas as Cotoname. Thus two
samples of Cotoname speech are now known. Berlandier's information in-

dicates that the Indians known as Carrizos represented remnants of two or more Indian populations who did not all speak the same language.

The preceding review of Cotoname-related documents makes it clear that, when living under native conditions, the Cotonames ranged over an area north of the Rio Grande, mainly in modern Hidalgo County. Very few observations of Cotoname behavior were recorded by Europeans, and these refer mainly to relationships with Spaniards. It may, however, be inferred from the vocabularies recorded by Berlandier and Gatschet that the Cotonames, like all other Indians along the lower Rio Grande, lived by hunting and gathering. Gatschet (in Hodge 1971, 2:352) equated the Cotonames with the Aranamas Indians who lived between the lower Guadalupe and Colorado rivers of Texas, some two hundred miles northeast of where the Cotonames were recorded as living. No connection between the two peoples has ever been demonstrated.

Guajolotes and Cacalotes

Two names of Nahuatl origin, Guajolotes ("turkeys") and Cacalotes ("ravens"), were applied by colonial Spaniards to several Indian groups of northeastern Mexico and southern Texas. The two names are here treated together because the documentary record is so confused that the specific population units to which the two names were applied can not be determined.

Guajolotes of Cerralvo. The name Guajolotes was first recorded in the seventeenth century and linked with the Cerralvo area of Nuevo León. In 1643 Alonso de León (León, Chapa, and Sánchez de Zamora 1961, 118, 191) and Bernardo García led their combined forces out to punish Guajolotes and Caujaguas, who were blamed for slaughtering many Spanish horses and killing two Indian women of the Cerralvo district. After this the name Guajolotes was not again mentioned in Spanish documents for some fifty years, and because of this documentary gap, it is not possible to relate the Cerralvo Guajolotes to Guajolotes and Cacalotes identified in later times.

Guajolotes of the Sierra de San Carlos. In and around the Sierra de San Carlos of central Tamaulipas, Guajolotes were frequently recorded after 1735, when Fernández de Jáuregui Urrutia (1963, 12–13) listed them among the various troublesome Indians of the eastern frontier who had, during the preceding twenty years, attacked various Spanish settlements near Linares, Hualahuises, Montemorelos, and Cadereyta. It is not known

if these Guajolotes were the same as the Guajolotes known earlier at Cerralvo, but they do not seem to have been confused at any time with the
Cacalotes who lived farther west on upper tributaries of the Río San Juan.

These Guajolotes were most often mentioned in documents of the later
eighteenth century, when they were reported to be living at various localities in and around the Sierra de San Carlos. Sometimes they were said to
be living in association with other groups, such as Borrados, Cadimas,
and Canaynas. In 1748 sixty families of Guajolotes were mentioned in one
document, and another document of 1757 said that they numbered three
hundred individuals (Saldívar 1943, 31; Escandón 1749a, 195; Organización de las Misiones 1946, 93; González n.d., 352, 362; López de la Cámara Alta 1946, 34, 133; Tienda de Cuervo 1929, 278). Some of the San
Carlos Guajolotes entered a mission to the west in the Pilón valley, apparently that known as Concepción, which was near modern Montemorelos
(Guimbardo 1768, 139; Luviaur 1773, 163–167; Noticias de los Conventos 1790–1814, 1–3, 5, 13, 219, 221, 237, 239; Barragán 1793a,
39–42).

Cacalotes of the Río San Juan.   Cacalotes were first recorded on the
upper tributaries of the Río San Juan about 1716–1717. These were also
called Pelones, apparently because they had a tonsure similar to other Indians known as Pelones. In 1730 they made peace with the government of
Nuevo León and, along with other Indian groups, were distributed in various localities near modern Montemorelos, General Terán, and Cadereyta
(Velasco 1715–1753, 285, 301–303, 310; Bueno de la Borbolla 1749,
208–209; Garza 1750, 218–219, 222–230, or 268–269, 272–280).

In 1735, however, Fernández de Jáuregui Urrutia (1963, 12–23) indicated that these Cacalotes had for some twenty years participated in Indian
attacks on Spanish settlements near Hualahuises, Cadereyta, and Cerralvo. Then in 1741 peace was again made with the Spaniards, and the
Cacalotes were among those who elected not to enter missions but to return to their native areas (Fundación de Presidios 1741, 9).

Some eight years later, in 1749, the Cacalotes of the upper Río San
Juan, along with the Aguatinejos and Tortugas, agreed to move northward
to the Rio Grande and settle at a mission near present-day Camargo. This
mission, known as Divina Pastora de Santillana, was not successful, was
abandoned two years afterward, and the Indians returned to the upper Río
San Juan (Velasco 1715–1753, 285–338; Escandón 1749a, 195–198,
1749b, 441, 1749c, 190–194; Bueno de la Borbolla 1749, 206–210;
Garza 1750, 218–219). A critical question here is whether or not some of

the Cacalotes remained in the vicinity of Camargo, and if so, how were they related to other Indians of the Camargo area also known as Cacalotes? As yet there is not enough documentary evidence to clarify these points.

In 1768 there was a quarrel among the Indians at missions near Montemorelos (Concepción and Purificación), and at least some of the Cacalotes seem to have participated in the squabble (Guimbardo 1768, 139; Correa 1768, 140–141; Luviaur 1773, 163–167). Later, in 1788, the Cacalotes were reported at Mission Cabezón de la Sal (Vidal de Lorca 1788, 33). Some of the Cacalotes were reported still living in the vicinity of Mission San Cristóbal de Hualahuises between the years 1790 and 1818 (Noticias de los Conventos 1790–1814, 1, 3, 5, 13, 219, 221, 237, 239; Bedoya 1816, table; Numana 1817, table; Antillón 1818, table). Throughout their entire history, the Cacalotes of the upper Río San Juan seem never to have been confused with the Guajolotes of the Sierra de San Carlos.

Guajolotes and Cacalotes of the Lower Rio Grande.   In 1750 José de Escandón (1751, 21; Valcarcel 1756, 106) made an official inspection of the newly established settlement of Camargo and reported Guajolotes as one of six Indian groups living in the vicinity. Escandón stated that these Guajolotes had been born and reared on the banks of the Rio Grande on the Texas side, opposite Camargo. According to Escandón, the Guajolotes numbered forty-three and were led by a man known as Blas de Santa María. Two years later, in 1752, some of the Guajolotes were said to have entered Mission San Agustín de Laredo of Camargo (Organización de las Misiones 1946, 88). They were still led by the same man, Blas de Santa María.

After 1752, documents pertaining to the lower Rio Grande no longer referred to Indians known as Guajolotes. Later documents all referred to Indians known as Cacalotes. It appears likely that the Guajolotes became known by a somewhat similar name, Cacalotes, but it is also possible that the Guajolotes, being small in numbers, lost their ethnic identity about the same time as Spaniards along the lower Rio Grande became aware of Indians known as Cacalotes. Additional evidence is needed for proper testing of these hypotheses.

Cacalotes of the lower Rio Grande were first noted by López de la Cámara Alta (1946, 119, 125) as living in the vicinity of both Camargo and Revilla, and some of them were also said to be living near salt lakes north of the Rio Grande delta. On López de la Cámara Alta's map, Cacalotes were placed near the salt lakes now known as La Sal del Rey and La Sal Vieja. Tienda de Cuervo (1929, 432), who accompanied López de la Cámara Alta to the lower Rio Grande in 1757, noted Cacalotes living in the vicinity of Revilla and said that they were also on the north side of the Rio Grande. A number of Cacalotes entries were made in the records of Mission San Agustín de Laredo for the period 1764–1808 (Bolton 1965, 450–451). A few Cacalotes were recruited by missionaries from San Antonio, particularly from Mission San Francisco de la Espada (Valverde and Menchaca 1767, 277–280). These were recruited from the salt lakes area near the delta of the Rio Grande. Thereafter, mainly between 1788 and 1818, Cacalotes were reported as being seen at or near Spanish towns along the Rio Grande, including Reynosa, Camargo, and Revilla (Vidal de Lorca 1788, 33; Sierra Gorda 1791, 292–294; Barragán 1793a, 39–42, 1793b, 344–345; Noticias de los Conventos 1790–1814, 1–2, 5, 13, 129, 136, 152, 219, 231, 237, 239; Bedoya 1816, table; Numana 1817, table; Antillán 1828, table).

In conclusion, it may be stated that Spaniards evidently applied the names Guajolotes and Cacalotes to diverse and widely distributed Indian groups in northeastern Mexico and southern Texas, and sometimes both names seem to have been applied to the same Indian group. In order to avoid confusion in identities, it is necessary to link these names with specific areas or localities.

Malaguitas

The name Malaguitas appears to be of Spanish origin, but it is not possible to link it with such Spanish words as *malaquita,* which refers to the mineral known as malachite, or to *malagaña,* which refers to a device used to trap swarms of bees. This is further complicated by the fact that the Malaguitas were first recorded in Spanish documents under the name Malahuecos.

The Malaguitas are of special interest because they represent a fairly clear case of an Indian group of Nuevo León that moved northward to the Rio Grande, then moved down that river to the coast, and eventually moved as far northward up the coast as Copano Bay. Documents strongly suggest that the original name Malahuecos changed to Malaguitas only after the group moved to their coastal territory. As the name Malaguitas was given to Padre Island in the second half of the eighteenth century, it has often been claimed that the Malaguitas were aboriginal to the coast of southern Texas, which is contradicted by information found in some of the primary documents.

The name Malahuecos was first recorded in 1728 by Pedro Rivera y Villalón (1945, 131–132) as one of the Indian groups known to missionaries of Nuevo León. But in 1735 Fernández de Jáuregui Urrutia (1963, 22) identified Malahuecos as participating in attacks on Spanish settlements near the present towns of Cerralvo, Agualeguas, and Sabinas Hidalgo. This seems to indicate that at that time these Malahuecos were living somewhere northeast of the Sierra de Picachos, and between the Río Sabinas and the Río San Juan. This area is not far from that section of the Rio Grande that lies between Mier and Revilla, where they were recorded after the colonization of Nuevo Santander. Various documents refer to place names south of the Rio Grande between Mier and Revilla that include the word Malahuecos, such as Arroyo Malahuecos (Ladrón de Guevara 1753a, 231, 234; López de la Cámara Alta 1758, map) and La Barranca de Malahueco (Mier Grants 1767, 19).

The Malahuecos seem to have moved northward and across the Rio Grande a few years after Escandón had established several settlements along the Rio Grande. They were mentioned in a document of 1756 (Valcarcel 1756, 108), which states that Malaguitas and Garzas Indians had been living in the vicinity of Mier, their combined populations being given as 132. A year later López de la Cámara Alta (1946, 122) visited Mier and referred to the same Malaguitas and Garzas, together numbering 220 (fifty families). They were said to be living on the north side of the Rio Grande. A map connected with this source shows Malaguitas just north of the Garzas, in a locality that seems to be near the present boundary line between Starr and Zapata counties, Texas. An account written by José Tienda de Cuervo (1929, 414–415, 1930, 115), who accompanied López de la Cámara Alta, noted thirty-two Malaguitas as living on the outskirts of Mier and added one important detail: the Malaguitas of Mier had come from Nuevo León (Hacienda del Alamo and Mission of Cantunes in Valle de Salinas mentioned). This strengthens the argument of the Malahuecos northward movement.

In 1757 Malaguitas were mentioned in a document referring to Revilla, but they were said to be living downstream toward Mier (Tienda de Cuervo 1929, 432). Much later, in 1770, it was reported that a few Malaguitas were living at Mission Ampuero of Revilla, also known as San Francisco Solano (Gómez 1942, 60). Two years later, Malaguecos were recorded at Mier for the last time. There the combined population of Malaguecos and Garzas was given as eighty-five (Estado de las Misiones 1946, 69). After 1772 succeeding documents fail to record the name Malaguecos or Malahuecos near the Rio Grande or at any other place. A decade earlier the name Malaguitas was used in documents associated with the coastal area neighboring the previous territory of the Malaguecos, which clearly suggests that the names Malaguecos and Malaguitas referred to the same population.

It is evident that Malaguitas moved on down the Rio Grande and ultimately reached the Gulf coast, and this is demonstrated by records of Diego Ortíz Parrilla's expedition of 1766 from Presidio San Juan Bautista of northeastern Coahuila across southern Texas to the coast just south of Corpus Christi Bay (Ortíz Parrilla 1767, 1–36; Cartografía de Ultramar 1953, map 112). At that time what is now Padre Island was referred to as Isla Blanca and also as Isla San Carlos de los Malaguitas. Ortíz Parrilla's map links the Malaguitas Indians with that part of Padre Island now included in Kleberg County and the northeastern part of Kenedy County. A later document of 1780 shows that some Malaguitas had moved farther north along the coastal islands, at least as far as Copano Bay (Cabello 1780a, 37–38).

Fairly abundant records demonstrate that the Malaguitas, at various times, entered Spanish missions over a large area. Prior to 1772 some of the Malaguitas moved up the Rio Grande as far as Guerrero, northeastern Coahuila. Missionary censuses record fifteen Malaguitas at Mission San Juan Bautista and two at Mission San Bernardo (Almaráz 1980, 29–33). It is known that some Malaguitas moved down the Rio Grande and entered Mission San Agustín de Laredo of Camargo after 1784 (Bolton 1965, 450–451), but no Malaguitas entered Mission San Joaquín del Monte of Reynosa until sometime after 1790 (Barragán 1793a, 39–42, 1793b, 344–345; Bolton 1965, 449).

Malaguitas are known to have entered at least three of the five missions at San Antonio: Nuestra Señora de la Purísima Concepción de Acuña, San Juan Capistrano, and San Francisco de la Espada, which were all established at San Antonio in the same year, 1731. There is no indication that any Malaguitas arrived at these missions prior to the colonization of the lower Rio Grande by Escandón shortly after 1747. It is very clear that the Malaguitas who entered San Antonio missions came from the coastal zone between Copano Bay and the Rio Grande delta. Documents pertaining to the San Antonio missions, particularly those written between 1760 and 1793 refer to Malaguitas in various connections: in recruiting plans, in actual recruiting, and in retrieving Malaguitas who had fled from the missions (Dolores et al. 1762, 171, 178; Concepción Marriage Register MS, entry of 1764; Riperdá 1772, 392–438; Cabello 1780a, 37–38, 1780b, 78–79; Ballí 1781, 1–3; Dabbs 1940, 9–10, 16; López 1793, 124–126; Revillagigedo 1966, 65–74). Apparently a considerable number of Malaguitas lived at the three San Antonio missions. The mission registers do not identify many Malaguita individuals, but this is because the registers are incomplete. Other documents refer to forty-three Malaguitas (including some Mulatos) who had fled from Missions Concepción and Espada, and eighteen others who had evidently been recruited for the first time. The localities from which the Malaguitas were collected were all in the area now covered by Cameron, Hidalgo, and Willacy counties.

A few Malaguitas entered Mission Nuestra Señora del Refugio, which was established at present-day Refugio, Texas, in 1794. Registers of this mission identify at least five Malaguitas for the years 1809, 1812, 1813, and 1815 (Refugio Registers MS). These were apparently among the last Malaguitas from the southern Texas coast to enter missions. Some Malaguitas appear to have continued living under native conditions near the coast as late as 1812. In that year Miguel Ramos Arizpe (Benson 1950, 4, 7) listed Malaguitas among the remnants of Indian groups still hunting and fishing along the Texas coast. He mentioned that Malaguita Island protected the seaport of Brazo Santiago (present Brazos Santiago Pass).

The information summarized above shows that the Malaguitas, originally from Nuevo León, became widely distributed along the Rio Grande (from Coahuila to the Gulf coast) and in late times moved northward along the southern coast of Texas to the vicinity of Copano Bay. They entered at least ten different missions, but some managed to survive under native conditions on the coast as late as 1812.

Mayapemes

The Mayapemes were first recorded in documents relating to the José de Escandón reconnaissance of 1747 (Escandón 1946, 60; Saldívar 1943, 35). They were named as one of fourteen Indian groups living on or adjacent to the delta of the Rio Grande. Ten years later, in 1757, López de la Cámara Alta (1946, 116, 1758, map) visited the delta area and listed Auyapemes as one of nine Indian groups encountered. His Auyapemes are undoubtedly the same as the Mayapemes of Escandón, and his map placed them on the south side of the Rio Grande in the vicinity of present-day Valle Hermoso, Tamaulipas. According to López de la Cámara Alta, the nine Indian groups had a total of seventeen hundred "warriors." All these Indians were tattooed (men on the face only, women on both face and body), fished by using the bow and arrow, and apparently spoke dialects of the same language. No words were recorded, and today it is not possible to determine whether it was related to the language now known as Comecrudo, recorded near Reynosa Díaz in 1886 by Gatschet (Swanton 1940, 55–118).

In an official report of 1780, Domingo Cabello (1780a, 37), then serving as governor of Texas, stated that, near the Gulf coast, "Maulipeños" lived on the north side of the Rio Grande and "Manyateños" on the south side. Both names are probably variants of the name Mayapemes (Indian names were often distorted through clerical error). The name "Manyateños" is known only from Cabello's report.

Between 1790 and 1798 various documents indicate that at least some of the Mayapemes continued to live on or near the Rio Grande delta, often camping near small Spanish ranching settlements in that area (Barragán 1793a, 39–42; Noticias de los Conventos 1790–1814, 68, 118, 136). In 1798 the Conde de Sierra Gorda (1798, 1–5) reported forty-three Mayapemes (twenty-six men, ten women, three boys, and four girls) as living at a locality called Carricitos, which may be connected with grants known as Concepción de Carricitos and San Pedro de Carricitos in southwestern Cameron County, or with San Juan de Carricitos in Willacy and Kenedy counties.

It is known that at least a few Mayapemes entered Spanish missions at Reynosa and Camargo. Early in the present century, Herbert E. Bolton (1965, 449–451) examined the registers of these missions and noted that the name Mayapemes was included in both sets of registers. The registers of Mission San Joaquín del Monte of Reynosa covered the years 1790–1806, and those of Mission San Agustín de Laredo covered the years 1764–1810. Bolton did not count the number of Mayapemes recorded at each mission.

Small remnants of various Indian groups from the lower Rio Grande entered missions at San Antonio during the second half of the eighteenth century (Cabello 1784, 20–21). Three adult Mayapemes (two men, one woman) were recorded in documents of 1789–1799 that pertain to Mission San José y San Miguel de Aguayo. The wife of one of these men was identified as Saulapaguemes, another Indian group from the lower Rio Grande. In the later documents of this series, most of the Indians from the lower Rio Grande were lumped under the general name Borrados (San José Registers MS, entry for 1789; Pedrajo 1793, 116–123; Huisar 1797, 73–75, 1798, 81, 1799, 187). Apparently only a few Mayapemes entered the missions of San Antonio.

Mayapemes were mentioned in various documents as living in the vicinity of both Reynosa and Camargo until as late as 1818 (Noticias de los Conventos 1790–1814, 13, 219, 221, 237, 239; Bedoya 1816, table; Numana 1817, table; Antillán 1818, table). After 1818 the Mayapemes apparently lost their ethnic identity through being absorbed by Spanish-speaking populations along the lower Rio Grande.

There has been considerable confusion among modern scholars about the identity of the Mayapemes. Hodge (1971, 1:795) referred to the Mayapemes as Mallopeme, but identified his Mallopeme as an Indian group from western Texas living at Mission San José of San Antonio. Gabriel Saldívar (1943, 45, map) and Wigberto Jiménez Moreno (1943, map) erred in identifying the Auyapemes and Mayapemes as two separate Indian populations and placing the Auyapemes on the Río San Juan of Nuevo León. T. N. Campbell (1983, 357) listed Mayapemes, Auyapemes, and Manyateños as three separate groups.

Mulatos

Ordinarily the Spanish word *mulato,* equivalent to mulatto in English, refers to individuals of hybrid origin, their parents being African blacks and Europeans. After 1750, however, in northeastern Mexico the name Mulatos was applied by Spaniards to two contemporary but geographically separated Indian groups who seem to have had little in common beyond the name Mulatos. It is possible that both populations were so called because their skin color was somewhat darker than that of their neighbors. One of these groups was associated with upper tributaries of the Río Soto la Marina, mainly northeast of modern Ciudad Victoria, in the western part of central Tamaulipas. The other Mulato group was associated with the lower Rio Grande, over 160 miles to the northeast. No native name for either group has been identified. Primary documents that refer to the Mulatos of the Río Soto la Marina do not refer to Mulatos living elsewhere, and the same is true of documents that refer to the Mulatos of the lower Rio Grande.

Mulatos of the Río Soto la Marina.   These Mulatos seem to have first been mentioned in a document of 1772 (Estado de las Misiones 1946, 65, 72), but this and later documents refer to them as living, as early as 1750, on Río Purificación and Río Santa Engracia, both of these streams being upper tributaries of Río Soto la Marina. The Mulatos, as well as other Indian groups of the area, intermittently attacked Spanish settlements as late as 1780. They were most frequently mentioned in documents referring to such Spanish towns as Guemes, Padilla, and Santillana (now Abasolo). After 1781 these Mulatos disappeared from the historical record, probably because of decline in numbers, and their ethnic identity was undoubtedly lost through absorption by the Spanish-speaking population of the upper Río Soto la Marina. There is no indication that any of them migrated to another area (Sierra Gorda 1780a, 1–12, 1780b, 361–363; Martínez Piñera 1781, 1–2; Quintanilla 1780, 1–17).

Mulatos of the Lower Rio Grande.   The Rio Grande Mulatos were first recorded in 1777 (Ballí, Trejo, and Cano 1777, 1–28) in connection with events that occurred on a Spanish ranch known as El Rosario. This ranch, owned by Pedro Cantú, appears to have been a short distance west of modern Matamoros (a map in the Archives of Matamoros shows that the Cantú family owned land there). A group of Mulato Indians was encamped near the ranch headquarters in 1777. In that year Abito Cantú, son of the landowner and foreman of the ranch, was imprisoned at Reynosa for abducting a Mulato boy. The court records contain considerable information about the Mulato Indians involved.

Abito Cantú had contracted for the purchase of a young girl, daughter of the Mulato leader, and had made an offer that included a horse, eleven sheep, some cloth and braid, blankets, beads, and earrings. When Cantú went to the Mulato camp to complete the transaction, he found that the girl's relatives were opposed to the deal and that all of the Mulatos had fled to the woods, leaving only an elderly woman, who was ill, and a young boy who was asleep. Cantú took the boy, and it was for this that he was later imprisoned. Kidnapping Indian children, or bartering for them, was illegal, but nevertheless not uncommon.

The case records contain a few details about Mulato culture. Their camp was near a thickly wooded area, into which they scattered when threatened. They had no real houses, only *ramadas,* which were merely brush arbors without walls. Ordinarily the Mulatos left the camp during the day to search for food, returning at nightfall. It is mentioned that they used the horse in hunting deer. There are references to deer hides, bows and arrows, and a gourd (the source and use of this gourd not given). The elderly woman, who was ill and thought to be dying, was said to have been ill because she had been bewitched by another Indian woman. Nothing was said about the functions of the leader who was willing to sell his young daughter to Spaniards.

In 1780 some of the Mulatos were reported to be living north of the Rio Grande. In that year Domingo Cabello (1780a, 37), then governor of Texas, listed the Mulatos as one of nine Indian groups living in the area lying between the lower Rio Grande and the lower Nueces River. He also listed Indian groups then living just south of the lower Rio Grande, but the Mulatos were not named on that list. Later in the same year, Cabello (1780b, 78–79) referred to a few Mulatos who had voluntarily entered missions at San Antonio. They had joined apostates from those missions who had fled southward and were being escorted back to San Antonio.

Apparently few of the Rio Grande Mulatos ever entered missions at San

Antonio. A few Mulatos were recorded in the registers of Mission San José y San Miguel de Aguayo (San José Registers MS). In 1784–1785 four Mulatos were recorded (one man, two women, and one boy). A mission census of 1793 (Pedrajo 1793, 120–121) identified at least nine Mulatos (three men, three boys, and three girls); one of the men was recorded as married to an Anda el Camino woman. In later censuses some of these same individuals were again recorded, although their identity had been changed from Mulatos to Borrados (Huisar 1797, 73–75, 1798, 82, 1799, 187). At this mission the name Borrados was consistently used in referring to Indians who had come from the lower Rio Grande area (Cabello 1784, 20–21). The Borrados recorded for the San Antonio missions of Nuestra Señora de la Purísima Concepción de Acuña and San Francisco de la Espada may have included a few Mulatos, but this is difficult to demonstrate (Cabello 1780b, 78–79). The registers of Mission San Antonio de Valero, for the period 1758–1785, record approximately forty individuals as *mulato* or *mulata* (Valero Registers MS). These were undoubtedly mulatto (hybrid) individuals who cannot be connected with the Mulato Indians of the lower Rio Grande. Some of these were recorded as having been born in such places as Guadalajara and Monclova.

In 1798 the Conde de Sierra Gorda (1798, 1–5) reported that sixty-eight Mulatos (twenty-five men, twenty-three women, ten boys, and ten girls) were living at a locality known as La Barranca, which was in what is now the northeastern part of the municipality of Matamoros. This account includes a limited amount of cultural information about the Mulatos and nine additional Indian groups then living on both sides of the Rio Grande.

According to Bolton (1965, 449–451), the registers of Spanish missions at Camargo and Reynosa, now missing, contained the names of individuals identified as Mulatos. The registers of San Agustín de Laredo of Camargo covered the years 1764–1810, and those of San Joaquín del Monte of Reynosa covered the years 1790–1816. Bolton did not specify the total number of Mulato individuals recorded at each of these missions, nor did he give a date for the earliest Mulato entry.

Small remnants of the Mulatos continued to live at various places on both sides of the lower Rio Grande during the nineteenth century. The baptismal registers of the Matamoros church known as Nuestra Señora del Refugio de los Esteros contain entries for at least eighteen Mulato individuals for the years 1810–1811. These entries refer to three men, five boys, nine girls, and one unclassified female. One marriage register entry of 1810 records the marriage of a Mulato man to a Como se Llaman woman who had been reared in a Spanish home of Matamoros (Matamoros Registers MS). Some of the Mulatos may have lived at the now extinct community of Mulatos, recorded as late as 1885 in the southeastern part of Willacy County, Texas (MacManus 1885, map).

It seems reasonably clear that the Rio Grande Mulatos, during their last days, were living as remnants in various localities. They were probably first recorded by one or more of the native names listed by Escandón in 1747. Perhaps the most important clue to the identity of these Mulatos is provided by linguistic evidence. In 1829 Jean Louis Berlandier, the French naturalist, collected a sample of Mulato speech (148 vocabulary entries). This sample has been studied by Ives Goddard (1979, 357, 367–371, 375–380), who identifies the language as Comecrudo, one of the better-documented languages of the lower Rio Grande area (Swanton 1940, 5, 55–118). The Rio Grande Mulatos, as recorded in primary documents, cannot be related to the Negros of the same area. At Reynosa and Matamoros, both groups were distinguished in the registers of Mission San Joaquín del Monte and the parish church known as Nuestra Señora del Refugio de los Esteros.

Negros

The word *negro* is Spanish for "black," but in this ethnohistoric context it refers to Negroes or blacks. In various documents pertaining to the delta of the Rio Grande, there is hearsay evidence that indicates that a considerable number of male African blacks survived a shipwreck near the mouth of the Rio Grande sometime prior to 1747. There is no eyewitness account of this wrecked ship, which may have been involved in the slave trade. The black castaways found wives among Indian groups living in the vicinity, and their descendants became known to Spaniards of the area as Negros.

In 1747 Indians living in the vicinity of present-day Matamoros apparently told Escandón about the black castaways. In 1749 Escandón learned from a Spanish soldier of Reynosa about a large settlement of blacks, with Indian wives and half-breed children (called *lobos*). They were said to live on an "island," but this island seems to have been an area lying between the main channel of the Rio Grande and one of its delta distributaries to the south. These Negros had stolen cattle from Spanish settlements farther up the Rio Grande (Escandón 1749d, 484–486). A year later, in 1750, Escandón mentioned in a letter written at Reynosa that the Negros presented no real threat to the Spanish settlements and that he hoped to induce them to enter the Spanish mission at Reynosa (Escandón 1750, 458; Altamira 1750, 463).

In 1757 additional information was recorded about the Negros. A map drawn in that year showed them as living between the main channel of the Rio Grande and a southern distributary, apparently the one now known as Arroyo Cajas Pintas. This area was said to have some hills, probably stabilized clay and sand dunes, that were high enough to escape inundation during floods. At this time the Negros were said to be at war with some of the neighboring Indian groups. Their men not only used the bow and arrow but also the spear, and it was noted that they used the spear with great dexterity. Again the original blacks were identified as shipwreck survivors (Tienda de Cuervo 1929, 384–385, 403; López de la Cámara Alta 1758, map, 1946, 117).

It seems evident that the Negros of the Rio Grande delta were the same as the Negros reported in 1793 as occasionally appearing in the vicinity of Reynosa (Barragán 1793a, 39–42). In a missionary report of 1797–1798, Negros were listed as one of ten Indian groups living somewhere east of Reynosa and occasionally visiting Mission San Joaquín del Monte at Reynosa (Noticias de los Conventos 1790–1814, 135–136). In 1798 another document referred to Negros as living on the Rio Grande about 104 miles (along its sinuous course) east of Reynosa Díaz. At that time Reynosa was 14 miles farther up the Rio Grande than its present location. These Negros were said to have a population of ninety-nine (fifty men, thirty-five women, eight boys, and six girls). They were also said to be at peace with Spanish settlers and sometimes to camp near Spanish ranches (Sierra Gorda 1798, 1–5).

Bolton (1965, 449) saw entries for Negros in the registers of Mission San Joaquín del Monte of Reynosa. These registers covered the years 1790–1816. Some Negros, however, continued to live near the mouth of the Rio Grande. The records of the Matamoros parish church, Nuestra Señora del Refugio, include register entries for Negros between the years 1801 and 1810. These entries refer to seven men, one boy, eight girls, and six unclassified females (Matamoros Registers MS). After 1810 the Negros seem to have lost their ethnic identity.

As the Negros appear to have been a hybrid population, it is regrettable that Spanish documents say so little about their physical characteristics, language, and culture. Their recorded use of both the spear and the bow and arrow in warfare, a combination that is unique in their area, suggests fusion of West African and American Indian weaponry. If a substantial sample of their language had been recorded, it would undoubtedly reflect their dual cultural heritage.

Pauraques

The Pauraques, although clearly linked with the lower Rio Grande area, were not recorded in Spanish documents prior to 1767. The name, apparently derived from some unrecorded Indian language, is today popularly used along the lower Rio Grande in referring to a bird, *Nyctidromus albicollis*, found in brushy and wooded areas along the river valley (Peterson 1963, 133–135; Peterson and Chalif 1973, 89, plate 15; Kutac 1982, 80, 83).

In 1767 Acisclos Valverde, a friar at Mission San Francisco de la Espada of San Antonio, recorded several names that resemble Pauraques: Huaraques, Taguariques, and Tuaraques. He made it clear that the Indians known by these names had arrived at the mission sometime between the years 1753 and 1767. The equation of these three names with Pauraques receives support from a document of 1772 (Riperdá 1772, 401) that refers to illegal recruiting of neophytes by the San Antonio missions. The missionaries at San Antonio had brought Indians from the lower Rio Grande, which was beyond the jurisdiction of any San Antonio mission. The document mentions the names of four Indian groups brought from the lower Rio Grande: Carrizos, Como se Llaman, Cotonames, and Pauraques. Campbell and Campbell (1985, 64, 66), who commented on probable linkages of Pauraques with Huaraques, Taguariques, and Tuaraques, had not seen this document.

The best linkage of Pauraques with the lower Rio Grande is found in a land survey document of 1777 (Copia Certificada 1790, 28; Davenport and Wells 1918–1919, 219), which mentions Pauraques who lived on lands of a grant known as Vicente de Llano Grande, which extended both east and west of the present boundary line between Cameron and Hidalgo counties. Some of these Indians served temporarily as guides for the 1777 survey party. It is known that at least a few Pauraques had entered Mission San Agustín de Laredo of Camargo after the year 1764 (Bolton 1965, 451).

As the Pauraques were not identified in documents pertaining to Escandón's colonization of the lower Rio Grande, they may not have been encountered at that time or may have been recorded under another name. The Pauraques evidently slowly declined in numbers during the later part of the eighteenth century; some, perhaps not very many, entered missions at Camargo and San Antonio; and they disappeared from the documentary record before 1800.

Pintos

The name Pintos seems to have been applied by Spaniards to two separate and distinct Indian groups who, when first seen living under native conditions, occupied areas near the Gulf coast, one associated with the lower Río San Fernando, the other with the lower Rio Grande. Both were apparently called Pintos (Spanish for things bearing marks or signs) because they were tattooed, although only sources pertaining to the Pintos of the lower Rio Grande actually refer to tattooing. The tattooing of both groups was probably not extensive enough for them to have been called Borrados, a name used in Nuevo León for referring to Indians with elaborate tattooing that obscured considerable portions of the skin surface. The two groups called Pintos occupied separate, nonoverlapping areas, and contacts between them are not indicated.

Pintos of the Río San Fernando. In earlier documents the name Pintos was consistently used to designate a specific set of Indians associated with that part of the Río San Fernando drainage that lies between the Sierra de Pamoranes and the Gulf coast. Pintos were distinguished from other Indian groups in that area, such as Comecrudos, Pamoranos, Quedejeños, and Quinicuanes. These Indians known by the Spanish name Pintos undoubtedly had a native name for themselves, and they may also have had native names for localized subdivisions. Whatever the case, in documents no native name has been equated with the Spanish name.

The Río San Fernando Pintos were known in Nuevo León before they were first visited in their homeland by José de Escandón in 1747. During the first half of the eighteenth century, they were recorded as one of numerous Indian groups on the eastern frontier who made raids on Spanish settlements along the mountain front between Cadereyta and Linares, and some of them had even been persuaded to enter Mission San Cristóbal de Hualahuises, which was near Linares and on one of the upper tributaries of the Río San Fernando (Copia de las Actas 1753, 1–12; Fernández de Jáuregui Urrutia 1963, 14, 17, 109; Fundación de Presidios 1741, 20, 25; Lozada 1732, 84–93; Villarreal A. 1969, 421). In some documents it was stated that the Pintos came from or lived in an area farther down the Río San Fernando, probably not far from the coast.

In 1747 Escandón (1946, 58, 93; Vedoia 1749, 153) encountered four Indian groups, consisting of 150 families, on the lower Río San Fernando just west of Salinas de la Barra, a series of saline lakes near the coast. These four groups—Pamoranos, Pintos, Quedejeños, and Quinicuanes—

were living together; and in the same area, but some distance away, lived a fifth group, the Comecrudos. The four associated groups, apparently because they wanted protection from their enemies, the Bocas Prietas, asked that a Spanish mission be established in their midst.

In 1749 Escandón (1749b, 435) was again on the lower Río San Fernando and noted that Pintos were camping at a spring adjacent to the Arroyo Chorreras, not far from its junction with the Río San Fernando. It was about this time that friars had established a mission, known as Cabezón de la Sal, for the Pintos and other Indians of the lower Río San Fernando (Yerro 1749, 281, 285–286; Organización de las Misiones 1946, 30, 40, 50, 52). The subsequent history of this mission can be traced through numerous documents. The next year, 1750, Escandón (1751, 104; Valcarcel 1756, 102) indicated that 101 Pintos (twenty-one families) were congregated at the mission. In 1752 Friar Silva (Organización de las Misiones 1946, 85) noted that a flood on the Río San Fernando had damaged the mission's irrigation canal and cultivated fields and that the Pintos and other Indians were out in the countryside searching for food.

In 1757 the lower Río San Fernando was visited by Agustín López de la Cámara Alta (1946, 111–112) and José Tienda de Cuervo (1929, 347–348, 351, 359, 362, 1930, 102, 302), and their accounts contain brief but informative general statements about local Indian populations and their cultures. They noted that Mission Cabezón de la Sal had been established on lands within the Pintos' territorial range. Although these accounts do not agree on the number of Pintos living in the area, the figure appears to have been between eighty and ninety-three.

Lino Nepomuceno Gómez (1942, 63) referred to the presence of Pintos at the same mission in 1770, by which time the mission was also known as Nuestra Señora del Rosario. Two years later the Conde de Sierra Gorda mentioned that Pintos and Tanaquiapemes were living at the mission, their combined population given as one hundred (Estado de las Misiones 1946, 18). In 1773 Vicente González de Santianés (1773, 380) reported that Pintos were only at the mission intermittently.

Shortly before 1774 Mission Cabezón de la Sal was abandoned by its missionaries, and in that year the Pintos were said to have petitioned the government to move them to another locality (González de Santianés 1774, 1–2; Vidal de Lorca 1774a, 228, 1774b, 233–234). Some Pintos of the lower Río San Fernando took their children westward to be baptized at the parish church of Cruillas (Cruillas Registers MS: entries for 1777, 1778, 1782). Later the Pintos asked that the provincial government move them to Burgos, a Spanish settlement north of the Sierra de San Carlos, but no action was taken (Serie de Documentos 1783–1800, 38–40; Lasaga 1783, 268, 1786, 336). The Pintos, who by this time were regarded as one of the most peaceful Indian groups of the province, continued to complain to the government about their isolation (Serie de Documentos 1783–1800, 7–31).

It was not until after 1790 that anything was done about the Pintos and other Indian groups of the lower Río San Fernando. About 1792 most of these Indians were moved to the rejuvenated Mission Helguera at Palmitos, near modern Jiménez (Serie de Documentos 1783–1800, 34–101; Puertollano 1793, 359; Sierra Gorda 1794, 356; Revillagigedo 1966, 85; González Salas 1979, 416–417). It is uncertain how long the Pintos remained at Mission Helguera, but it is evident that most of them eventually returned to the lower Río San Fernando. They are referred to in various documents of the early nineteenth century, the last one dated 1818 (Noticias de los Conventos 1790–1814, 1, 3, 13, 219, 221; Bedoya 1816, table; Numana 1817, table; Antillán 1818, table).

Pintos of the Lower Rio Grande. The name Pintos was not included on the lengthy list of Indian groups recorded by Escandón in 1747 for the Rio Grande delta area. It is possible that the Spanish name Pintos referred to one or more of the native names on that list, for in 1750 Escandón (1751, 49; Valcarcel 1756, 106) was in Reynosa and referred to Pintos as one of the Indian groups living in the vicinity. These Pintos, Escandón said, had been born and reared on the north side of the Rio Grande, and he gave their population as forty-one (sixteen men, twenty-five women and children). Later, in 1753, when Escandón was again in Reynosa, he also mentioned Pintos as living in the vicinity (Ladrón de Guevara 1753c, 325, 327).

The Pintos figure prominently in Spanish documents of 1757. Tienda de Cuervo (1929, 381) noted that Pintos from north of the Rio Grande came to Reynosa to trade with Spaniards. López de la Cámara Alta (1946, 116, 1758, map) recorded Pintos as living about sixteen miles east of Reynosa, which clearly links them with the Rio Grande delta. His map of 1758 shows Pintos on the north side of the Rio Grande, apparently in what is now eastern Hidalgo County, Texas. Evidently some Pintos were still living north of the Rio Grande in 1780, when Cabello (1780a, 36–37) listed them among Indians living near the coast between the Rio Grande and the Nueces River. During the last thirty years of the eighteenth century, most references to Pintos link them with the area immediately surrounding Reynosa, or with its mission, San Joaquín del Monte (Gómez 1942, 61; Sierra Gorda 1790a, 81, 1790b, 83; Ballí and Hinojosa 1785,

1-3; Barragán 1793a, 39–42, 1793b, 344; Bolton 1965, 449; Noticias de los Conventos 1790–1814, 1, 3, 5, 125). It is of interest to note that no Pintos were identified as living on the Rio Grande above Reynosa.

After 1800 there are numerous references to surviving Pintos, mainly at or near Reynosa (e.g., Ballí 1809, 1–5; Noticias de los Conventos 1790–1814, 22; Berlandier 1980, 2:590). At times some of these surviving Pintos were identified as Carrizos (Hodge 1971, 1:209, 1972, 2:237). Probably the last Pintos were recorded by Powell (1891, 6), who noted that Gatschet's unpublished records of 1886 mention two Pinto women living at La Bolsa on the Rio Grande midway between Reynosa and Matamoros.

In 1886 Gatschet obtained a lengthy list of words from Comecrudos living at Las Prietas near the site of the first Reynosa. His Comecrudo informants told him that the Pintos were all gone, but that they had spoken the same language as the Comecrudos (Swanton 1940, 59, 70, 85, 105, 135). The difficulty with this information is that it was obtained so late. The Pintos may not originally have spoken the Comecrudo language. Gatschet's informants may have referred to remnants of Pintos who had given up their own language and used Comecrudo because it was, in late times, spoken by most of the surviving Indians of their community.

There is, however, circumstantial evidence suggesting that the Pintos of the lower Río San Fernando did not speak the same language as that of the Pintos of the lower Rio Grande. In 1747 Escandón (1946, 58, 93; Vedoia 1749, 153) recorded the following information. None of the San Fernando Indians, including the Pintos, could tell him how far it was from the Río San Fernando to the Rio Grande, nor could they provide him with guides who knew a route northward to the Rio Grande. Six Indians from the Río San Fernando accompanied Escandón northward to the Rio Grande, and when that river was reached, these Indians were unable to serve as interpreters. This seems to indicate that the San Fernando Indians did not speak the same language as any of the Rio Grande Indians actually encountered by Escandón. Perhaps there was a linguistic boundary between the two areas.

Saulapaguemes

The Saulapaguemes were one of the numerous groups recorded in 1747 by Escandón (1946, 65–66; Saldívar 1943, 34) as living in the Rio Grande delta area. They were said to live on the south side of the river, and the order of listing suggests that they lived fairly close to the Gulf shoreline. In 1757 López de la Cámara Alta (1946, 116, 1758, map) again listed the Saulapaguemes as living in the same area, and his map placed them on the south side of the Rio Grande, apparently in the area just south of modern Matamoros. In 1757 Tienda de Cuervo (1929, 375–376) said that Saulapaguemes lived on the south side of the Rio Grande and sometimes came to exchange their deer hides at Reynosa. Some two decades later, in 1770, Gómez (1942, 62) listed the Saulapaguemes as living about sixteen miles from Reynosa Díaz, but on the north side of the Rio Grande.

A few Saulapaguemes were among Indians recruited from the lower Río Grande by missionaries from San Antonio. The late registers of Mission San José y San Miguel de Aguayo identify a Saulapaguem woman in 1785 and a man in 1793 (San José Registers MS). In a San José mission census of 1793 (Pedrajo 1793, 116–123), five Saulapaguemes (four men and one woman) were enumerated. One of the four men was later recorded by name in a census of 1796 (Huisar 1796, 163) but classified as Borrados. In the last censuses taken at San Antonio missions, most of the Indians who had come from the lower Rio Grande were collectively referred to as Borrados. In 1783 Cabello (1784, 20–21) had mentioned that a large number of Borrados from the southern coastal zone entered Mission San José.

Most of the Saulapaguemes remained in the lower Rio Grande area. In 1793 Francisco Nepomuceno de Barragán (1793a, 39–42) noted that Saulapaguemes were among the various Indian groups who frequently visited the village of Reynosa. In 1797–1798 a mission report listed Saulapaguemes as one of ten coastal groups that lived near Spanish ranches in the area east of Reynosa (Noticias de los Conventos 1790–1814, 136). And in 1798 the Conde de Sierra Gorda (1798, 1–5) reported ninety-two Saulapaguemes (thirty-nine men, thirty-six women, six boys, and eleven girls) living at Rancho Nuevo about thirty-six miles east of Reynosa.

Although details are lacking, it is clear that at least some of the Saulapaguemes had entered Mission San Joaquín del Monte of Reynosa after 1790, and others had entered Mission San Agustín de Laredo of Camargo after 1764 (Bolton 1965, 449–451). Other sources indicate that Saulapaguemes were at both missions in 1801 (Noticias de los Conventos 1790–1814, 152). Early in the nineteenth century, three Saulapagueme children were identified in the church register of Nuestra Señora del Refugio de los Esteros at Matamoros. These are connected with the years 1809 and 1814.

Except for those who entered Mission San José at San Antonio, the Saulapaguemes evidently remained in the lower Rio Grande area. They managed to maintain their identity during the period when Spanish ranches were being established in the delta area and survived into the early nineteenth century.

Tampacuas

Tampacuas appears to be a name derived from the Comecrudo language, but this does not mean that the Tampacuas themselves spoke that language. The Comecrudo vocabulary collected by Gatschet in 1886 (Swanton 1940, 85, 97) includes the words *tom* and *pakahuai/pakawai,* which together are probably best translated as "tattooed people." Gatschet's Comecrudo informants indicated that the Tampacua Indians spoke "another language." The identity of that other language remains unknown.

The Tampacuas were first recorded on a map of the Texas coast that was prepared shortly after Ortíz Parrilla visited the Corpus Christi Bay area in 1766. The name is placed on the mainland near the Gulf coast, apparently somewhere between modern Baffin Bay and the mouth of the Rio Grande (Cartografía de Ultramar 1953, map 112). There is no clear documentary evidence to prove that Ortíz Parrilla actually saw the Tampacuas in that area. Information on the location of the Tampacuas was probably obtained from local Indians or from a Spaniard who had explored the coast by sea. Later maps, evidently based on the Ortíz Parrilla map, place the Tampacuas in the same area (Cartografía de Ultramar 1953, maps 7, 113). None of these maps show enough coastline detail to determine just how far north of the lower Rio Grande the Tampacuas were ranging in 1766.

In a census of 1772, a few Tampacuas were recorded as living at Mission San Juan Bautista on the south side of the Rio Grande in northeastern Coahuila, some 175 miles northwest of the Tampacuas location on the Ortíz Parrilla map of 1766. It appears likely that missionaries of San Juan Bautista were recruiting Indians disturbed by Spanish ranching activities along the lower Rio Grande. The census of 1772 recorded nineteen Tampacuas at San Juan Bautista: four men, nine women, two boys, and four girls (Almaráz 1980, 28–33). Two of the Tampacua women were married to men identified as Pastaloca and Pampopa, and the children of these marriages were identified by missionaries as Tampacuas. A third Tampacua woman at Mission San Juan Bautista was also identified as Borrados, a name often applied to Indians who were tattooed.

In 1780 Cabello (1780a, 37) named the Tampacuas as one of nine Indian groups still living near the Gulf coast between the Nueces River and the Rio Grande. Nearly two decades later, missionary reports of 1797–1798 (Noticias de los Conventos 1790–1814, 135–136) listed Campaquazes (Tampacuas) as one of ten Indian groups that lived near Spanish ranching settlements east of Reynosa. These groups were considered by missionaries as living within the jurisdiction of Mission San Joaquín del Monte of Reynosa.

In 1798 the Conde de Sierra Gorda (1798, 1–5) reported Tampacuas living at a place known as Carricitos, said to be about sixty miles east of present-day Reynosa Díaz. The name Carricitos may refer to any one of three land grants known as San Pedro de Carricitos, Concepción de Carricitos, and San Juan de Carricitos. The first two were in present-day Cameron County, Texas, and the third covered all of Willacy County, as well as much of Kenedy County. The Tampacuas at Carricitos were said to number eighty-three (thirty-three men, twenty-six women, eleven boys, and thirteen girls). They were one of ten Indian groups recorded in this document, which contains a few observations on the culture of all eight groups as a whole.

Some of the Tampacuas undoubtedly lived for a time at Mission San Joaquín del Monte of Reynosa. Bolton (1965, 449) noted the names of an unspecified number of Tampacuas in the mission registers, which cover the years 1790–1816. Their presence at the mission is confirmed by other documents (Noticias de los Conventos 1790–1814, 152). The names of two Tampacuas individuals, one boy and one girl, are found in the baptismal register of the parish church at Matamoros. The entries are dated as 1801 and 1811 (Matamoros Registers MS).

The Tampacuas were recorded at or near Reynosa until the middle nineteenth century. A report of 1831 (Guerra Cabasos 1831, 1–7) refers to twelve Tampacuas men at Reynosa, and in 1834 Berlandier (1980, 2:590) mentioned the Tampacuas as one of five Indian groups still living on the outskirts of Reynosa. Berlandier recorded observations made on these Indian groups as a whole. The Tampacuas identity was maintained as late as 1853–1855, when Tampaquash (Tampacuas) and Carcese (Carrizos) were cited in reports of raids made on Anglo-American ranches located in present Hidalgo County (Winfrey and Day 1966, 260–262).

In the later part of the nineteenth century, the names Tampacoas, Tampacuos, and Tampaguas were recorded as place names on various maps (Llano Grande Grant 1879, no. 723; MacManus 1855, map; Trowbridge 1923, map). Gatschet mentioned a locality known as Tampacuas in Hidalgo County and suggested that the name may have been a variant of the name Karankawa (Gatschet 1891, 44, 51). Davenport and Wells (1918–1919, 141–142) made the same suggestion, but no documentary evidence has been found that equates the names Tampacuas and Karankawa.

Tanaquiapemes

In Spanish documents covering almost a century, the name Tanaquiapemes seems to have been recorded in about forty different ways, and a few
variants have been mistaken for names of separate Indian groups. The Tanaquiapemes are of special interest because various documents indicate
that they were associated with the coastal zone in two areas: one along the
lower Rio Grande, the other along the lower Río San Fernando. They appear to be the only Indian group that can be clearly associated with both
areas, which raises questions about where they may originally have lived
and about their linguistic and cultural affiliations.

The name Tanaquiapemes was first recorded in 1732 as one of the numerous Indian groups on the eastern frontier of Nuevo León (Lozada
1732, 85). The document does not indicate just where they were living at
the time, but recorded circumstantial evidence suggests that it was somewhere on the Río San Fernando northeast of Linares. In 1738 Ladrón de
Guevara (1738, 49–65) wrote an account of his visit to an Indian encampment that included some of the Tanaquiapemes, but he failed to give its
location. Other Indians (group names not recorded) came to the encampment to trade with the Spaniards. Ladrón de Guevara, in referring to all
Indians present, noted facial tattooing and briefly described a few items of
material culture, such as drills for making fire, bows, arrows, and quivers.
He also recorded three words which appear to be from the language spoken by the Rio Grande Comecrudos.

As the Tanaquiapemes were associated with two areas, they will here
be discussed for each area separately. In 1747 Escandón (1946, 65–66)
listed the Tanaquiapemes as one of the Indian groups living on the south
bank of the Rio Grande, apparently not far from the coast, and he made
brief general notes about cultural traits observed in the area. An anonymous, undated document, believed to have been compiled about 1748
(Saldívar 1943, 33–34) placed some of the Tanaquiapemes in the same
area. Then in 1757 López de la Cámara Alta (1946, 116, 1758, map)
placed them in the same area, and he too commented on shared cultural
traits. In 1770 Gómez (1942, 62–64) recorded them living on the north
side of the Rio Grande some sixteen miles east of Reynosa. Later, in 1790,
Cabello (1780a, 37) listed them for the south bank of the Rio Grande. Still
later, in 1792, José Nepomuceno Gallo (1792, 9; Revillagigedo 1792,
28–29) referred to Tanaquiapemes as living at places named La Tijera and
La Amargosa south of modern Matamoros, where they were working for
Spanish ranchers as cowboys and shepherds. Some Tanaquiapemes sur-

vived in the Matamoros area until the early part of the nineteenth century. Registers of the parish church, Nuestra Señora del Refugio de los Esteros, identify three individuals in entries for 1804, 1808, and 1811 (Matamoros Registers MS). The late registers of Mission San José y San Miguel de Aguayo of San Antonio identify three Tanaquiapemes under such names as Tinacape and Taniacapeme (San José Registers MS, entries for 1785). These Tanaquiapemes were evidently recruited from the lower Rio Grande area, as were other groups at Mission San José.

An anonymous, undated document, probably written about 1748, not only recorded Tanaquiapemes for the lower Rio Grande (south bank) but also recorded them for the lower Río San Fernando (Saldívar 1943, 33–34). On the Río San Fernando, the Tanaquiapemes were associated with the Comecrudos of that area, and on the Rio Grande they were also associated with Comecrudos, who apparently were different from the Comecrudos of the lower Rio Grande and seem to have spoken a different language. This situation suggests that the Tanaquiapemes may have been native to an area lying between the two river drainages.

Various documents show that at least some of the Tanaquiapemes entered Mission Cabezón de la Sal shortly after it was established on the lower Río San Fernando in 1749. An inspection report, written in 1752 (Organización de las Misiones 1946, 85), stated that Tanaquiapemes and Comecrudos of the lower Río San Fernando were the last two local groups to congregate at Mission Cabezón de la Sal, but they, along with the other Indians, had abandoned the mission because of a disastrous flood on the Río San Fernando and were out searching for food in the surrounding area. Later Friar José Joaquín García (1766, 132; Villaseñor E. 1967, 1187–1189), who had served at the mission during its first five years, noted that the Tanaquiapemes, who were said to be numerous, had helped dig the mission's irrigation canal. In 1757 Tienda de Cuervo (1929, 360) stated that the Tanaquiapemes were among the Indians who frequently visited the Spanish village of San Fernando, but he did not mention them as among the resident mission Indian groups.

In 1792 some of the Tanaquiapemes, along with other Indian groups of the abandoned Mission Cabezón de la Sal, moved to Mission San Francisco de Helguera at the site of Palmitos, about five miles northeast of present-day Santander Jiménez. A census taken at the time listed sixty Tanaquiapemes (Barragán 1793a, 39–42, 1793b, 344–345; Sierra Gorda 1794, 356; Serie de Documentos 1783–1800, 30–40). The Tanaquiapemes did not remain long at Mission Helguera and returned to the Río San

Fernando area, where probably some of them had remained (Noticias de los Conventos 1790–1814, 1, 3, 5, 68). In 1798 the Conde de Sierra Gorda (1798, 1–5) reported fifty-seven "Queniapemes" (twenty-four men, nineteen women, six boys, and eight girls) living at Santa Teresa, about thirty-five miles northeast of San Fernando and about forty miles south of Matamoros. At the time he recorded a few cultural details. Some Tanaquiapemes continued to be reported in the San Fernando area until 1814 (Noticias de los Conventos 1790–1814, 13, 219, 221, 237, 239).

The information recorded for the Tanaquiapemes poses questions that are difficult to answer. Analysis of the numerous name variants seems to show that all variants refer to the same population, but certain documents indicate that the Tanaquiapemes were divided into two groups: one associated with the Rio Grande; the other, with the Río San Fernando. Some observers saw the two groups in both areas during the same year. Presumably the two groups originally lived together in a single area, but this must have been at some time prior to 1732, when some of them were recorded on the Nuevo León frontier. The name Tanaquiapemes contains a suffix, *apem,* as do ten additional group names recorded for the lower Rio Grande area, and this suffix appears to be from the langauge spoken by Comecrudos of the lower Rio Grande recorded by Gatschet in 1886 (Swanton 1940, 63). The three words recorded in 1738 by Ladrón de Guevara (1738, 64) for the Tanaquiapemes and their associates can be equated with Rio Grande Comecrudo words recorded by Gatschet. These words are: *payauyape* (horse), *atanaguay* (sea), and *zepin* (salt). Although the evidence is by no means satisfactory, it would appear that all the Tanaquiapemes originally lived south of the Rio Grande and spoke the Rio Grande Comecrudo language. How far south of the Rio Grande toward the Río San Fernando their area may have extended remains speculative.

Apparently the Tanaquiapemes never entered the missions at Reynosa and Camargo as supposed by Bolton (in Hodge 1971, 2:729). He also erroneously suggested that the Tanaquiapemes were the same as the Saulapaguemes. Some modern maps mistakenly present variations of this group name (Tanniaquiapen, Tanaquiapem, and Queniacapem) as different groups in different locations (Saldívar 1943, map; Jiménez Moreno 1943, map; Eguilaz de Prado 1965, 55, 57, 73, map 2).

Tejones

The word *tejón* is Spanish for the animal known as badger, but in Mexico it was applied to the raccoon (*Procyon lotor*). After 1750 the name Tejones was used in referring to certain Indians living along both sides of the lower Rio Grande, particularly at and near the Spanish settlements of Camargo and Reynosa. No native name for these Indians has yet been identified. As far as is now known, the Tejones always lived in this area; they were never recorded as living anywhere else.

The Tejones were first recorded under that name in 1750 when Escandón (1751, 48–49) visited the new settlement of Reynosa. Escandón noted that these Indians were living along both sides of the Rio Grande west of Reynosa (present Reynosa Díaz). At that time some of the Tejones were sharing an encampment with Zacatiles Indians, and this encampment had a population of sixty individuals (twenty-four men, thirty-six women and children). Escandón further stated that the two groups were native to that area, but it is now known that the Zacatiles were migrants from eastern Nuevo León. Although Escandón also visited Camargo, some twenty-three miles farther up the Rio Grande, he mentioned no Tejones being seen there.

Two years later, in 1752, Tejones were recorded as one of seven Indian groups living in the vicinity of Camargo, their combined population being given as 359. The leader of the Tejones was identified as a Capitán Juan de Dios (Organización de las Misiones 1946, 87–88). In 1753 they were listed as one of four Indian groups seen at Reynosa; their combined population was estimated to be about 200 (Ladrón de Guevara 1753c, 325).

An official inspection of Spanish settlements in 1757 reported the presence of Tejones at both Reynosa and Camargo (Tienda de Cuervo 1929, 373, 376, 381, 396–398, 402, 1930, 108, 302; López de la Cámara Alta 1946, 116). At Mission San Joaquín del Monte of Reynosa, the Tejones numbered some thirty-four to thirty-seven (seventeen men, seven or eight women, and ten or twelve children) and then were said to be living on mission land at a locality known as El Desierto. They were led by a Tejón man identified as Capitán Antonio Francisco. The number of women was said to be low because more women than men had previously died in an epidemic of measles. At Mission San Agustín de Laredo of Camargo, the Tejones numbered thirty-three (fifteen men, eighteen women and children).

Gómez visited Camargo and Reynosa in 1770. At Mission San Agustín de Laredo of Camargo, he reported the Tejones as one of five Indian groups with a combined population of 246, and at Mission San Joaquín del Monte of Reynosa, he also reported the Tejones as one of three groups with a total population of 122 (Gómez 1942, 56, 61). Two years later, in

1772, the Indian population at the Camargo mission had increased slightly to 259, and that of the mission at Reynosa had increased to 249. The latter would indicate not a natural increase but entry of additional Indians (Estado de las Misiones 1946, 68–69).

In 1780 Cabello (1780a, 36–37) said that three groups, including the Tejones, were still represented at Mission San Joaquín del Monte of Reynosa, and in the same document he listed the Tejones as one of eight Indian groups then living near the coast south of the Rio Grande. In 1785 Juan Antonio Ballí (Ballí and Hinojosa 1785, 1–3) referred to the same three groups at Mission San Joaquín, whose total Indian population was given as 258, showing some growth since 1772.

Miscellaneous documents indicate the continued presence of Tejones at Mission San Joaquín between 1788 and 1800 (Vidal de Lorca 1788, 33; Noticias de los Conventos 1790–1814, 1, 3, 5, 135–136, 152). In 1793 Barragán (1793a, 39–42) reported the Tejones as one of thirteen Indian groups then roaming the neighborhood of Reynosa, and some of these at times visited Mission San Joaquín. Bolton (1965, 449–451), who examined the registers of the missions at Reynosa (1790–1816) and Camargo (1764–1810), noted the presence of Tejón individuals at both. Because of extensive flooding of the Rio Grande, Reynosa was moved in 1802 to its present location from its original location at Old Reynosa, or Reynosa Díaz; and the Indians living at the original site were left without a missionary or a Spanish protector. It is said that these Indians visited churches at both Reynosa localities, and in 1814 they were said to have continued living at the original site of Reynosa (Noticias de los Conventos 1790–1814, 221; Ballí 1809, 1–5).

In 1886, when Gatschet was recording Indian languages at Las Prietas, near present Reynosa Díaz, his Indian informants knew of the Tejones but said that none were still living (Swanton 1940, 64, 85, 87, 93, 96). These informants claimed that the Tejones had spoken the same language as that spoken by Comecrudos and Pintos. This is all that was ever recorded about the Tejón language, and it suggests that they spoke a dialect of the Comecrudo language recorded by Gatschet in 1886. Bolton (in Hodge 1971, 2:724–725), who was at Las Prietas in 1907, stated that a few Tejones were still living there. This contradicts what Gatschet's informants had said in 1886, some twenty years earlier. At any rate, it is clear enough that the Tejones lost their ethnic identity either late in the nineteenth century or early in the twentieth century.

Conclusions

Despite the confusion in ethnic names and the limited amount of information recorded for some groups, it seems fairly clear that, during the greater part of the historic period, the Rio Grande delta was occupied by a large number of separately named Indian groups. All of these groups subsisted on the relatively abundant food resources of the delta area. At least forty-nine groups can be linked with the Rio Grande delta, and there may have been others whose names were never recorded. Prior to 1747 refugee groups displaced by Spanish colonists from other areas, particularly northeastern Nuevo León and northwestern Tamaulipas, do not seem to have entered the delta area. Thus most of the Indian groups recorded in the years 1747 and 1757 were probably native to the delta. Although earlier documents, going back as early as 1519, did not record the names of delta Indian groups, they do indicate the presence of numerous groups, noting that some forty Indian encampments were distributed along both banks of the Rio Grande.

Analysis of documents shows that, after 1747, there was an increase in the number of Spanish names for Indian groups, and a corresponding decrease in the number of native names. In 1747, of thirty-one groups recorded in one set of documents, all but one (Comecrudos) had names of native origin. In 1757, of thirteen names recorded, four had Spanish names. By the close of the eighteenth century, of fifteen groups still represented in the delta area, nine had Spanish names. These figures seem to indicate that, as Indian populations declined in size, two or more groups often shared encampments or lived near each other in the same locality, and Spanish colonists simplified the identity problem by applying descriptive Spanish names to sets of associated Indian groups. Failure to recognize the overlaps in native and Spanish names has led to considerable confusion among ethnohistorians. This is further complicated by the fact that some Spanish names applied to Indians of the delta area were also applied to unrelated groups in other areas. Unfortunately, the documentary record does not yield enough information to permit recognition of synonymous native and Spanish names.

It is difficult to identify the small refugee groups that, after 1747, moved down the Rio Grande to live in the delta area or near its margins. Most of those that can be identified are known to have lived originally in northeastern Nuevo León, from which they had been displaced by the expanding colonial frontier. Few migrants seem to have actually moved into the delta area to live for any length of time, probably because they arrived during the period when Spanish ranches were being established.

When Indian groups native to the delta area began to enter Spanish missions, most of them went to the nearest missions, particularly San Joaquín del Monte of Reynosa. Fewer went to missions farther up the Rio Grande. Some were recruited by missionaries from more distant missions, particularly those at San Antonio. The last surviving delta Indians were recorded in 1886 as living in the vicinity of Reynosa Díaz.

CHAPTER 5

Coastal Areas North and South of the Rio Grande Delta

THE NAMES of few Indian groups were ever recorded for extensive areas both north and south of the Rio Grande delta. As noted in chapter 2, these areas lacked perennial streams and, to hunting and gathering populations accustomed to the abundant water and food resources of the delta, these lands must have been regarded as marginal. The lack of natural harbors prevented these areas from being approached by European ships, and until José de Escandón established Spanish towns along the lower Rio Grande in 1747, there was little land travel across these areas. Northward from the delta, there were no recorded concentrations of Indian groups except in the area near Baffin and Corpus Christi bays; and southward from the delta, the only concentration was found along the lower Río San Fernando. These concentrations, both north and south of the delta, were not comparable to that of the Rio Grande delta. These contrasts in population density undoubtedly reflect the attractiveness of the delta environment.

North of the Delta

The area lying between the Rio Grande delta and Corpus Christi Bay was distant from all Spanish administrative centers of northeastern Mexico and Texas, and there was little travel across any part of it. In 1747 Escandón recommended that a Spanish settlement and a mission be established near present-day Corpus Christi. The settlement was to be named Villa de Vedoya, and the mission, Nuestra Señora del Soto. The mission was to administer to Indians of that area whom Orobio Basterra had identified as Apatin, Ippantapajeis, Nacuap, Pajasequeis or Carrizos, and Zuncal. Neither the Spanish settlement nor the mission was ever established, and no identity has been determined for the Indian groups named by Orobio Basterra. Except for the Apatin (see below), no documents refer to recognizable variants of these names, and it is not now possible to determine if they were actually native to the area or were refugees from another area. The only clue is linkage of the Spanish name Carrizos with the native name Pajasequeis, which suggests a connection with the various groups called Carrizos living along the Rio Grande upstream from Camargo (Escandón 1946, 68–71, 95; Bolton 1970, 293).

Diego Ortíz Parrilla (1767, 1–36; Cartografía de Ultramar 1953, map 112) crossed southern Texas in 1766, traveling from Presidio San Juan Bautista of northeastern Coahuila to a point just south of Corpus Christi Bay. On a map that was drawn for him are found the names of six Indian groups. According to his diary, a party of soldiers traveled southward along present Padre Island to a locality southeast of Baffin Bay, and the six Indian groups seem to be referable to this section of the south Texas coast. The names include Maquites or Malaguitas, Manos de Perro, Pasnacas (Pasnacanes), Patun, Piguisas or Piguicanes (Piguiques), and Pimaraqui. The Malaguitas named are evidently the Malaguitas first recorded in northern Nuevo León who later migrated eastward to the Texas coast. The five remaining groups seem to have been native to the area. Three of them—Manos de Perro, Pasnacanes, and Piguiques—are known from other documents pertaining to the area (Campbell in Branda 1976, 3:570, 707, 733–734; Campbell and Campbell 1981, 48–49, 54–55). The name Pimaraqui is probably a variant of Pamaques, also known from other documents. The Patun were apparently the Apatin mentioned living in the neighborhood of Corpus Christi Bay in 1747, but no other documents refer to this name. Of these groups only the Malaguitas can be associated with the delta of the Rio Grande. Ortíz Parrilla also referred to Indian groups considered to be of Karankawan affiliation, but these were linked with areas farther north along the Texas coast.

The information presented above seems to indicate that the area lying between Baffin Bay and the Rio Grande delta was sparsely occupied during the middle eighteenth century. Ortíz Parrilla's map, which is somewhat distorted, shows Tompaqueses (Tampacuas) on the mainland near the Gulf coast, somewhere between Baffin Bay and the lower Rio Grande. Their territory apparently did not extend far from the margin of the delta. There is no indication that any of the Indian groups native to the delta area had moved northward.

South of the Delta

Much more is known about the Indian groups of the area south of the Rio Grande delta than north of it, mainly because Escandón established a Spanish town and a mission on the lower Río San Fernando. But the area lying between the delta and the lower Río San Fernando was evidently not frequented by Indian groups. Only the Tanaquiapemes can be associated with this area, and this appears to be explained by the fact that Tanaquiapemes were associated with both the Rio Grande delta and the lower Río San Fernando.

Of special interest for this area are early European observations made about the northern extent of agriculture during the sixteenth century. Francisco Garay and four hundred men traveled by land southward from the Rio Grande delta in 1523 and arrived at the Río San Fernando near its mouth. Between the two rivers, the terrain, as described in documents, agrees well with the terrain as known today. No Indians were seen on the Río San Fernando, but a short distance to the south, less than twenty miles, the Spaniards came to a village where agriculture was practiced. The Indians had deserted the village before the Spaniards arrived, and Garay and his men helped themselves to stored corn, guava (*guayava*) fruit, and some sort of hens (*gallinas*). Farther south, before arriving at the Río Soto la Marina, two similar villages were also seen (Mártir de Anglería 1944, 570–573; Díaz del Castillo 1955, 1:106; Herrera 1945, 4:265; López de Gómara 1954, 2:282).

This recorded information seems to indicate that, in 1523, the northern limit of Mesoamerican agriculture on the Gulf coast was some sixty or seventy miles farther north than it was thereafter reported. Escandón and other Spaniards who visited the lower Río San Fernando in 1747, and later, said nothing about native agriculture in the area. At present it is not possible to determine whether marginal agricultural populations were replaced by hunters and gatherers, or whether they gave up agriculture, possibly for environmental reasons, and themselves became hunters and gatherers.

The Cacolotes and Comecrudos are discussed in chapter 4.

Pamoranos

The Pamoranos were first recorded in the Cerralvo area of Nuevo León early in the eighteenth century. Later they joined other displaced Indian groups in eastern Nuevo León and eventually became associated with that section of the Río San Fernando that lies within what is now Tamaulipas. The first recorded Pamoranos may have been an amalgamation of remnant groups displaced from the Cerralvo area in the second half of the seventeenth century. Juan Bautista Chapa (León, Chapa, and Sánchez de Zamora 1961, 190) listed the native names of some seventy Indian groups known to Spaniards in the Cerralvo area prior to 1700, but no name on his list resembles the name Pamoranos. In Tamaulipas the Pamoranos were clearly associated with the Sierra de Pamoranes, an isolated mountain mass just northeast of Méndez, and the Pamoranos were last recorded near a Spanish mission on the lower Río San Fernando.

In 1715 Francisco de Barbadillo y Victoria (1715, 65) wrote that the Pamoranos lived somewhere to the north of Cerralvo, and he briefly described an episode in which the Pamoranos had killed three shepherds near the presidio at Cerralvo. Soldiers from the presidio pursued some of the Pamoranos and killed three or four. The remaining Pamoranos fled to the rugged mountainous area nearby, probably the present Sierras de Picachos and Papagayos west and southwest of Cerralvo. The presidial commander tried to persuade the Pamoranos to submit peacefully to Spanish control. Envoys from the Pamoranos seem to have ambushed some Spanish soldiers. Further details were not clearly recorded (see also Hoyo 1963, 16). Later some of the Pamoranos entered Mission San Cristóbal de Hualahuises, but probably did not remain there very long (Copia de las Actas 1753, 14–21).

Maps drawn by Francisco Alvarez Barreiro, an engineer who accompanied the frontier presidial inspection party of Pedro Rivera y Villalón in 1724–1728, placed the Pamoranos north of the modern Río San Fernando in an area that includes the Sierra de Pamoranes, but these mountains are not shown on the map (Alvarez Barreiro 1729, map; Wheat 1957, 82–84, map 115c).

During the decade of 1730–1740, Spanish settlements were frequently attacked by numerous remnants of displaced Indian groups living in eastern Nuevo León. The Pamoranos were involved in these attacks, and for a time the various Indian groups were led by a Pamorano known to Spaniards as Capitán Pedro Botello, who claimed to have been the leader of twenty-six Indian groups, ten of which are identified in one document. Botello responded to overtures by missionaries to negotiate peace, but nothing permanent developed (Lozada 1732, 84–102; Fernández de Jáuregui Urrutia 1963, 16–22, 106–108; see also Troike 1961, 30, 1962,

59). Attacks on frontier settlements continued until 1741, when a treaty of peace was finally negotiated with the provincial government of Nuevo León. The leaders of the various Indian groups were granted amnesty and allowed to return to their respective areas (Fundación de Presidios 1741, 20–22; 25–26).

In 1747 Escandón (1946, 58, 93; Vedoia 1749, 153) mentioned Pamoranos as living with Pintos, Quedejeños, and Quinicuanes west of the Salinas de la Barra on the banks of the lower Río San Fernando. The combined population of these groups was given as 150 families, led by Marcos Villanueva, a Christianized Pinto Indian who was married to a Tlaxcaltecan woman of Hualahuises. These Indians asked that a mission be established for them as soon as Spanish settlers occupied the area. Their petition for a mission seems to have been prompted mainly by a desire for protection from their enemies, the Bocas Prietas.

A document believed to have been written in 1748 (Saldívar 1943, 32–33) refers to movements of the Pamoranos, along with other Indian groups, such as Pintos and Quinicuanes. The Pamoranos were living some twenty-one to twenty-six miles from Las Presas (present San Fernando). From this locality they are said to have ranged as far westward as the upper tributaries of the Río San Juan. Together with the Quinicuanes, they sometimes visited Linares during the harvest season. Some twenty families of Pintos and Pamoranos were seen near Las Presas, these groups being led by their respective leaders Gerónimo (de Villarreal) and Salvador.

In 1749, when Escandón's colonization party traveled up the north side of the Río San Fernando in search of a westward route leading to the Río San Juan, the Spaniards were for a time guided by Pamorano Indians. These Indians guided the Spaniards upstream as far as some rainwater ponds named San Macario, but declined to travel any farther westward (Yerro 1749, 281).

Three years later, in 1751, Escandón (1751, 51, 58, 104; Valcarcel 1756, 102) recorded the presence of 108 (thirty-two families) Pamoranos and Quinicuanes at Mission Cabezón de la Sal of present-day San Fernando. Both groups were led by a Quinicuan known as Capitán Isidro.

The next year, 1752, Friar Silva (Organización de las Misiones 1946, 85) observed some of the Pamoranos at the site of Mission Cabezón de la Sal, which had recently been destroyed by a flood. At that time the Pamoranos and other Indians of the mission were out searching for food. A later account by Friar José Joaquín García (1766, 131, 156; Villaseñor E. 1967, 1187, 1202), who had served five years at Mission Cabezón de la Sal, referred to Pamoranos as being among the resident Indian groups. One Indian, probably a Pamoranos, is reported to have expressed his resentment of Spanish attempts to take their lands, their women, and their children.

The Pamoranos ceased to be recorded in Spanish documents after 1757. In that year José Tienda de Cuervo (1929, 360, 362, 1930, 102) referred to Pamoranos as one of the Indian groups that sometimes visited the Spanish settlement of San Fernando. He noted that the Pamoranos occasionally encamped with Pintos at a new mission site about a quarter of a league from San Fernando. These Indians remained at the mission only as long as food was available there. Their population was recorded as mixed with other groups of these missions, such as Pintos and Quinicuanes. Evidently very few Pamoranos were present. Later Spanish documents do not refer to actual encounters with Pamorano Indians. It appears likely that their diminished population was absorbed by remnants of other Indian groups along the lower Río San Fernando.

No evidence has been found that corroborates Manuel Orozco y Berra's statement that the Pamoranos once lived in Texas north of Laredo (Orozco y Berra 1864, 299; Hodge 1971, 2:197). He seems to have misinterpreted Barbadillo y Victoria's reference to the Pamoranos as living north of Cerralvo. Laredo is about one hundred miles north of Cerralvo, and north of Laredo there are no sierras in which the Pamoranos could have taken refuge after being attacked by the presidial soldiers of Cerralvo.

The language spoken by the Pamoranos remains unknown, and what little is known about their culture occurs in references that include other Indian groups. The name Pamoranos survives today in the place name Sierra de Pamoranes, and also as the name of a ranch in the municipality of General Bravo, Nuevo León. In the Sierra de Pamoranes area, there is a species of ants called *pamoranas*. It is not known which name came first, that for the Indian group or that for the mountains.

The Pintos are discussed in chapter 4.

Quedejeños

Just where the Quedejeños originally lived is uncertain, but it was probably somewhere in the drainage of the Río San Fernando. According to Eugenio del Hoyo (1960, 502, 504, 509), *quedejeños* is a Quinigua word meaning prickly pear. This does not necessarily mean that the Quedejeños spoke a dialect of the Quinigua language (no words from the language spoken by Quedejeños were ever recorded). As the Quinigua language appears to have been spoken in the Monterrey-Cadereyta-Cerralvo area of Nuevo León, Quedejeños could be a Quinigua name applied to a more easterly Indian group that did not speak Quinigua. This suggests that perhaps the Quedejeños originally lived on upper tributaries of the Río San Fernando in eastern Nuevo León. It is of interest to note that no names resembling Quedejeños are found in Juan Bautista Chapa's lengthy lists of Nuevo León Indians known to Spaniards in the seventeenth century (León, Chapa, and Sánchez de Zamora 1961, 190–191).

The Quedejeños first became known during the period 1715–1723 as one of the Indian groups recorded at Mission San Cristóbal de los Hualahuises near Linares (Copia de las Actas 1753, 14–21). It is doubtful that there were very many Quedejeños at this mission or that they remained there very long. In 1732 Quedejeños were identified as one of numerous remnant Indian groups who attacked Spanish settlements in Nuevo León. These groups were said to be based somewhere between Linares and the Gulf coast, probably near the Río San Fernando (Lozada 1732, 85). At that time the leader of these Indians, a Pamorano chief known as Pedro Botello, negotiated a temporary peace with the provincial government of Nuevo León through a missionary at Linares. A more lasting peace was negotiated in 1741 (Fundación de Presidios 1741, 20–22), when the Quedejeños were led by a Pinto Indian known as Marcos Villanueva.

In 1747 Escandón (1946, 58, 93) found the Quedejeños to be living just west of Salinas de la Barra, along both sides of the Río San Fernando near the Gulf coast. There they were closely associated with Pamoranos, Pintos, and Quinicuanes. These four groups, claiming that they needed protection from the Bocas Prietas Indians, asked that a Spanish mission be established near them. An anonymous document, apparently written shortly after 1747 (Saldívar 1943, 33), stated that sixty families of Quedejeños and Quinicuanes were living at Las Presas, a place near the modern town of San Fernando.

In 1750 Escandón (1751, 104; Valcarcel 1756, 102) revisited the lower Río San Fernando area and recorded fifty-six Quedejeños (twenty-one families) living at the mission, which had become known as Cabezón de la Sal. Shortly thereafter the Quedejeños left the mission because a flood had damaged mission farmlands (Organización de las Misiones 1946, 85, 91; García 1766, 131; Villaseñor E. 1967, 1187).

The Quedejeños seem to have been in and out of Mission Cabezón de la Sal during the next few years, but their main encampment sites were farther

down the Río San Fernando near the coast, where they supported themselves by fishing, hunting, and gathering plant foods. In 1757, when the
area was visited by López de la Cámara Alta (1946, 112) and José Tienda
de Cuervo (1929, 349–351, 360, 1930, 102–103), the Quedejeños population was said to consist of seventy-three individuals (twenty-three men,
fifty women and children). Agustín López de la Cámara Alta's map (1758)
placed the Quedejeños north of the Río San Fernando and also east of
Arroyo Chorreras.

  After 1757 the Quedejeños continued to be reported along the lower
Río San Fernando. At some unspecified time prior to 1773, a number of
Quedejeños had gone southward to live for a time at Mission Purísima
Concepción de Infiesto of Soto la Marina, but these were eventually sent
back to the Río San Fernando (Sierra Gorda 1773, 1–15; Gómez 1942,
63; Estado de las Misiones 1946, 68). Various sources indicate that the
Quedejeños continued to live at or near modern San Fernando between
1788 and 1793 (Vidal de Lorca 1788, table; Noticias de los Conventos
1790–1814, 1, 3, 5). Together with other Indians of Mission Cabezón de
la Sal, the Quedejeños had been seen several times at Cruillas and Burgos.
They had tried to settle at the latter (Serie de Documentos 1783–1800,
30–40; Barragán 1793a, 39–42). For a short time (1792–1794), the
Quedejeños, along with other Indian groups of the Río San Fernando,
lived at Mission San Francisco de Helguera at Palmitos, near modern Santander Jiménez. At that time the Quedejeños seem to have consisted of
only fifteen families (Barragán 1793a, 39–42, 1793b, 344–345; Sierra
Gorda 1794, 357).

  Evidently all surviving Quedejeños ended up near modern San Fernando. Various mission reports place them there between 1808 and 1818
(Noticias de los Conventos 1790–1814, 13, 219, 221, 237, 239; Bedoya
1816, table; Numana 1817, table; Antillán 1818, table). Apparently the
Quedejeños were absorbed by the Spanish-speaking population of the
lower Río San Fernando area. Thus, throughout most of their history,
the Quedejeños were associated with the Río San Fernando. In late times
some of them lived temporarily to the south as far as Río Soto la Marina, but
none at any time were reported along the lower Rio Grande to the north.

Quinicuanes

The Quinicuanes are known by this name only in documents in the first
half of the eighteenth century, and they were not recorded after 1757.
Throughout this period they seem to have been linked with some part of
the drainage of the Río San Fernando between the Linares-Hualahuises

area and the mouth of the river. There is no indication that any Quinicuanes ever lived along the lower Rio Grande.

In the later part of the seventeenth century Chapa (León, Chapa, and Sánchez de Zamora 1961, 190–191) compiled the names of numerous Indian groups known to Spaniards of Nuevo León. He linked these with four areas: Monterrey, Cadereyta, Cerralvo, and Nuevo León in general. A few of these names bear some resemblance to the name Quinicuanes, such as Quiniguales and Yaquinigua (Cadereyta), Quinegaayos (Cerralvo), and Quiniquijos (Nuevo León in general). As the name Quinicuanes was first recorded after 1700, it is not now possible to equate any of these seventeenth-century names with Quinicuanes. Eugenio del Hoyo (1960, 495–496) and Karl-Heinz Gursky (1964, 325) have indicated that the Quinicuanes spoke the language known as Quinigua, but they failed to cite any supporting documentary evidence. It seems best to withhold judgment on the linguistic affiliation of the Quinicuanes.

The Quinicuanes were first recorded during 1715–1723, when some of them were said to have entered Mission San Cristóbal de Hualahuises just west of Linares (Copia de las Actas 1753, 17). In the 1730s the Quinicuanes were identified as one of numerous remnant Indian populations that attacked Spanish settlements in Nuevo León (Lozada 1732, 85; Fernández de Jáuregui Urrutia 1963, 17–18). In 1740 the Quinicuanes were among the Indian groups who made peace with the government of Nuevo León and who were allowed to return to their respective areas (Fundación de Presidios 1741, 20–22, 25–26).

In 1747, when Escandón (1946, 58, 93) made a reconnaissance of the coast of northern Tamaulipas, he found Quinicuanes as one of four groups living near the coast just west of Salinas de la Barra on the banks of the Río San Fernando. These groups—Pamoranos, Pintos, Quedejeños, and Quinicuanes—had apparently migrated from some part of the Río San Fernando drainage to the west or southwest. They were concerned about attacks from their enemies, the Bocas Prietas, and asked Escandón to establish a mission for them on the lower Río San Fernando.

Shortly after 1747, documents show that Indian groups then living along the lower Río San Fernando, particularly Pamoranos, Quedejeños, and Quinicuanes, frequently went to the Linares area during the harvest season, probably to work for Spaniards, after which they returned to the lower Río San Fernando (Copia de las Actas 1753, 14, 17, 20; Saldívar 1943, 32–33). One source gave the combined population of Quedejeños and Quinicuanes as sixty families.

In 1750 Escandón (1751, 104; Valcarcel 1756, 102) revisited the lower

Río San Fernando, where Mission Cabezón de la Sal had been established. He noted that the combined Quinicuanes and Pamoranos population at the mission consisted of 108 individuals, or thirty-two families.

In 1752 Friar Silva, a missionary, wrote about difficulties at Mission Cabezón de la Sal. This mission had suffered from a disastrous flood, and the Indians had to leave it and support themselves by hunting and gathering in the surrounding area (Organización de las Misiones 1946, 85). The same facts were recorded by another missionary (García 1766, 131; Villaseñor E. 1967, 1187).

When López de la Cámara Alta (1946, 112) visited the lower Río San Fernando in 1757, he listed the combined population of Pintos and Quinicuanes as 173. Tienda de Cuervo (1929, 347–348, 351, 360, 1930, 102), who accompanied López de la Cámara Alta, gave additional information on population size. He stated that the eighty-four Quinicuanes (twenty-one to twenty-seven of these referred to as men) were actually congregated at Mission Cabezón de la Sal. He commented on the relatively large number of women and said that an epidemic had killed fifty-four Quinicuanes (a figure he compiled from the mission registers). These population figures suggest that disease was an important factor in the decline of the Quinicuanes population. After 1757 the name Quinicuanes disappeared from the historical record. It seems reasonable to conclude that later in the eighteenth century they declined further in numbers and were probably absorbed by other groups larger in size.

The Tanaquiapemes are discussed in chapter 4.

Conclusions

The areas immediately to the north and south of the Rio Grande delta appear to have been sparsely occupied throughout the historic period. The only notable concentrations of Indian groups were distant from the delta: near Baffin and Corpus Christi bays to the north (eleven groups) and along the lower Río San Fernando to the south (seven groups).

Except for the Malaguitas, the Indian groups recorded for Baffin and Corpus Christi bays seem to have been native to that area. The Malaguitas had migrated from northern Nuevo León eastward to the coast during the second half of the eighteenth century. On the lower Río San Fernando, the Pintos, Quedejeños, and Quinicuanes were probably native to the area surrounding the Spanish village of San Fernando. The Comecrudos and Tanaquiapemes lived closer to the Gulf coast. The Pamoranos and Cacalotes of the lower Río San Fernando were migrants from Nuevo León. The Tanaquiapemes are of special interest because they were recorded as living in the delta area and also along the lower Río San Fernando. It appears likely that they were a coastal people who ranged the shoreline between the Rio Grande and the Río San Fernando.

CHAPTER 6

Northeastern Nuevo León

THIS CHAPTER is concerned with certain Indian groups who were displaced by Spanish colonists in Nuevo León (see chap. 3). Remnants of these groups later migrated eastward to the Gulf coast or northeastward to the lower Rio Grande. All originally lived in northeastern Nuevo León, or that part of Nuevo León lying northeast of the Sierra Madre Oriental. As many of these groups were at some time either associated with the Rio Grande delta or were associated with delta Indians in Spanish missions along the lower Rio Grande, their recorded histories must be reviewed in order to clarify what has long been a very confused situation. Most of these Indian groups are known only by Spanish names, and several names, such as Borrados, Pelones, and Pintos, were so indiscriminately used by Spaniards that it is now impossible to sort out their connotations in successively dated documents. The summaries presented of what is known about specific groups is preceded by interpretive statements about the route followed by Cabeza de Vaca in 1535 while traversing what is now northeastern Nuevo León. Although Cabeza de Vaca recorded no names for Indian groups that he visited in Nuevo León, his description of terrain, his comment on distances between Indian encampments, and his statements about Indian behavior seem to indicate an area between the Río San Juan and the mountains now known as Sierra de Picachos and Sierra Papagayos.

Early Spanish Contact: Cabeza de Vaca in Northeastern Mexico, 1535

Numerous scholars have attempted to trace the route used by Alvar Núñez Cabeza de Vaca in crossing the southern part of North America on foot during the years 1529–1536. Most of these have not interpreted the documentary evidence as indicating that Cabeza de Vaca traversed any part of northeastern Mexico. But others, better informed about northeastern Mexico and its former Indian populations, have argued that Cabeza de Vaca traveled from the great bend of the Gulf coast in Texas more or less southwestward to cross the Rio Grande somewhere between its mouth and the upper end of Falcon Reservoir. In the seventeenth century, Alonso de León (León, Chapa, and Sánchez de Zamora 1961, 15) had already speculated that Cabeza de Vaca and his companions had passed just north of present Cerralvo in order to get where they later arrived. Among the modern proponents of a route across northeastern Mexico are Bethel Coopwood (1899–1900), Harbert Davenport and Joseph K. Wells (1918–1919), Alex D. Krieger (1955, 1961), and Leroy Johnson, Jr. (1983). They are not in agreement about Cabeza de Vaca's route of travel from his crossing of the Rio Grande to the point where he ceased traveling in a southerly direction and turned westward into Coahuila. Their interpretations of the route are based mainly on scattered statements made in the documents about terrain features, distances between Indian encampments, and alterations in the direction of travel. The distribution of Indian encampments visited by Cabeza de Vaca and the environmental implications of this distribution were not considered.

The four interpretations of Cabeza de Vaca's route identified above may be briefly summarized as follows:

Coopwood: Rio Grande crossed near its junction with the Rio Salado (near Zapata, Texas); travel was southeastward to a point near the Sierra de Pamoranes.

Davenport and Wells: Rio Grande crossed near Reynosa Díaz; travel was southwestward to cross the Río San Juan near China, Nuevo León, and reach a point near Cerralvo.

Krieger: Rio Grande crossed near its junction with the Río Alamos, not far from Mier; travel was southward to the Río San Juan, which was followed upstream, presumably along its western bank, to a point south of the Sierra Papagayos.

Johnson: Rio Grande crossed near Reynosa; travel was southwestward to a point near the Sierra de San Carlos.

Of these four interpretations, only that of Krieger has Cabeza de Vaca traveling west of the Río San Juan. The others have Cabeza de Vaca traveling in various directions across a large area east of the Río San Juan that, as noted in chapter 2, is notable for its complete lack of perennial streams. This area, which consists of over four thousand square miles, extends from the Rio Grande valley southward to the Sierra de Pamoranes, and it extends eastward from the Río San Juan almost to the Gulf coast. In documents written after Cabeza de Vaca's time, this area was avoided by Spanish travelers, and no documents identify Indian groups with it except along its margins. In 1749 during the colonization march between the Río San Fernando and the Rio Grande, Escandón's party avoided this area, traveling inland along the Río San Fernando (Conchas) and one of its tributaries (Arroyo San Lorenzo). Then they turned northwestward, passing along a series of rain-water ponds to reach the Río San Juan, which was followed downstream to its juncture with the Rio Grande, a route which later became the road between the villages of Camargo and San Fernando. Friar Simón del Hierro (Yerro 1749, 281–284), who wrote the journal of this expedition, said that only salt lakes and rain-water ponds existed in the coastal territory both south and north of the lower Rio Grande. López de la Cámara Alta (1758, map) showed the road used by Escandón and also showed a more direct route between San Fernando and Reynosa Díaz. The latter may have been used as an alternative route during periods of greater rainfall, since only four widely separated rain-water ponds were shown on the map. Even today the greater part of this area is marked by a low population density.

According to the primary documents, Cabeza de Vaca crossed the Rio Grande and visited in succession five Indian encampments as he traveled southward before turning to the west. No names were recorded for these Indians. For three of the encampments, Cabeza de Vaca estimated the number of houses seen, the number ranging from forty to one hundred. The largest encampment must have contained several hundred individuals. The encampments visited by Cabeza de Vaca were inhabited by Indians who lived by hunting and gathering, and these temporary settlements were distributed along a line of travel at least eighty miles in length. The area occupied must have had sufficient water and food resources to support its population. When these points are considered, it appears doubtful that Cabeza de Vaca's route traversed any part of northeastern Mexico lying between the Río San Juan and the Gulf coast.

Although Cabeza de Vaca does not seem to have crossed the Río Pesquería, Krieger's interpretation of the route is the most realistic of the four here reviewed. He has Cabeza de Vaca passing southward between the Río San Juan and two ranges of mountains to the west, the Sierra de Picachos and the Sierra Papagayos. It is in this area that the early Spanish colony of Cerralvo was established, and in the latter part of the seventeenth century, Juan Bautista Chapa recorded the names of seventy Indian groups associ-

ated with the Cerralvo area. In a generalized way, Alonso de León described the culture of these and neighboring groups, and some of his statements are similar to those made by Cabeza de Vaca. It seems likely that
the Indians of the five encampments visited by Cabeza de Vaca were an-
cestral to some of the Indian groups later named by Chapa. The interpretations of Coopwood, Davenport and Wells, and Johnson are not acceptable
because they are based on the assumption that all parts of northeastern
Mexico offered essentially the same amounts of water and food resources
and that its hunting and gathering Indian populations were more or less
evenly distributed.

Named Indian Groups

Aguatinejos

It is clear that the Aguatinejos were one of the Indian groups of Nuevo
León known to early Spaniards as Pelones, which without much question
indicates that their customary hair dress involved removal of considerable
head hair. As early as 1716–1717, some of the Aguatinejos entered Mission Nuestra Señora de Purificación in the Pilón valley of the upper Río
San Juan (vicinity of modern Montemorelos). In 1730 they were said to be
one of eight Indian groups, led by Capitán Francisco de la Garza of the
Tortugas (also known as Pelones), who made peace with the governor of
Nuevo León and were afterward settled at various localities in eastern
Nuevo León (Garza 1750, 218–219 or 222–230; Velasco 1715–1753,
301–303, 310).

By 1735 Aguatinejos were listed as one of numerous Indian groups
who attacked Spanish settlements in areas near such places now known as
Montemorelos, General Terán, Cadereyta, and Cerralvo (Fernández de
Jáuregui Urrutia 1963, 12–23). In 1741 at Monterrey, the Aguatinejo
leader, Domingo Juan de León, received amnesty for his people (Fundación de Presidios 1741, 15–16). An anonymous document, probably written about 1748, mentioned that twenty families of Aguatinejos were living
somewhere in the Pilón valley (Saldívar 1943, 32).

It is known that a number of Pelones Indians (Aguatinejos, Cacalotes,
and Tortugas) accompanied José de Escandón during his exploration and
colonization of the Gulf coast in 1747 and 1749. It was this contact with
Escandón that led the three Pelones populations to move northward to the
Rio Grande in 1750 and settle at the short-lived Spanish mission, Divina
Pastora de Santillana, established at present Camargo. In 1751, however,
the mission and its Indians moved southward to the Pilón valley (Velasco

1715–1753, 285–338; Escandón 1749a, 195–199, 1749b, 441; Bueno de la Borbolla 1749, 206–210).

The last mention of the Aguatinejos was in a document of 1774, which indicates that at least some of the Aguatinejos were living close to the Sierra de Picachos near Cerralvo (Barragán 1774, 1–3). These could have been Aguatinejos who had chosen to live near the Rio Grande after Mission Divina Pastora de Santillana had been moved to the upper Río San Juan. It is possible that these Aguatinejos may later have merged their identity with surviving Indian groups of the Cerralvo area known by various Spanish names. It is, of course, also possible that the Aguatinejos were originally native to the Cerralvo area.

Blancos

The Blancos (Spanish for "whites") are known only from a few documents of the seventeenth century. In 1646 Mission Santa Teresa de Alamillo was established for three Indian groups—Axipayas, Blancos, and Mimioles—near present Agualeguas, Nuevo León. Agualeguas is about seventeen miles north of Cerralvo and approximately the same distance east of the Sierra de Picachos (Hoyo 1972, 2:410). These three groups probably ranged over parts of an area lying between the Sierra de Picachos and the Río San Juan to the east. Blancos were again recorded in 1686 in connection with Spanish concern about La Salle's French fort on the Gulf coast. A Pelón Indian, who had visited the Blancos and Pajaritos, learned that Europeans similar to Spaniards had been seen somewhere to the north, and this information was passed on to Spanish authorities in Nuevo León (Paredes 1686, 77–82; Weddle 1973, 57–58).

This is all that is definitely known about the Blancos. It is possible, however, that these Blancos were the same people seen in 1535 by Cabeza de Vaca (1542, 48a–48b; Oviedo y Valdés 1959, 4:306–307) when he was traversing an area east of the Sierra de Picachos. He said that these people were lighter in skin color than any Indians he had previously seen. He also said that more than half of them had a clouded eye (*eran tuertos de nubes*), and others were completely blind (*son ciegos*). According to Claud A. Bramblett, professor of physical anthropology at the University of Texas at Austin (personal communication), this description strongly suggests a high incidence of albinism, or absence of normal pigment in skin, hair, and eyes. If albinos do not have devices for reducing the amount of sunlight that enters the eyes, they lose much of their vision or become blind.

Borrados

Spaniards of what is now northeastern Mexico and southern Texas applied the Spanish name Borrados to numerous, widely distributed Indian groups during a period of some two hundred years. It can be assumed that all Indians referred to as Borrados had one thing in common, the practice of tattooing, since this was the reason why they were so named. It cannot, however, be assumed that all Indians sharing the name Borrados also shared the same tattoo patterns. If one considers the wide distribution of Indian groups called Borrados, and also keeps in mind the time span of two hundred years, it appears naive to assume that all Indians known as Borrados were closely related linguistically and culturally.

In any particular area for which Borrados were recorded, the native names of various Indian groups were also recorded. Spanish documents occasionally indicate that a specific Indian group with a native name was classified as Borrados, but there are not enough of these equations to permit assemblage, for any particular area, of all the Indian groups with native names who were also called Borrados by Spaniards. A satisfying treatment of the Borrados identity question is not at present achievable.

After 1600, and continuing as late as 1800, the name Borrados was applied to various apparently unrelated Indian groups in at least three areas: the Monterrey-Cadereyta-Cerralvo area of Nuevo León, the Sierra de San Carlos area of central Tamaulipas, and the lower Rio Grande area of northern Tamaulipas and southern Texas. This has led to considerable confusion, and sometimes scholars have assumed that all Indians called Borrados were either related or were actually the same people. No previous attempt has been made to sort out the recorded data on each of the groups called Borrados and thereby clarify the identity problem.

Borrados of Nuevo León.   Spanish documents reveal that the name Borrados was applied by Spaniards to numerous Indian groups living in the general vicinity of Monterrey late in the sixteenth century, when that area was initially colonized. All of these Indians lived by hunting and gathering and had separate native names for themselves, far too many for the colonists to keep track of. Many of these Indian groups, but certainly not all of them, apparently shared one highly visible cultural trait, extensive tattooing, which leaves permanent marks on human skin that is fairly light in color. As tattooing is a word of Polynesian origin, and had not yet passed into European languages, the Spaniards of early Nuevo León referred to these tattooed Indians as Borrados. Borrados is derived from the Spanish verb *borrar,* which in Spain seems initially to have been connected with writing on paper. *Borrar* refers to striking out or crossing out, to rubbing or blotting out, to erasing, and to smearing with ink. Its more abstract connotations include clouding, darkening, and obscuring. Eugenio del Hoyo (1960, 494, 1972, 1:2) has suggested that the early Spaniards of Nuevo León called certain Indians Borrados because tattooing on face and body was so extensive that it seemed to obscure the natural skin color (he also includes painting, but painting is impermanent and therefore not pertinent). This is a plausible hypothesis, but it is difficult to test because the Spanish documents do not contain detailed descriptions of tattoo patterns or clearly indicate the amount or extent of tattooing on the individual Indian.

Nuevo León documents of the seventeenth century occasionally refer to Borrado Indians in the area that extends from Monterrey and Cadereyta northward as far as Cerralvo. These refer mainly to Indian attacks on Spanish settlements and to Indians associated with the haciendas under the *encomienda* system. Analysis of such information as was recorded in Spanish documents shows that some Indians of this area were classified as Borrados and that others were not (for specific details, see Cavazos Garza 1966, passim, 1973, 188; González 1975, 8–18; Hoyo 1963, 8–9, 13, 1972, 149–153, 351–360; León, Chapa, and Sánchez de Zamora 1961, 81–83, 85–88, 165; Pérez-Maldonado 1947, 14–19; Villarreal A. 1969, 75). In these documents a few Indian groups are referred to by a native name and also referred to as Borrados (Alazapas, Camasanes, and Maciguaras); one Borrado leader's name (Suimiguara) may also have been the name of the group that he led; and other group names are recorded in contexts which seem to indicate that the Spaniards did not regard them as Borrados (Guacacameguas and Cacamacaos). These recorded statements suggest that Indians known as Borrados shared the same areas with Indians who differed in language and culture.

It is not necessary to go further into the matter of identifying specific Borrado groups in the Monterrey-Cadereyta-Cerralvo area. Chapa, an early historian of Nuevo León (León, Chapa, and Sánchez de Zamora 1961, 189–191) has listed the names of approximately 250 Indian groups known prior to 1700, and it will probably never be possible to determine how many of these the Spaniards classified as Borrados. These Nuevo León Borrados do not seem to be related to Borrados known elsewhere, especially the Borrados of the lower Rio Grande area.

Borrados of the Sierra de San Carlos.   As early as 1665, Borrados, apparently different from the Borrados of the Monterrey-Cadereyta-Cerralvo area, were reported as living in the area surrounding the Sierra de San Carlos of central Tamaulipas. One document refers to Auguistiguaros as a group from the Sierra de San Carlos known as Borrados, apparently because they were tattooed (Cavazos Garza 1966, entry 354). Alonso de León (León, Chapa, and Sánchez de Zamora 1961, 158) mentioned that he had led several parties out to punish the Borrados of the Sierra de San Carlos. One of these Borrado groups seems to have entered Mission San Cristóbal de Hualahuises, at modern Hualahuises, between the years 1715 and 1723, where they were referred to as Antiguos Borrados (Copia de las Actas 1753, 14, 17, 20; Razón de los Utencilios 1753?, 3).

In 1735 Fernández de Jáuregui Urrutia (1963, 12–23) listed the Borrados of the Sierra de San Carlos among the groups who had attacked settlements of Nuevo León during the previous twenty years. They had attacked Galeana, Hidalgo (Tamaulipas), Linares, and Hualahuises. Hoyo (Fernández de Jáuregui Urrutia 1963, 105–110) has expressed the opinion that the Borrados of the Sierra de San Carlos included such groups as Amiyayas, Bazaguaniguaros, Bocas Prietas, and Camiopajamaras.

The Borrados of the Sierra de San Carlos were later mentioned in connection with a mission at Burgos, just north of the mountains (Yerro 1749, 287, 299, 301; Organización de las Misiones 1946, 93; López de la Cámara Alta 1946, 113). Borrados at Mission San Cristóbal de Hualahuises continued to be recorded in 1753, 1754, 1759, and 1775 (Copia de las Actas 1753, 1–17; Razón de los Utencilios 1753?, 1–4; Barrio Junco y Espriella 1979, 13; Ladrón de Guevara 1969, 110; González de Santianés 1783, 289–292). They were last recorded in various routine missionary reports during the period 1790–1818 (Noticias de los Conventos 1790–1814, 1, 3, 5, 13, 219, 221, 237, 239; Bedoya 1816, table; Numana 1817, table; Antillán 1818, table).

Although it is not certain, the Borrados of the Sierra de San Carlos seem not to have been the same as the Borrados farther west in Nuevo León, and there is no indication that they were the same Borrados as those recorded for the lower Rio Grande area.

Borrados of the Lower Rio Grande.   After José de Escandón began the Spanish colonization of the lower Rio Grande after 1747, remnants of various Indian groups referred to as Borrados, presumably because they were tattooed, began to be recorded at various places along the Rio Grande

as far west as Guerrero in northeastern Coahuila and as far north as San
Antonio and Goliad in Texas. These Borrados seem to have gathered near
Spanish settlements, particularly at missions. This gravitation toward
Spanish centers suggests that by this time the expansion of Lipan and
other Apache Indians into southern Texas was having its effect. Such in-
formation as happened to be recorded seems to show that these various
Borrados were primarily from the lower Rio Grande, including the delta,
and were in no way connected with the various Borrados of central Nuevo
León or those farther south in the San Carlos area of Tamaulipas.

The first indication that these Borrados had moved away from the lower
Rio Grande was recorded in 1754, prior to which year some Borrados had
fled from Mission San Francisco de la Espada of San Antonio to Mission
San Juan Bautista at present-day Guerrero in northeastern Coahuila. They
were sent back to the San Antonio missions (Guadalupe 1754, 178; Oliva
and Ortíz de Posada 1756, 12). This is the earliest report of Borrados at
either mission. Three years later, in 1757, Borrados were mentioned as
one of several Indian groups said to be living in the vicinity of Hacienda
de Dolores, near the Rio Grande about thirty miles downstream from
Laredo (Tienda de Cuervo 1929, 436, 1930, 302).

In 1760 Bartholomé García (1760, title page) listed Borrados as one of
the Indian groups represented at unspecified San Antonio missions who
did not speak the language now known as Coahuilteco. In 1762 Borrados
from the lower Rio Grande were recorded as living at Mission San Francisco de la Espada of San Antonio and also at the two missions near modern Goliad, Espíritu Santo de Zúñiga and Nuestra Señora del Refugio (Dolores et al. 1762, 171, 178b, 182b). The surviving marriage register of
Mission Nuestra Señora de la Purísima Concepción de Acuña of San Antonio indicates that at least six Borrados were living there between the
years 1767 and 1788 (Concepción Marriage Register MS).

Nicolás Lafora, in 1768, named Borrados among the Indians then
living at the missions of both Guerrero and San Antonio (Kinnaird 1967,
160, 185, 187). In 1768 the Marqués de Rubí (1768, 40) wrote that the
Borrados of the missions at San Antonio and Goliad had been recruited
from the lower Rio Grande to replenish the declining Indian populations of
those missions. It is known that sometime after 1764 Borrados entered
Mission San Agustín de Laredo of Camargo (Bolton 1965, 450–451). In
1772 the Conde de Sierra Gorda (Estado de las Misiones 1946, 70) referred to the homeland of these Borrados as being toward the coast from
Laredo just north of the Rio Grande, and a census of the same year identi-

fied six Borrados at Mission San Juan Bautista in northeastern Coahuila
(Almaráz 1980, 29–33). The same census also identified nineteen Tampacuas, one of whom was also identified as Borrados.

In 1780 Domingo Cabello (1780a, 37–38) referred to Borrados as one
of eleven Indian groups from the coastal region of southern Texas who had
entered Mission San Francisco de la Espada of San Antonio. A document
signed by Cabello (1784, 20–21) also noted that three years later (1783)
112 Borrado Indians from the Camargo area had entered one of the San
Antonio missions, San José y San Miguel de Aguayo. Some of these Borrados had fled from the mission in 1784, but part of them were found
by soldiers and returned. In small parties they continued fleeing from the
missions, according to records of 1788 (Martínez Pacheco 1788a, 74–
75; 1788b, 82). This association of Borrados from the lower Rio Grande
with San Antonio missions is confirmed in 1785 (actually 1789) by José
Francisco López, who reported thirty-two Borrados at San José and an unspecified number of Borrados at Concepción (Dabbs 1940, 6–10, 16).
López also referred to the Malaguitas of Mission San Francisco de la
Espada as being Borrados from the southern coast of Texas.

The clearest indication that the name Borrados was used collectively in
referring to specific Indian groups of the lower Rio Grande is found in
records pertaining to Mission San José of San Antonio. The same Indian
individuals identified in mission registers as Anda el Camino, Casas Chiquitas, Mayapemes, Mulatos, and Saulapaguemes were in later annual
mission censuses referred to only as Borrados (San José Registers MS;
Pedrajo 1793, 116–123; Huisar 1796, 161–165, 1797, 72–76, 1798, 80–
84, 1799, 186–189). Thus the Borrados, or tattooed Indians of the Rio
Grande delta and vicinity, identified under specific names by Escandón in
1747 and 1749, were widely dispersed and eventually identified in records
pertaining to two Spanish missions along the Rio Grande, three at San Antonio, and two at Goliad.

Carrizos

Carrizos (Spanish for "canes" or "reeds") is a descriptive name that was
applied after 1700 to various widely distributed Indian groups of northeastern Mexico and Texas, apparently because they lived in houses whose
frames were covered by canes or reeds. As some of the groups called Carrizos were unrelated, it is not realistic to speak of Carrizos as a specific
ethnic unit. Here treatment is restricted to groups called Carrizos who
lived along both sides of the Rio Grande between the Laredo area and the

Gulf coast. One set of Carrizos will be referred to as Western Carrizos, the other as Eastern Carrizos. It is not possible to draw a boundary line between the two sets, but for practical purposes the division is made about midway between Revilla and Camargo.

Western Carrizos. The earliest record of Western Carrizos seems to be a reference in 1715 to an orphaned Carrizo girl baptized at Mission Nuestra Señora de los Dolores de la Punta de Lampazos, near modern Lampazos, Nuevo León (Lampazos Baptism Register MS). A map compiled about 1728 shows Carrizos on the north side of the Rio Grande near its junction with the Río Alamos (Alvarez Barreiro 1729, map, 1730, 108–118; Wheat 1957, 82–84, map 115c). This would place them in either Starr or Zapata counties. In 1735 Fernández de Jáuregui Urrutia (1963, 22) recorded Carrizos among the various Indian groups who had attacked the Spanish settlement of Cerralvo during the preceding twenty years.

In 1752 José Joaquín de Solís (Organización de las Misiones 1946, 89) noted that Carrizos were living about eighteen miles from Revilla (no direction indicated). These Carrizos were said to have connections with the Hacienda del Alamo de los Garzas on the Río Alamos. Two years later, in 1754, a group of Carrizos said to number twenty-seven were reported as having asked for work at Hacienda de Dolores, which was downstream from Laredo (Valcarcel 1754, 341–342). Still later, in 1757, José Tienda de Cuervo (1929, 432, 436, 440) noted that Carrizos brought animal skins to Hacienda de Dolores for trade.

A few Carrizos, also referred to as Tusan, were recorded in 1762 as living at Mission San Juan Bautista on the Rio Grande near modern Guerrero, northeastern Coahuila (Ximénes 1762, 106; Naranjo 1934, 54–55). A year earlier these Carrizos were said to have come from an unspecified locality farther down the Rio Grande. These were probably Carrizos from the lower Río Salado, near its junction with the Rio Grande. Other records reported a few Tusan Indians at Mission San Miguel de Aguayo of Monclova and continued to mention them at San Juan Bautista (Almaráz 1980, 32; Barrios y Jáuregui 1760–1762, 229–230). Gaspar José de Solís in 1768 found Carrizos living along the lower Río Salado and also on the Rio Grande about twenty-six miles downstream from Laredo. He mentioned some of their foods: maguey bulbs, snakes, rabbits, rats, and other unspecified animals (Kress and Hatcher 1931, 35).

In 1774 Western Carrizos were said to be living in the vicinity of Hacienda del Alamo, but their male population was given as less than thirty.

At this time they were accused of having communicated with the Apache who were raiding in northern Nuevo León (Barragán 1774, 1–3). In 1775, however, Vidal de Lorca (1775a, 248–251) stated that no Carrizos were living in Nuevo León. Again, in 1782, the Carrizos were accused of giving aid to the Apache who were raiding Spanish ranches in northern Nuevo León (Causas Criminales 1782–1787, 1, 3 7–8, 13, 23, 42, 116).

A missionary report of 1788 (Vidal de Lorca 1788, 33) recorded the presence of 102 Carrizos at Laredo (40 men, 30 women, 17 boys, and 15 girls). The next year a census taken at Laredo indicates a congregation of 110 Carrizos (Wilcox 1946, 349). Another document of 1788 also referred to Carrizos at Laredo (Lacomba 1788, 400–401). In 1790 Mescalero and Lipan Apache attacked Laredo, and this time the Carrizos received credit for assisting the Spaniards (Muñoz 1790, 39; González 1790, 45). Again in 1791 and 1792 the Western Carrizos aided Spaniards against the Apache (Díaz de Bustamante 1791, 79–81, 1792, 151).

The registers of the parish church at Laredo, known as San Agustín, also recorded the presence of Carrizos in the Laredo area. Between the years 1789 and 1823, these registers show that thirty-two boys and thirty-four girls were baptized; sixty-two persons were buried (twenty-two men, fifteen women, nineteen boys, and six girls); and twelve adults were married (Laredo Registers MS).

The last informative observations of Western Carrizos were written by Berlandier (1980, 1:244–246, 262, 2:421, 429) during the years 1828–1829. He visited a Carrizo encampment near Hacienda Mamulique in northern Nuevo León and learned that these Indians moved seasonally. During winter they moved to localities near Spanish settlements in northern Nuevo León and along the Rio Grande. It was at this time that the Comanche from Texas raided southward across the Rio Grande. In spring and summer, these Carrizos ranged along the Río Salado east of Lampazos, Nuevo León. These same Carrizos were known to local Garzas Indians as Yemé, to distinguish them from Carrizos of the Camargo area, known as Yué. Berlandier collected a vocabulary from the Yemé, whose language is now thought to be related to the language known as Comecrudo (Goddard 1979, 370–371, 378–381).

Eastern Carrizos. The Eastern Carrizos were first recorded by López de la Cámara Alta (1946, 119, 125) in 1757, when they were said to be living near a salt lake close to the Gulf coast. On López de la Cámara Alta's map these Carrizos were shown near a salt lake that seems to be the one later known as La Sal del Rey in present Hidalgo County, Texas. In the same year Tienda de Cuervo (1929, 432, 1930, 204) placed these Carrizos north of the Rio Grande between Revilla and Camargo.

Various documents written between 1764 and 1780 associate the Eastern Carrizos with the Camargo area, particularly the Texas side of the Rio Grande between Camargo and the Gulf coast (Bolton 1965, 450–451; Barragán 1770a, 1–3, 1770b, 131; Riperdá 1772, 392–438; Cabello 1780a, 37). During this period missionaries from San Antonio recruited Carrizo neophytes from this area.

In 1791 Conde de Sierra Gorda (1791, 292–294) noted that some of the Carrizos of the Camargo area had assisted Spaniards against raiding Indians from the north, probably Apache from the coastal plain between the Nueces River and the southern margins of the Edwards Plateau. In 1793 Barragán (1793a, 39–42, 1793b, 344–345) noted that Carrizos were in the vicinity of Camargo, where they subsisted by hunting, fishing, and gathering wild plant foods. Thereafter, as late as 1823, Carrizos were reported in the Camargo area (Noticias de los Conventos 1790–1814, passim; Bedoya 1816; Numana 1817; Antillán 1818; Nava 1816–1823). A few Carrizos also entered Mission San Joaquín del Monte of Reynosa after 1790 (Bolton 1965, 449), and at least one Carrizo was recorded in Matamoros (Matamoros Registers MS).

In 1829 Berlandier (1980, 2:429–431) recorded a separate name Yué, for the Carrizos of the Camargo area. From these Yué he collected a vocabulary of 104 entries. According to Goddard (1979, 369–371, 377–380), the Yué spoke the Cotoname language.

It is evident that the name Carrizos was applied to various Indian groups associated with the Rio Grande delta. At various times documents refer to the following groups as Carrizos: Comecrudos, Pintos, Tejones, Cotonames, and Casas Chiquitas. Without much question, Indians referred to as Carrizos included remnants of numerous unrelated groups along the Rio Grande from Laredo to the Gulf coast.

Carvios

The name Carvios is known only from a document of 1757 that mentions the presence of three Carvios (two women and one infant) at Mission San Agustín de Laredo of Camargo. These three individuals were said to have recently arrived at the mission (Tienda de Cuervo 1929, 397). As most of the Indian groups represented at this mission came from areas west of the Río San Juan, it is possible that Carvios is a distorted rendition of the name Caurames.

Caurames

The Indians known as Caurames were recorded only in documents for the period 1686–1735, and they appear to have been native to an area that included the Sierra de Picachos (west of Cerralvo) and extended eastward as far as the Río San Juan.

In 1686, during an expedition to the mouth of the Rio Grande in search of La Salle's Fort St. Louis, Alonso de León (León, Chapa, and Sánchez de Zamora 1961, 194–202) encountered forty-four Caurames (all warriors) who were out checking on their enemies (unspecified). He met them just east of the Río San Juan, apparently near the present boundary line between Nuevo León and Tamaulipas. On his return from the lower Rio Grande, León again encountered the Caurames, but at a locality farther up the Río San Juan, somewhere near modern China, Nuevo León.

Much later, in 1700, several documents refer to Caurames as raiding Spanish frontier settlements and mention that a Spanish military party from the vicinity of present-day Sabinas Hidalgo went to the Sierra de Picachos area to punish the Caurames (Hoyo 1963, 77–78; Cavazos Garza 1964, 148).

Two maps drawn about 1728 place the Caurames on the south bank of the Rio Grande just west of its junction with the Río San Juan at Camargo (Alvarez Barreiro 1729, map; Wheat 1957, 82–84, map 115a). Two years later, in 1730, the Caurames were listed as one of numerous Indian groups who made peace with Spaniards in Monterrey (Garza 1750, 224 or 274; Velasco 1715–1753, 303). The last record of the Caurames was in 1735, when they were listed as one of many Indian groups who had previously made raids on Spanish settlements near modern Montemorelos, General Terán, and Cadereyta (Fernández de Jáuregui Urrutia 1963, 12–23).

Chinitos

Chinitos, a Spanish diminutive form of the name for Chinese, is recorded as the name of an Indian group only in late missionary documents covering the period 1790–1818. According to these brief reports, the Chinitos lived at or near Revilla and supported themselves mainly by hunting (Noticias de los Conventos 1790–1814, passim; Bedoya 1816; Numana 1817; Antillán 1818). Although Israel Cavazos Garza (1973, 190) has shown that Chinese immigrants were in Nuevo León as early as 1718, it does not appear likely that the Chinitos represent a hybrid Chinese-Indian population. The Chinitos were probably merged remnants of several Indian groups who had formerly lived somewhere in the Cerralvo area.

Cueros Quemados

The Cueros Quemados (Spanish for "burned skins") were first mentioned in 1735 as one of the Indian groups that had attacked Spanish settlements at or near Cerralvo (Fernández de Jáuregui Urrutia 1963, 22, 107). Later records link the Cueros Quemados with both sides of the Rio Grande between Camargo and Revilla.

During the visit of 1750, Escandón (1751, 21; Valcarcel 1756, 106) referred to the Cueros Quemados as native to the Camargo area, and he further stated that they had been born and reared on the north bank of the Río Grande near its junction with the Río San Juan at Camargo. At that time thirty-three individuals (ten men, twenty-three women and children) were congregated at Camargo. Two years later, in 1752, the Cueros Quemados were listed as one of seven Indian groups at Mission San Agustín de Laredo of Camargo (Organización de las Misiones 1946, 88).

Tienda de Cuervo (1929, 397–398, 402, 432, 1930, 302) visited Camargo in 1757 and reported the presence of twenty-three Cueros Quemados (six men, seventeen women and children). He noted that the Cueros Quemados were sometimes seen on the north side of the Rio Grande farther upstream near Revilla. Later documents also indicate the presence of Cueros Quemados at Camargo and Revilla (Gómez 1942, 56; Estado de las Misiones 1946, 69; Bolton 1965, 450–451).

A few sources appear to link the Cueros Quemados with areas near the Gulf coast, but these are questionable. In 1780 Cabello (1780a, 37) listed the Cueros Quemados among the Indian groups living south of the Rio Grande near the Gulf coast, but this probably refers to the Cueros Quemados of the Camargo area. Vidal de Lorca (1788) compiled a table that listed Cueros Quemados as one of the Indian groups represented at Mission Cabezón de la Sal on the lower Río San Fernando. This is probably a clerical error. No other documents link the Cueros Quemados with the Rio Grande delta or with the lower Río San Fernando.

The last references to Cueros Quemados occur in documents written near the close of the eighteenth century. These indicate that at least some Cueros Quemados families or individuals were still living along the Rio Grande at Camargo and near Mier (Barragán 1793a, 39–42, 1793b, 344–345; Noticias de los Conventos 1790–1814 129–130, 136, 152).

Garzas

The name Garzas (Spanish for "herons") was applied to combined remnants of various Indian groups who originally lived in the Cerralvo region of Nuevo León, and its use can be traced back to the year 1715, when Indians called Garzas were reported as living at Mission San Nicolás de Agualeguas north of Cerralvo (González de Santianés 1783, 289–292; Causas Criminales 1782–1787, 152–153). From 1756 until as late as 1829, Garzas were reported as living at or near Mier, and some of these were said to be living on the north bank of the Rio Grande. In 1770 the Garzas at Mier were reported to number 101, and shortly after 1793 the number was given as 300. This increase was not natural increase, but increase due to absorption of additional Indian group remnants of the area (Tienda de Cuervo 1929, 411–414, 432; López de la Cámara Alta 1758, map, 1946, 122; Gómez 1942, 59–60; Estado de las Misiones 1946, 69; Vidal de Lorca 1775b, 252, 1778, 1–19; Noticias de los Conventos 1790–1814, passim; Barragán 1793b, 344–345; Bedoya 1816; Numana 1817; Antillán 1818; Revillagigedo 1966, 85).

Garzas were sometimes reported as visiting Mission San Francisco Solano of Revilla (Gómez 1942, 59–60), farther up the Rio Grande, but they were never seen farther down the Rio Grande than Mier. Garzas were also recorded as living as far west as modern Vallecillo and Sabinas Hidalgo (Causas Criminales 1782–1787, passim). It thus appears clear enough that Indians known to Spaniards as Garzas were connected with the area between Cerralvo and the Rio Grande.

In 1829 Berlandier (1980, 1:263, 2:428–429, 431) noted the presence of Garzas at Mier and said that they had intermarried with Carrizos (Yué division), who spoke a different language. Berlandier collected about twenty words from the Garzas. Goddard (1979, 357, 369–371, 377–380) suggests that the language of the Garzas may have been related to the language of the Comecrudos and Carrizo Yemé. Goddard also tries to associate the Garzas with the Rio Grande delta group Atanaguaypacam (Comecrudo for the Spanish word *garza* or the English word "heron"), but this appears doubtful when one considers that the people called Garzas by the Spaniards were an amalgam of Indian group remnants of the Cerralvo area and that they were never recorded farther down the Rio Grande than Mier.

The Guajolotes and Cacalotes are discussed in chapter 4.

Gualeguas

Little is known about the Gualeguas, but the name became known rather early, sometime between 1625 and 1664, as representing one of numerous Indian groups living in the vicinity of Cerralvo (León, Chapa, and Sánchez de Zamora 1961, 189–191). It appears that Mission San Nicolás de Agualeguas, located about seventeen miles north of Cerralvo, probably received its name from the Gualeguas Indians (Cadena 1942, 27). In 1730 Gualessuegues (Gualeguas) were noted as one of the troublesome Indian groups of eastern Nuevo León (Garza 1750, 274; Velasco 1715–1753, 303). The Gualeguas were last recorded at Mission San Francisco Solano de Ampuero of Revilla in 1770 (Gómez 1942, 60). Evidently only a few Gualeguas were then living at Revilla, for the total mission Indian population, consisting of Gualeguas, Malaguitas, and Garzas, was given as twenty-five.

Guapes

This name is known only from the registers of Mission San Agustín de Laredo of Camargo, which are now lost, but Bolton (1965, 450) compiled a list of Indian groups represented when he examined the registers early in the present century. As the name Guapes has not been found in other documents, no ethnic identity can be established.

The Malaguitas are discussed in chapter 4.

Malnombre

The Spanish phrase *mal nombre* ("bad name" or "bad reputation") seems to have been consistently linked with a group of Indians, probably the combined remnants of several groups, that lived in various parts of the area surrounding Cerralvo. When first actually recorded in 1675, the Malnombre were associated with Mission San Nicolás de Agualeguas, which was seventeen miles north of Cerralvo (Barragán 1774, 1–3; Cadena 1942, 29). Between 1715 and 1748, the Malnombre were occasionally mentioned as one of numerous hostile Indian groups in eastern Nuevo León (Garza 1750, 224; Velasco 1715–1753, 303). A document written about 1748 referred to twenty families living in the valleys known as Salinas and Pesquería southwest of Cerralvo and north of Monterrey (Saldívar 1943, 33).

The Malnombre were not noted on the Rio Grande until the second half of the eighteenth century, sometime after 1764 at Camargo and in 1772 at Mier (Estado de las Misiones 1946, 69; Bolton 1965, 450–451), but other Malnombre were reported to be living elsewhere, particularly west and north of the Sierra de Picachos (Vidal de Lorca 1775b, 252, 1778, 1–19; Causas Criminales 1782–1787, passim). For these more westerly Malnombre, a few cultural details were recorded: eating broiled yucca flower buds, prickly-pear fruit, and honey; one family that at least temporarily lived in a cave or rock shelter; use of both flint and metal (iron) for arrow-points; and ceremonial dances. There is no indication that Malnombre ever moved farther down the Rio Grande than Camargo, where a few of them may have remained until 1818 (Noticias de los Conventos 1790–1814, passim; Bedoya 1816; Numana 1817; Antillán 1818).

Narices

Narices ("noses") has never been equated with a recorded name of Indian origin. Various documents identify the Narices as one of many Indian groups that originally lived in eastern Nuevo León on the upper Río San Juan. After displacement by Spanish colonists, some of the Narices eventually ended up living near the Rio Grande in the vicinity of Reynosa.

Although the record is none too clear, it appears that some of the Narices may have entered Mission Purificación near modern Montemore-los prior to 1720 (Fundación de Presidios 1741, 22–24). If so, they probably did not remain there very long. In 1730 the Narices were one of eight Indian groups led by a Tortuga Indian chief, Francisco de la Garza, all said to be living along the upper Río San Juan and its tributaries (Velasco 1715–1753, 303; Garza 1750, 224). Between 1730 and 1740, the Narices were sometimes identified as one of the Indian groups who attacked Spanish settlements in the upper part of the Río San Juan drainage, particularly those near present-day Montemorelos and General Terán. They were also associated with the villages of Cadereyta and Cerralvo (Fernández de Jáuregui Urrutia 1963, 17–18; Ladrón de Guevara 1969, 18).

In 1741 the Narices were listed among the remnants of various Indian groups who went to Monterrey and concluded a treaty of peace with the provincial government. At that time Francisco Galván was identified as leader of the Narices. The Narices and other Indian groups were granted amnesty and given presents (money, crystal beads, raw-sugar loaves, ribbon from Naples, and bundles of tobacco). It is said that these pardoned Indians did not thereafter enter missions but chose to live under native conditions in their respective areas (Fundación de Presidios 1741, 22–24). According to an anonymous document written about 1748, the Narices of Río Pilón, apparently living near modern Montemorelos, were said to consist of twenty families (Saldívar 1943, 32).

Although some of the Narices appear to have remained in Nuevo León, others evidently moved northward to the Rio Grande and after 1747 were recorded as living near Reynosa. In 1751 Escandón (1751, 49–50; Valcarcel 1756, 106) identified the Narices of Reynosa as having come from eastern Nuevo León and gave their population as thirty-one (thirteen men, eighteen women and children). In 1753 the Narices of Reynosa were mentioned as one of four Indian groups said to number about two hundred (Ladrón de Guevara 1753c, 325). The continued decline of the Narices of Reynosa is further documented by José Tienda de Cuervo, who, in 1757, saw only six men and one woman, but the resident missionary at Reynosa said that in the area there were fifteen surviving Narices (López de la Cámara Alta 1946, 116; Tienda de Cuervo 1929, 372, 376, 381, 1930, 108).

As Narices is a name of Spanish origin that was applied to an Indian group after 1700, it may refer to one or more of the forty-four native group names recorded by Juan Bautista Chapa for the Cadereyta area in the second half of the seventeenth century (León, Chapa, and Sánchez de Zamora 1961, 291). Since no specific culture traits are recorded, and no samples of their speech have been identified, no positive statements can be made about the cultural and linguistic affiliations of the Narices.

Nazas

The Spanish word *nasa* refers to several kinds of containers, including the netted fish trap. It is possible that the Indians called Nazas by Spaniards were so called because they used netted traps to take fish. The Nazas are of special interest here because they originally lived in eastern Nuevo León, were displaced by Spaniards, migrated northeastward to the lower Rio Grande, and then later returned to their homeland area in Nuevo León. Their movements are fairly well documented. As the Nazas have sometimes been regarded as native to the lower Rio Grande, it is evident that caution must be used when attempting to identify the original homeland of any Indian group displaced by Europeans.

It seems likely that a native name for the Nazas appears on the list of forty-four Indian groups recorded by Juan Bautista Chapa as associated with the Cadereyta area in the second half of the seventeenth century (León, Chapa, and Sánchez de Zamora 1961, 291). Under the name Nazas, many of these Indians appear to have been represented at Mission Purificación (near modern Montemorelos) prior to 1720 (Fundación de Presidios 1741, 11–12). How many Nazas entered that mission or how long they remained is unknown. In 1732 Nazas were named as one of twenty-six displaced Indian groups under the nominal leadership of a Pamorano Indian known as Pedro Botello (Lozada 1732, 85). Between 1730 and 1740, the Nazas were sometimes named as one of the Indian groups who attacked Cerralvo, Cadereyta, and various haciendas in the valleys of San

Mateo del Pilón and Mota, near modern Montemorelos, and General Terán (Fernández de Jáuregui Urrutia 1963, 17–18; Ladrón de Guevara 1969, 18).

In 1741 various rebellious Indian groups, including the Nazas under a leader known as Tomás, concluded a treaty of peace with the provincial government of Nuevo León and were allowed to return to their respective areas (Fundación de Presidios 1741, 11–12). According to an anonymous document probably written about 1748, the Nazas, lead by Capitán Juan de Medina, were said to consist of twenty families who lived by hunting and gathering in the Pilón valley (Saldívar 1943, 32).

In 1750 we have the earliest clear reference to Nazas on the lower Rio Grande. Escandón (1751, 49; Valcarcel 1756, 106) reported that the Nazas of Reynosa had previously lived at a locality known as Las Sierritas de los Nazas about twenty-five miles southwest of Reynosa Díaz. The locality appears to be identifiable with La Sierrita in the present municipality of General Bravo, Nuevo León. Escandón noted that some of the Reynosa Nazas were away hunting and gathering in eastern Nuevo León. The total Nazas population was given as forty-five (nineteen men, twenty-six women and children). Escandón also noted that three of the male Nazas at Reynosa had previously been baptized at "Pueblo del Pilón," which probably means Mission Purificación near modern Montemorelos. The Nazas had evidently moved from the vicinity of Montemorelos northeastward along the Río San Juan to reach Reynosa.

In 1757 Tienda de Cuervo (1929, 373, 376, 381; López de la Cámara Alta 1946, 116) gave the Nazas population at Reynosa as thirty-six (eight men, twenty-eight women and children). These Nazas told Tienda de Cuervo that they had left the Reynosa mission because they could not get along with the resident missionary and had returned to Reynosa only because they had heard of Tienda de Cuervo's arrival. They hoped to have their grievances settled, but apparently this hope was not realized. They left the Rio Grande area for good, and thereafter no documents refer to Nazas as living anywhere along the Rio Grande. They must have returned to their homeland in Nuevo León, for they are mentioned in records that pertain to the missions of Purificación and Concepción (González n.d., 349; Guimbardo 1768, 139; Luviaur 1773, 165). They were last recorded in missionary reports of that area in 1790 and 1792 (Noticias de los Conventos 1790–1814, 1, 3).

The above statements indicate that the Nazas, known only from documents of the eighteenth century, were Indians of eastern Nuevo León who only temporarily resided on the lower Rio Grande. There are no recorded statements about the language they spoke, and all that is known about their culture is that they lived by hunting and gathering and may have used netted traps in fishing.

Paisanos

The name Paisanos (Spanish for "countrymen" or "peasants") seems to have referred to two unrelated Indian groups. One of these groups, more commonly recorded as Pausanes, lived mainly in northeastern Coahuila and the adjacent part of Texas (Espinosa 1708, 42, 1746, 463, 481–482; Sevillano de Paredes 1727, 49–50). These entered missions in Coahuila and at San Antonio, Texas (Giraldo de Terreros 1734, 23; Garza Falcón 1737, 383–385; García 1760, title page). The other Paisanos, those being considered here, were connected with the lower Rio Grande. They were first noted by Miguel Sevillano de Paredes (1727, 50), who placed them on the north bank of the Rio Grande, apparently in what is now southeastern Starr County, Texas. It was probably while living in this territory that some Paisanos had caused trouble in the Cerralvo area (Garza 1750, 224; Velasco 1715–1753, 303; Fernández de Jáuregui Urrutia 1963, 22, 108).

It is clear that these Paisanos entered Mission San Agustín de Laredo of Camargo, for in 1750 Escandón (1751, 20) noted the presence there of eighteen Paisanos (seven men, eleven women and children). He said that they were native to the Camargo area and had lived on both sides of the Rio Grande. The Paisanos at Camargo continued to be recorded in documents up to the year 1793 (Bolton 1965, 450–451; Vidal de Lorca 1788; Noticias de los Conventos 1790–1814, 1; Barragán 1793a, 39–42, 1793b, 344–345).

Pajaritos

This Spanish name ("little birds") was applied to Indian groups in various areas, but the Pajaritos under consideration here were encountered by Alonso de León (León, Chapa, and Sánchez de Zamora 1961, 194–202; see also Reyes 1944, 159–180) in the Río San Juan valley not far from present China, Nuevo León. These appear to have been the same Pajaritos listed among Indian groups who frequently attacked Spanish settlements of Nuevo León in the early eighteenth century (Garza 1750, 224; Velasco 1715–1753, 303), including Cerralvo (Fernández de Jáuregui Urrutia 1963, 22, 108). A document written about 1748 noted that Pajaritos often peacefully visited Cerralvo (Saldívar 1943, 321.)

These were evidently the Pajaritos who entered Mission San Agustín de Laredo of Camargo. In 1751 there were seventeen Pajaritos (six men, eleven women and children) at the Camargo mission (Escandón 1751, 20), said to have come from Ciénega de Pajaritos, a marsh sixteen miles southeast of Camargo, apparently near present Valadeces. In 1757 Tienda de Cuervo (1929, 396–398, 402, 1930, 111) reported fifty-six Pajaritos (nineteen men, thirty-seven women and children) at the Camargo mission, and thereafter, at least until 1809, Pajaritos were recorded as being at the mission (Bolton 1965, 450–451; Gómez 1942, 56; Estado de las Misiones 1946, 69). In 1780 Cabello (1780a, 37) listed Pajaritos among the Indian groups living south of the Rio Grande near the Gulf coast, but this probably referred to the Pajaritos of Camargo. As other documents refer to Pajaritos up the Rio Grande as far as Mier (Noticias de los Conventos 1790–1814, passim; Bedoya 1816; Numana 1817; Antillán 1818), they probably never went down the Rio Grande as far as the delta.

The Pamoranos are discussed in chapter 5.

Pelones

Pelón is a Spanish word whose basic meaning is "hairless" or "bald." In at least three widely separated areas of northeastern Mexico and Texas, Spaniards referred to certain Indian populations as Pelones. Although for two of these areas descriptive details are lacking, it is clear enough that the word Pelones was used because adult Indian males removed substantial portions of the head hair in a patterned way, producing a tonsure. The reference is to a cultural phenomenon, not to congenital baldness in males or to pathological loss of head hair. As the Pelones of the three areas appear not to have been linguistically or culturally related, it is necessary to be very careful not to confuse one set of Pelones with another, particularly in situations involving migration of one set of Pelones nearer to the area occupied by another.

In the middle eighteenth century, a specific Indian group of southern Tamaulipas was referred to as Pelones in Spanish documents that cover a very short period (1749–1752). In 1749 this group was said to be living at a place known as Paso del Metate, which was about twenty-six miles northwest of Tampico (Yerro 1749, 300; Eguilaz de Prado 1965, 54). In 1752 they were again mentioned, along with two other groups (Anacanas and Pachimas), as living temporarily at Mission San Juan Capistrano de Suances of Altamira, twenty miles north of Tampico (Organización de las

Misiones 1946, 80). The tonsure of these Pelones was never described. It would appear that in southern Tamaulipas the name Pelones was briefly used to refer to an Indian group later recorded by a native name. No information has been found that in any way links these Pelones with those of central Nuevo León, who ranged over an area at least 250 miles to the northwest.

In Texas, during the first half of the eighteenth century, a Plains Apache band was frequently identified in Spanish documents as Pelones (Dunn 1911, passim; Tunnell and Newcomb 1969, 141–176 passim). These Pelones were first recorded as living in northern Texas, and they moved southward with the Lipan and other Apaches. After 1760 their identity was merged with that of the Lipan, and their name began to disappear from the historical record. These Texas Pelones, according to Spanish sources, spoke an Athapascan language that was either similar to, or identical with, that spoken by the Lipan. They are thus not to be confused with the Pelones of northeastern Mexico, who were not only identified in other Spanish documents of the same period but also in earlier documents.

The Pelones of Nuevo León first become known in documents pertaining to the 1660s, which indicate that they became troublesome by stealing Spanish horses, sheep, and goats and by occasionally killing a shepherd. These Pelones were said to be living in the vicinity of the Sierra Papagayos, a small range of mountains midway between Cadereyta and Cerralvo. León, who lived at Cadereyta, indicated that he had led several Spanish parties out to punish the raiding Pelones. In 1667 the Pelones seem to have staged a small revolt against the Spaniards, and this led the governor of Nuevo León, Diego Pruneda, to order out four companies of soldiers. Troubles with the Pelones evidently continued, for in 1683 Spanish punitive expeditions were still being sent into their area (León, Chapa, and Sánchez de Zamora 1961, 19, 158, 185, 188; Hoyo 1960, 493). León briefly described the hair removal patterns of the Nuevo León Pelones. Hair was removed from the top of the head down to the forehead hair line. The band of exposed scalp varied in width from one group of Pelones to another. The hairless band was tattooed, lines of tattooing extending from the crown of the head forward as far as the nose.

It was from a Pelón Indian that Spaniards in Nuevo León first heard about La Salle's French colony on what is now the Texas coast (Matagorda Bay area). In 1686 a party of Pelones visited a Spanish ranching settlement about fifty-two miles northeast of Monterrey. One Pelón man claimed that he had heard about the French colony from two neighboring Indian groups, Blancos and Pajaritos. This same Pelón Indian also said that he had later seen an Indian "from the north" who was wearing European trousers, coat, and hat (Paredes 1686, 77–82). This news soon led to León's being sent from Cadereyta northeastward to the coast on the first of several attempts to find the French colony.

Later, in a document of 1704, brief mention is made of continued hostilities between Spaniards and Pelones in Nuevo León (Hoyo 1963, 79). Shortly before 1707 some Pelones, apparently not many, crossed the Rio Grande into what is now southern Texas, hoping to persuade Indians of that area to aid them in their conflict with the Spaniards of Nuevo León. News of this reached Spanish authorities, and in 1707 Sergeant Diego Ramón led a party of Spanish soldiers from Presidio San Juan Bautista (northeastern Coahuila) into the area now covered by Duval and Webb counties of Texas, his orders being to find and punish the Pelones. He learned that Pelones were at two encampments of local Indians, which he found, attacked, killed three Pelones, and took a few Indian captives back to Presidio San Juan Bautista (Ramón 1707, 53–71). This seems to be the only early record of Nuevo León Pelones anywhere north of the Rio Grande.

After 1707 Spanish documents began to refer to specific names for Indian groups classified as Pelones. About 1716, or shortly thereafter, some of the Pelones entered Mission Nuestra Señora de la Purificación near present-day Montemorelos, and these were identified as Aguatinejos, Cacalotes, and Tortugas (Velasco 1715–1753, 285, 301–303, 310; Bueno de la Borbolla 1749, 208–209; Garza 1750, 218–219, 222–230). Thereafter, for about two decades, the same three groups identified as Pelones were named among numerous Indian groups who ranged over eastern Nuevo León and repeatedly attacked Spanish settlements (Lozada 1732, 84–93; Fernández de Jáuregui Urrutia 1963, 17–18; Fundación de Presidios 1741, 1–26).

In 1749 the same three groups identified as Pelones agreed to enter a new mission on the Rio Grande, Divina Pastora de Santillana, established at El Tepextle near modern Camargo. Some of them had accompanied Escandón in 1747 and 1749 on two expeditions to what is now northern Tamaulipas. Two years later, however, this Camargo mission was moved southward to the vicinity of present-day Montemorelos. Some of the three Pelón groups seem to have followed the mission, but later documents pertaining to the lower Rio Grande refer to some of them who must have remained on that river (Velasco 1715–1753, 285–338; Escandón 1749a, 195–199, 1749b, 441, 1749c, 190–194; Bueno de la Borbolla 1749, 206–210; Garza 1750, 218–219).

The Indians of Nuevo León referred to by Spaniards as Pelones were, when first clearly recorded under that name, living in a mountainous region lying between Cadereyta and Cerralvo. The area occupied by these Pelones drains into the Río Pesquería, an important western tributary of the Río San Juan, a river that flows northeastward to join the Rio Grande at Camargo. Throughout their recorded history the Pelones of Nuevo León were associated with the Río San Juan drainage and with the Rio Grande both above and below Camargo. The last remnants of the Pelones seem to have lost their identities near Spanish missions of Montemorelos on the upper Río San Juan, and near the missions of Camargo and Reynosa on the lower Rio Grande.

Of the three Indian groups that Spanish documents clearly identify as Pelones, only one, the Aguatinejos, is known by a name that appears to be of native origin. The Cacalotes and Tortugas had names that were given to them by Spaniards. It appears likely that some of the native names recorded for the Cadereyta and Cerralvo areas by Chapa (León, Chapa, and Sánchez de Zamora 1961, 190) refer to groups with tonsures and thus might have been identified as Pelones. For lack of evidence, however, none of Chapa's native names can be equated with Aguatinejos, Cacalotes, and Tortugas. The modern historian, Eugenio del Hoyo (1963, 105–110), has identified certain other Indian groups as Pelones (Aguanos, Carrizos, Guajolotes, Lomisaaguas, Quiguaguanes, and Yupimanes) and has suggested that still others also may have been Pelones (Lumbres, Nazas, Paisanos, Pajaritos, and Piguanos). Unfortunately, no documentary evidence was presented in support of these statements, and thus far none has been found.

Pistispiagueles

Although mentioned in very few documents, the Pistispiagueles were evidently native to the Cerralvo area of Nuevo León. In 1728 Pedro Rivera y Villalón (1945, 129, 131–132) listed them as one of thirteen Indian groups then represented at the Spanish missions of Nuevo León. They were not linked with any particular mission. In 1735 Fernández de Jáuregui Urrutia (1963, 22, 109) identified them as one of the Indian groups that had made attacks in the Cerralvo area. In 1757 some of the Pistispiagueles were said to be living along the Rio Grande in the vicinity of Revilla (Tienda de Cuervo 1929, 432). Presumably their ethnic identity was lost shortly thereafter by merging with another surviving Indian group larger in number.

Tareguanos

The earliest documents that refer to Tareguanos connect them with the Cerralvo area of Nuevo León (Garza 1750, 224; Velasco 1715– 1753, 303; Fernández de Jáuregui Urrutia 1963, 22, 110). One document written about 1748 refers to some thirty families who frequently visited the Spanish settlement at Cerralvo (Saldívar 1943, 33). Tareguanos also entered Mission San Nicolás de Agualeguas north of Cerralvo, but remained there only fifteen days (Escandón 1751, 20).

At least seventy-six Tareguanos (twenty-five men, fifty-one women and children) entered Mission San Agustín de Laredo of Camargo as early as 1751, and documents of the time claimed that they were native to the Camargo area. As Camargo is only about fifty miles from Cerralvo, it appears likely that the Tareguanos originally ranged over the intervening area (Escandón 1751, 19–20; Organización de las Misiones 1946, 87–88; Tienda de Cuervo 1929, 396–398, 402, 1930, 111). The Tareguanos who entered the Camargo mission seem to have remained there until as late as 1818, when records ceased to refer to Indians by their ethnic group names (Gómez 1942, 56; Estado de las Misiones 1946, 69; Vidal de Lorca 1788; Barragán 1793a, 39–42, 1793b, 344–345; Revillagigedo 1966, 85; Noticias de los Conventos 1790–1814, passim; Bedoya 1816; Numana 1817; Antillán 1818; Bolton 1965, 450–451).

Tortugas

The Tortugas ("tortoises" or "turtles") originally lived on the upper tributaries of the Río San Juan in eastern Nuevo León. After being displaced by Spanish colonists, some of them migrated northward to the Rio Grande. The identity of the Tortugas is complicated by the fact that their original native name has not been identified and also by the fact that they were one of several Indian groups of Nuevo León who were often referred to as Pelón or Pelones ("bald" or "hairless"). In the eighteenth century, a number of Indian groups in Nuevo León were called Pelón because of peculiarities in hairdress. The males removed substantial amounts of head hair in several patterned ways. Thus some apparently related and unrelated Indian groups of Nuevo León became known to Spaniards as Pelones.

In eastern Nuevo León, the Tortugas were first recorded under that name in 1716–1717, when they and other rebellious Indian groups were settled at Mission Purificación in the Pilón valley (near modern Montemorelos). Prior to that time, they were probably known by a native name. By 1723 most of these Indians had deserted the mission and had become involved in attacks on Spanish settlements (Garza 1750, 218–219, 222–230, or 268–269, 272–280; Velasco 1715–1753, 285, 301, 310). It was apparently about this time that some of the Tortugas moved to the Rio Grande.

The only clear indication that some of the Tortugas were seen north of the Rio Grande comes from a map drawn by Francisco Alvarez Barreiro, an engineer who accompanied Pedro Rivera y Villalón on his inspection of frontier presidios during the years 1724–1728 (Alvarez Barreiro 1729, map, 1730, 108–118; Wheat 1957, 82–84, map 115c). This map shows the Tortugas on the north side of the Rio Grande northeast of, and near, its junction with the Río San Juan (near modern Camargo). It is possible that some of the Tortugas may have been included among the Pelones recorded in 1707 by Diego Ramón (1707, 53–71) in the area lying between the Nueces River and the Rio Grande. Ramón had set out to punish these Indians because they had been involved in a Pelón revolt in Nuevo León that had begun in 1704 (Hoyo 1963, 79).

Between 1730 and 1748, the Tortugas were recorded frequently in documents pertaining to Spanish-Indian hostilities and peace negotiation in eastern Nuevo León, particularly along the upper tributaries of the Río San Juan. The Indians raided as far south as Montemorelos, as far west as Cadereyta, and as far north as Cerralvo (Velasco 1715–1753, 302–303, 310; Garza 1750, 223–224, or 273–274; Ladrón de Guevara 1969, 18; Fundación de Presidios 1741, 7–8; Saldívar 1943, 33).

In 1749 Escandón proposed to settle some of the troublesome Pelón groups on the Rio Grande at a site where Camargo was later established. This site was called El Tepextle, and a mission, Divina Pastora de Santillana, was established for various Pelón groups, including Tortugas, Cacalotes, and Aguatinejos. The Tortugas were led by a man known as Capitán Francisco de la Garza. According to Escandón, there were 359 Indians at this mission, but the Tortuga leader gave the number as 187 (there had been a recent epidemic). The Indians were dissatisfied with Mission Divina Pastora and wished to return to the upper Río San Juan in Nuevo León. In 1751 this mission was transferred to the Pilón valley on the upper Río San Juan, and apparently most of the Rio Grande Tortugas went with it (Escandón 1749a, 195–196, 1749c, 190–194; Bueno de la Borbolla 1749, 206–210; Garza 1750, 218–219, 222–230; Velasco 1715–1753, 285–338).

Most of the surviving Tortugas continued to live in eastern Nuevo León after 1751. By 1756 they were transferred to Mission Purificación also in the Pilón valley (Ladrón de Guevara 1969, 69–70). In 1768 they were still said to be living in the Pilón valley when the Indians of Missions Purificación and Concepción quarreled among themselves (Guimbardo 1768, 139; Correa 1768, 140–141; Luviaur 1773, 165). Some Tortugas were reported as living near Mission San Cristóbal de Hualahuises between 1790 and 1814 (Noticias de los Conventos 1790–1814, 1, 3, 5, 13, 219, 221, 237, 239), and undoubtedly some of these, or their descendants, continued to live near modern Hualahuises (west of Linares) until later in the nineteenth century.

Some Tortugas, however, seem to have remained in the lower Rio Grande valley. Bolton (1965, 450–451), who examined the registers of Mission San Agustín de Laredo at Camargo, noted an unspecified number of Tortuga entries. The registers examined covered the years 1764– 1810. It is possible that Berlandier (1980, 2:590), who visited Reynosa in 1834, saw some Tortugas among the Pelón Indians he reported as living in small huts on the outskirts of Reynosa.

It seems evident that the Tortugas were native to the upper Río San Juan in eastern Nuevo León and that most of them lived there until their ethnic identity was lost in the nineteenth century. A few, however, remained on the Rio Grande and lost their identity in the Camargo-Reynosa area. At no time did the Tortugas penetrate very far into southern Texas and, so far as is now known, were in no way related to the Tonkawa Indians of Texas. A few references to a vaguely located topographic feature in Texas, a hill said to be known as Tortugas, has led to suggestions that the Tortuga Indians may have been a subdivision of the Tonkawa Indians (Gatschet 1891, 36; Hodge 1971, 2:786; Krieger, in Webb 1952, 2:791). No connection between the Tortugas and Tonkawa can be established.

Venados

The name Venados (Spanish for "deer") was applied by Spaniards to several widely scattered Indian groups, only two of which are considered here. One group was associated with an area southeast of San Antonio, Texas, and some of these entered missions at San Antonio. The other group was connected with an area south of the Rio Grande, extending westward from the lower Río San Juan to the vicinity of Cerralvo, Nuevo León, and a considerable number of these entered Mission San Agustín de Laredo of Camargo. Some writers have suggested that these two groups represented a single population (e.g., see Campbell and Campbell 1985, 43–44), but no clear documentary evidence supports this view. It seems more reasonable to conclude that the same Spanish name was applied to two separate and probably unrelated Indian groups.

The Venados who entered the mission at Camargo were first noted in 1735 as one of the Indian groups who had at times attacked the Spanish settlement of Cerralvo (Fernández de Jáuregui Urrutia 1963, 22, 110). An anonymous document written about 1748 referred to thirty families of Venados who in previous years had peacefully visited Cerralvo (Saldívar 1943, 33). In 1749 it was recorded that these Venados were expected to enter the short-lived Mission Divina Pastora de Santillana near present Camargo, but this never happened (Escandón 1749a, 196, 198; Bueno de la Borbolla 1749, 207). They did, however, enter Mission San Agustín de Laredo when it was established at Camargo, and fifty-six individuals (seventeen men, thirty-nine women and children) were recorded there in 1750 (Escandón 1751, 20; Valcarcel 1756, 106). They were said to be Indians native to the area surrounding Camargo. Two years later, in 1752, Venados were again reported at this mission (Organización de las Misiones 1946, 88). A document of 1757 (Tienda de Cuervo 1929, 396–398, 402, 1930, 111) gave the number of Venados at the Camargo mission as fifty-one (twenty-three men, twenty-eight women and children).

The same Venados were still living at Mission San Agustín as late as 1772 (Gómez 1942, 56; Estado de las Misiones 1946, 69), but apparently all of the Venados had not entered this mission. In 1774 Venados were reported among the remnants of various Indian groups who visited El Pantano, an hacienda of northern Nuevo León, where they sought jobs (Barragán 1774, 1–3). Several missionary reports indicate that, as late as 1818, a few Venados were still living in the vicinity of Camargo. These reports note that some of the Venados cultivated fields of corn and that others worked for Spaniards of the area. They often went out to hunt deer and peccaries in the countryside (Vidal de Lorca 1788, table; Noticias de los Conventos 1790–1814, passim; Barragán 1793a, 39–42; Bedoya 1816; Numana 1817; Antillán 1818).

Zacatiles

Most of what is known about the Indians called Zacatiles pertains to their location at various times. Their language remains unknown, and nothing was recorded about their culture other than that they lived by hunting and gathering.

Throughout their recorded history the Zacatiles seem to have been associated with the drainage of the Río San Juan, a stream that heads in the

Sierra Madre Oriental of Nuevo León, mainly between Cadereyta and Montemorelos, and flows northeastward to join the Rio Grande near Camargo in northern Tamaulipas. When first recorded in 1686, the Zacatiles were said to be living at two widely separated localities. Some were associated with a Spanish hacienda near Cadereyta; and others, apparently much more numerous, were living under native conditions along the Río San Juan near the present Nuevo León–Tamaulipas boundary line. It appears likely that the Zacatiles had originally lived on the upper Río San Juan and had been displaced by Spanish colonists along the mountain front, but this cannot be clearly demonstrated by documentary evidence.

Zacatil seems to be related to *zacate,* a word of Nahuatl origin that early Spaniards in Mexico had applied to certain American grasses (Santamaría 1978, 1139). Zacatiles is evidently not the native name that the group used when referring to themselves. As far as is now known, the name Zacatiles was first recorded in 1686 when León and seventy-five soldiers set out from Cadereyta to verify a rumor that the French had established a fort on the Gulf coast. This expedition did not go far enough to find the French fort, which was La Salle's Fort St. Louis on Matagorda Bay, Texas (León, Chapa, and Sánchez de Zamora 1961, 196).

In 1686 León owned land near Cadereyta, and some of the Zacatiles Indians were attached to his land in accordance with the Spanish *encomienda* system. One of these Indians, a leader referred to as Alonso, served as León's guide on the expedition. A study of León's route of travel has been published by Candelario Reyes (1944, 159–180), who traces the route downstream along the Río San Juan and shows that other Zacatiles, living under native conditions, were seen in the vicinity of a town known today as Doctor Cos. An earlier name for Doctor Cos was Paso del Zacate. About ten miles east of Doctor Cos is a tributary of the Río San Juan known as Arroyo Zacate, on which some modern maps show a small community known as El Zacate. The word *zacate* in these place names is probably connected with the ethnic name Zacatiles, but it is not possible to determine which came first, the place names or the ethnic name.

Today Zacatiles cannot be linked with the native name of any Indian group recorded at an earlier date. The names of forty-four Indian groups who originally lived in the general vicinity of Cadereyta were compiled by Chapa (León, Chapa, and Sánchez de Zamora 1961, 190) in the second half of the seventeenth century. Most of these Indian groups lost their identities after being displaced by Spanish colonists. Remnants of some of these displaced populations probably survived as late as 1686, when León recorded the Zacatiles Indians, and an amalgam of some of the remnants may be represented by the Indians that León referred to as Zacatiles.

Zacatiles were next recorded between the years 1724 and 1728, when Rivera y Villalón inspected presidios along the entire northern frontier of Nueva España. Maps drawn by an engineer, Alvarez Barreiro (1729, map, 1730, 108–118; Wheat 1957, 82–84, map 115c) show Zacatiles as living farther down the Río San Juan, east of this river and not far from its junction with the Rio Grande. It would appear that these mapped Zacatiles were not very far from the 1686 location recorded by León, perhaps no more than thirty or forty miles. The Zacatiles were still associated with the same drainage system, that of the Río San Juan.

During the 1730s there was considerable unrest among the surviving Indian groups of eastern Nuevo León, and a few documents refer to Zacatiles as being among the Indian groups who raided Spanish settlements as far north as Cerralvo and as far south as Montemorelos. These sources do not mention any particular locality where Zacatiles were seen in native encampments during the period (Velasco 1715–1753, 303; Garza 1750, 274; Fernández de Jáuregui Urrutia 1963, 17–18).

An undated, anonymous document (Saldívar 1943, 32) believed to have been written about 1748, refers to a small group of Indians, some identified as Zacatiles, others as Cacalotes, as living in Nuevo León on the Río Pilón, an upper tributary of the Río San Juan. This Río Pilón is also known as Río Montemorelos, and it passes through Montemorelos, which was once known as San Mateo del Pilón. These Río Pilón Indians were said to consist of thirty families. As most of the Zacatiles at this time were living on the lower Río San Juan near the Rio Grande, the anonymous document may be referring to a less conservative subdivision of the Zacatiles who chose to remain near the older, better-established Spanish settlements. Some confusion has developed concerning the location of these Zacatiles on the Río Pilón of Nuevo León. In Tamaulipas there is also a stream still known as Río Pilón, and Wigberto Jiménez Moreno (1943, no. 60 on map) has placed Zacatiles on that stream instead of the former Río Pilón of Nuevo León.

After Escandón established various Spanish settlements in what is now northern Tamaulipas just before 1750, Zacatiles were mentioned as living on both sides of the Rio Grande in that area. Escandón (1751, 48–49) named Zacatiles among the Indian groups living near Reynosa. He listed Zacatiles and Tejón Indians as sharing a settlement near Reynosa; their combined population was given as sixty (twenty-four men, thirty-six women and children). Both groups were said to have previously lived immediately west of Reynosa Díaz. The Zacatiles, when ranging north of the Rio Grande, must have been in present-day Hidalgo and Starr counties of Texas.

No records indicate that Zacatiles individuals entered the Spanish missions at Reynosa and Camargo, or missions anywhere else. Presumably the Zacatiles of northern Tamaulipas declined in numbers during the late eighteenth century and eventually lost their ethnic identity through absorption by the Spanish-speaking population of the lower Rio Grande.

Zalayas

In 1688 Zalayas were mentioned in connection with the Convent of San Francisco of Cerralvo, which indicates that they lived somewhere in the Cerralvo area (Cavazos Garza 1973, 99). In 1735 Fernández de Jáuregui Urrutia (1963, 23, 108) identified Zalayas as one of the Indian groups that had caused trouble at the Spanish village of Agualeguas, some seventeen miles north of Cerralvo. The only indication that any Zalayas lived as far north as the Rio Grande is a statement made by Tienda de Cuervo (1929, 411) that a Zalayas woman, one of the last survivors of her group, was living with Garzas at Mier. She had been baptized at Mission San Nicolás de Agualeguas and at the time was serving as leader of the Garzas. This seems to be the only record of women leaders anywhere along the lower Rio Grande.

Conclusions

In Nuevo León, Spanish colonization began in the Monterrey-Cadereyta-Cerralvo area, which was occupied by numerous Indian groups, nearly all of which were hunters and gatherers. Several hundred native names for Indian groups have been recorded for the area now known as Nuevo León, but there has never been a systematic attempt to sort out the Indian populations of Nuevo León in a meaningful way. The earliest Spanish colonists in Nuevo León began to apply descriptive Spanish names to associated groups of displaced Indians, and this practice continued throughout the historic period. This makes it very difficult to identify Indian groups from Nuevo León who migrated eastward to the Gulf coast and northward and northeastward to the valley of the Rio Grande. In this chapter, twenty-four Indian groups, most of them known only by names of Spanish origin, have been identified as migrant groups. Of these, five groups can be linked with the upper headwaters of the Río San Juan in eastern Nuevo León, and the remaining nineteen can be linked with the lower Río San Juan and the Cerralvo district immediately to the west. Only a few migrant groups reached the Gulf coast, either north or south of the Rio Grande delta. Most of them seem to have drifted northward to the Rio Grande and down that stream toward the delta. Of these, only a few actually lived in the delta area at any time.

CHAPTER 7

Culture

THIS CHAPTER summarizes miscellaneous bits of information recorded about Indian cultures of the study area. These come from documents covering a long span of time, from 1519 to 1886. Some of this descriptive information can be linked with one specific Indian group; some can be linked with two or more Indian groups of a particular locality or area; and some can be linked only with a particular area, no Indian group names having been recorded. The information is presented under topical headings commonly used by ethnographers.

Subsistence

Hunting

In northern Tamaulipas and southern Texas the same game animals were available nearly everywhere and were undoubtedly hunted by most of the Indian groups. In documents written by Europeans, very few kinds of animals hunted by Indians were identified. No European ever bothered to list the names of all animals, large or small, that were hunted by a particular Indian group, or by various Indian groups associated with some specific area. The various animals actually named in documents are presented in Table 2, which reflects the casual recording of game animals. The Rio Grande delta area has more identified animals merely because of the relative abundance of documents.

Nearly every recorded list of animals hunted by Indian groups contains the name of deer, which was undoubtedly the principal game animal everywhere. During the period of record, bison were rarely seen south of the Rio Grande east of Coahuila. A smaller game animal, the peccary, was

Table 2
Animals Hunted

Animals	Rio Grande Delta	Lower Rio San Fernando	Cerralvo Area
Deer	1, 2, 3, 8, 9	6	7, 9
Peccary	2	6	7
Rabbits	—	6	5
Rats, mice	3, 8	—	5
Turkey	—	6	—
Birds, unspecified	4	—	—
Snakes	—	—	5
Wild horses	8	—	—
Spanish livestock	8	—	—

Key:
1. Ballí, Trejo, and Cano 1777, 1–28.
2. Barragán 1793a, 39–42, 1793b, 344–345.
3. Berlandier 1980, 1:244, 2:590.
4. Escandón 1946, 65.
5. Kress and Hatcher 1931, 35.
6. Ladrón de Guevara 1969, 29.
7. Noticias de los Conventos 1790–1814, 68, 118, 131, 136, 152.
8. Sierra Gorda 1798, 1–5.
9. Tienda de Cuervo 1929, 375, 381, 385, 396–398, 402, 411–414, 432.

also widely hunted. Still smaller animals, such as rabbits, rats, and mice, were occasionally mentioned but were probably hunted by all Indian groups. The hunting of wild horses and Spanish livestock, which is recorded for the Rio Grande delta, was a late phenomenon, occurring after Spanish ranches had been established in that area.

Fishing
Most of the information on fishing is recorded for Indian groups living near the Gulf coast and along the Rio Grande above the delta.

Fishing was probably the main source of food for Indians of the Rio Grande delta area. In 1688, while searching for La Salle's Fort St. Louis, Andrés de Pez and Manuel Rivas explored the area at the mouth of the Rio

Grande, where the Indians gave them fish (Rivas 1688, 7–17). Over fifty years later, during his reconnaissance of 1747, José de Escandón (1946, 65), found that fish were an important source of Indian food, and the local Indians provided fish for his men to eat. The Indians probably also collected clams for food, since Escandón was told that the river *ostiones* sometimes contained pearls, which were of no interest to the Indians.

Ten years later, in 1757, Agustín López de la Cámara Alta (1946, 116) commented on bow and arrow fishing in the coastal lagoons near the mouth of the Rio Grande. The Indians waded out into water that was sometimes waist deep, quickly taking large numbers of fish. Another source covering the same expedition noted that fishing was seasonal and that fish were dried and stored for later use (Tienda de Cuervo 1929, 403).

On the lower Río San Fernando, Antonio Ladrón de Guevara (1969, 29), writing in 1738, said that the Indians fished during the winter when plant foods were scarce. He referred to long nets made from soft yucca fibers with a mesh so fine that even the smallest fish were caught. In 1747 Escandón (1946, 34–35, 43, 57–58) reported that the San Fernando Comecrudos kept fish alive by means of netted pens, which may refer to a form of fish weir. He also noted the use, in fishing, of a plank boat salvaged from a wrecked French vessel that had been moved on log rollers to an inland lake. These Indians provided Escandón and his men with both raw and cooked fish.

Along the Rio Grande above the delta, various Indian groups were reported to have taken fish from the river. These reports refer mainly to Indians living at various Spanish missions upstream from Camargo and date up to 1818 (Organización de las Misiones 1946, 88; Barragán 1793a, 39–42; Noticias de los Conventos 1790–1814, passim; Bedoya 1816; Numana 1817; Antillán 1818). The reports say nothing about the fishing methods in use.

Food Gathering

The documentary sources examined refer frequently to wild plant foods gathered by Indian groups. Sometimes specific plants and plant parts are named, but often the food resources are merely referred to by such general terms as fruits, roots, and herbs. Table 3 summarizes the recorded data for three areas. The sources make it clear that the three most widely used plants were prickly pear (mainly the fruit), mesquite (bean pods), and maguey (root crowns). Of these, the prickly pear was by far the most commonly mentioned food plant, probably because of its wide distribution and tendency to grow in dense thickets. In 1535 Alvar Núñez Cabeza de Vaca

(1542, 42a–42b; Oviedo y Valdés 1959, 4:305–306) observed its use by Arbadaos, Cuchendados, and various unnamed Indian groups living on both sides of the Rio Grande in southern Texas and northern Nuevo León. Among the Arbadaos and Cuchendados north of the Rio Grande, green prickly-pear fruits and pads were said to have been roasted in some sort of earthen oven. During the first half of the seventeenth century, Alonso de León (León, Chapa, and Sánchez de Zamora 1961, 20) observed pit barbecuing of flowers and small fruits of prickly pear by the groups of the Monterrey-Cadereyta-Cerralvo area. In a ranchería of seventy or eighty huts south of the Rio Grande, Indians gave Cabeza de Vaca twenty loaves of bread made of mesquite-bean flour. The linkage of palm use with the Rio Grande delta is probably explained by the fact that palms were either rare or absent elsewhere. The clustered fruit of the Rio Grande palm was probably used for food. The unspecified roots often mentioned probably included the roots of a considerable number of plants in each area, but the unspecified fruits must refer mainly to prickly pear and mesquite. Very little information was recorded about methods of plant food collection, or how such foods were processed or otherwise prepared for human consumption.

Agriculture

Although documents of the seventeenth and eighteenth centuries indicate that the Indians of eastern Nuevo León and northern Tamaulipas were all hunters and gatherers, two separate expeditions in the sixteenth century refer to maize agriculture. In 1523 Francisco Garay and his people (Mártir de Anglería 1944, 573; Díaz del Castillo 1955, 1:106; Herrera 1945, 3:265; López de Gómara 1954, 2:282) observed clear evidence of maize being grown near the Gulf coast just south of the Río San Fernando. There they also observed guava and some sort of hens. In 1535 Cabeza de Vaca (1542, 49a) encountered two Indian women carrying loads of ground maize, apparently in an area southeast of Cerralvo. The women said that more of this flour could be obtained where they had come from, but thereafter Cabeza de Vaca did not mention seeing maize while traversing Nuevo León. This evidence of maize agriculture is less convincing than that of Garay, for it must be assumed that Cabeza de Vaca was able to recognize maize in a pulverized form. Nevertheless, there is enough evidence to suggest that in the early sixteenth century some maize was being grown farther north in northeastern Mexico than in later times.

Table 3
Wild Plants Used for Food

Plants	Rio Grande Delta	Lower Rio San Fernando	Cerralvo Area
Prickly pear: fruits, pads	1, 3	8, 10, 11	4, 5, 14
Mesquite: bean pods	1, 3	8	5
Maguey: root crowns	1	8, 12	7
Garlic, onions: bulbs	6	—	—
Yucca: flower buds	—	—	5
Palm: unspecified part	6	—	—
Roots: unspecified	1, 2, 3, 6, 13	12	2
Fruits: unspecified	2, 13	8	2, 3, 11
Herbs: unspecified	2, 13	12	2

Key:
1. Ballí and Hinojosa 1785, 1–3.
2. Barragán 1793a, 39–42, 1793b, 344–345.
3. Berlandier 1980, 2:590.
4. Causas Criminales 1782–1787, 83.
5. Cabeza de Vaca 1542, 41a–42b, 46a–48; Oviedo y Valdés 1959, 4:305–307.
6. Escandón 1946, 85.
7. Kress and Hatcher 1931, 35.
8. Ladrón de Guevara 1753b, 166.
9. Ladrón de Guevara 1969, 29.
10. Noticias de los Conventos 1790–1814, 131.
11. Saldívar 1943, 32–33.
12. Serie de Documentos 1783–1800, 119–121.
13. Sierra Gorda 1798, 1–5.
14. Tienda de Cuervo 1929, 411–412.

Domesticated Animals

Although most of the Indian peoples of northern Tamaulipas and southern Texas probably kept dogs, European documents rarely mention them. The vocabulary collected in 1886 from Comecrudos who still lived in the vicinity of Reynosa contains numerous words and phrases pertaining to dogs (Swanton 1940, 73–74). In 1535 Cabeza de Vaca (1542, 111a; Oviedo y Valdés 1959, 4:305) had mentioned dogs kept by the Arbadaos of southern Texas (vicinity of modern Hebronville). He and his companions bartered for two dogs, which they ate, but Cabeza de Vaca said nothing about the Arbadaos themselves eating dogs. In 1828 Berlandier (1980, 1:245) found numerous dogs among the surviving Western Carrizos (Yemé), who originally lived south of that section of the Rio Grande lying between Laredo and Mier.

Horses seem to have been rare among the various Indian groups of the area here being considered. The first mention of horses in the Rio Grande delta area was in connection with Garay's attempt to establish a Spanish colony near the mouth of the Rio Grande. In driving the Spaniards from that area, the Indians killed some of their horses (Díaz del Castillo 1955, 1:421, 2:105; Cervantes de Salazar 1971, 2:111, 281; Fernández de Navarrete 1955, 3:98–102; Mártir de Anglería 1944, 570). In 1747 Escandón (1946, 85) noted that horses and cattle were living wild along the lower Rio Grande, but he said nothing about Indian interest in them. Only after Spanish ranches began to be established on the Rio Grande delta, after 1760, did Indians become interested in European livestock. There are records of some groups, such as Malaguitas, Como se Llaman, and Mulatos, that refer to parents trading their children for horses and other livestock. The sheep and goats mentioned were probably eaten by the Indians, but horses were probably kept for use. The Mulatos are said to have used the horse in hunting deer (Riperdá 1772, 392–438; Ballí, Trejo, and Cano 1777, 1–28). Elsewhere there is little indication of Indians keeping European animals, except collectively in Spanish missions. On one occasion Escandón (1751, 105), as a gesture of good will, presented a few horses to Comecrudos of the lower Río San Fernando.

Food Preservation and Storage

The only records of food preservation and storage are connected with areas near the Gulf coast. In 1757 Tienda de Cuervo (1929, 403) wrote that Indian groups of the Rio Grande delta had a structure in which fish were dried and stored. Earlier, in 1739, Joseph Antonio Ladrón de Guevara (1969, 29) had noted that Indians along the Río San Fernando not only consumed quantities of wild fruits when ripe but also dried and stored these fruits for later use. He did not describe the storage structure.

Excavated Wells

In 1747 wells were seen in the area lying between the Nueces River and the northern margin of the Rio Grande delta (Escandón 1946, 72), and in 1777 a Spanish land surveying party in the delta area made use of a well that had presumably been dug by Pauraques encamped nearby (Copia Certificada 1790, 28; Davenport and Wells 1918–1919, 219). Escandón (1946, 58) also noted in 1747 that Indians in the vicinity of Salinas de la Barra, near the mouth of the Río San Fernando, obtained drinking water from small holes they had dug with their hands. Escandón said that water from these shallow wells tasted brackish. At that time the locality was occupied by Comecrudos of the Río San Fernando. Along the Texas coast northward from the Rio Grande, similar shallow wells were also reported. In 1767 Diego Ortíz Parrilla (1767, 1–36) noted them near abandoned Indian campsites on Padre Island southeast of Baffin Bay, and much farther up the coast, on the shores of Matagorda Bay, Damian Massanet in 1689 wrote that Indians of that area dug wells for drinking water (Bolton 1965, 363).

Houses

For this area the recorded information on houses is notable for lack of useful information on house form and size and on the spatial arrangement of houses in encampment areas. So far as the Rio Grande delta is concerned, the scanty data seem to indicate that none of its Indian populations lived in completely enclosed structures. The only kind of structure now identifiable is the brush arbor (*ramada*), which consists of support poles for a flat roof covered by leafy tree branches or some other kind of locally available vegetative material. In 1777 the Mulatos of this area were said to have no real houses, only *ramadas* erected in wooded areas (Ballí, Trejo, and Cano 1777, 14). In 1798 Conde de Sierra Gorda (1798, 1–5) noted that the Indians still living along both sides of the Rio Grande below Reynosa either lived in wooded localities without houses of any kind or under *ramadas*. In the rare and short periods of freezing weather, these Indians kept fires burning continuously. More than a century earlier, in 1686, León (León, Chapa, and Sánchez de Zamora 1961, 200) had noted abandoned Indian camps near the coast south of the Rio Grande and referred to "sticks" that may have been the remains of *ramada* structures.

A. S. Gatschet (1891, 63), who in the late nineteenth century visited the Tonkawas at Fort Griffin in northern Texas and the Comecrudos on the lower Rio Grande, described their houses together, as though there were no significant differences: "[Their houses] are cane or willow stick lodges, flat on top, open on one or two sides and covered with brushwood and sailcloth, old blankets, etc., on the top and closed-up sides. They average in height from five to seven feet." Although this is not ideal reporting, it does appear that the Comecrudos of Gatschet's time were continuing the lower Rio Grande *ramada* tradition.

For the lower Río San Fernando, all we know is that in 1757 the Indians of that area were living in structures that Tienda de Cuervo (1929, 352) referred to as *toritos*. Just west of Sierra de Picachos, the Carrizo Yemé were said to live in huts built of palm fronds in 1829 (Berlandier 1980, 1:244), but no details were given about the structure. In the same area, families of Malnombre sometimes lived in a cave during the prickly-pear season (Causas Criminales 1782–1787, 90).

There is some information on houses of Garzas and Malaguitas, who are linked with an area north of Cerralvo, Nuevo León. In 1757 some of these were seen on the Rio Grande at Mier, and Tienda de Cuervo (1929, 414, 1930, 115) stated that their houses were covered with mats and thatch and that when a camp was moved these houses were dismantled and the materials moved to the new location. The use of mats for covering portable houses by the Garzas and Malaguitas is of interest because, in 1535, Cabeza de Vaca (1542, 41a) noted the same material and probably the same kind of structure among the Arbadaos who, according to Campbell and Campbell (1981, 38), lived somewhere in the vicinity of Hebronville, Texas, which is about sixty miles from Mier. Unfortunately, after leaving the Arbadaos and crossing the Rio Grande into the Cerralvo area, Cabeza de Vaca failed to mention any details of house construction.

The information summarized above suggests that at least two housing traditions existed along the Rio Grande: a brush arbor, or *ramada*, tradition near the coast and an enclosed house tradition much farther up the river. The *ramadas* were probably rectangular in floor plan, and the enclosed houses, probably round. An environmental factor may partially explain these differences in housing. The climate of the Rio Grande delta is characterized by short, mild winters, whereas farther up the Rio Grande, winters are longer and colder.

Clothing

The only information on clothing comes from the Rio Grande delta area. In 1747 Escandón (1946, 66) reported that Indian men wore no garments of any kind and that women wore only a skirt of animal skin or grass. Sometime between 1783 and 1796, males of an unnamed Indian group observed at the mouth of the Rio Grande were still wearing no garments (Evia 1968, 165). By 1798, probably after being influenced by Spanish disapproval of complete nudity, the men were said to be wearing breech-clouts of any suitable material and the women, skirts of animal skin (Sierra Gorda 1798, 1–5). At Mission San Joaquín del Monte of Reynosa, Indians from the delta area were said to be dressed in deer skin (Ballí and Hinojosa 1785, 1–3).

In 1828 Berlandier (1980, 1:245) briefly described clothing worn by surviving Western Carrizos (Yemé), who originally lived south of that section of the Rio Grande lying between Mier and Laredo. In summer the men wore a breechclout consisting of a square piece of cloth, presumably attached to a cord around the waist, but in winter a more closely fitting breechclout was worn. The women wore either a wrap-around skirt that extended from the waist down to the knees or an inexpensive Spanish housedress.

Early in the nineteenth century, Berlandier (1969, 165, fig. 17) observed that the Western Carrizos had gone barefooted near Laredo. Some Indians also referred to as Carrizos, living near the mouth of the Rio Grande sometime before 1886, were said to have gone barefooted (Gatschet 1891, 79). Words for moccasins (*zapatos*) and sandals (*sandalias* or *huaraches*) were mentioned in the Comecrudo vocabulary of 1886 (Swanton 1940, 82, 100). In 1535 Cabeza de Vaca (1542, 47b) observed moccasins (*zapatos*) among the possessions taken from the second ranchería visited after crossing the Rio Grande; they were taken by Indians who were escorting the Spaniards. In the Monterrey-Cadereyta-Cerralvo area, León (León, Chapa, and Sánchez de Zamora 1961, 19) observed sandals, which he described as soles with leather straps that protected the feet from thorns.

Ornamentation

Hair Dress
Spanish observers seem to have had little interest in styles of Indian hairdress, and most of what they noted is connected with partial removal of

head hair. Any Indian group that removed some of the head hair, apparently males only, was likely to be referred to as Pelones. The only descriptive information is connected with Pelones of the Cerralvo area in northern Nuevo León. These Pelones removed a band of hair from the top of the head down to the forehead hair line.

Ornaments

Ornaments of native manufacture were mentioned only by Cabeza de Vaca (1542, 47a–48b), who in 1535 saw beads among three Indian groups living south of the Rio Grande in an area that today lies between Camargo and Cerralvo.

Tattooing

It seems clear enough that tattooing was widely practiced among the Indian groups of northeastern Mexico and adjacent areas, but references to tattooing are usually vague and generalized (Ruecking 1955b). It is not possible to prepare a list of all Indian groups who tattooed, or a list of those who did not. No particular tattoo pattern was ever described. In some cases it is not even possible to determine whether a passage refers to permanent tattooing or to temporary body painting.

In 1757 López de la Cámara Alta (1946, 116) noticed tattooing among the various Rio Grande delta Indians that he encountered, and he said that men were tattooed on the face; women, on both face and body. He also said he could not tell one group from another on the basis of tattoo patterns, which probably means that tattooing was not primarily for purposes of ethnic identification. López de la Cámara Alta (1946, 119) also gave essentially the same information for several groups later seen farther up the Rio Grande, among them Cacalotes, Carrizos (eastern), and Cotonames. He noted, however, that these groups added to their tattooing every year. Gatschet's Comecrudo vocabulary of 1886 refers to the Rio Grande Pintos, then extinct, as having been tattooed.

In 1738 Ladrón de Guevara (1738, 65) commented on tattooing among the Tanaquiapemes of the lower Río San Fernando, noting that the lines of tattooing were narrow like the mark left by a lash (*verdugón*). Among other Indians of that coastal region, he said, the tattoo lines were somewhat broader. This seems to indicate significant stylistic differences, but not much else can be deduced from his remarks.

Face and Body Painting

Face and body painting was probably done by all Indian groups on special occasions, but documents are barren of descriptive detail.

Pigments

The pigments used for body painting and tattooing are rarely mentioned. In 1535, after he had crossed the Rio Grande and was apparently in what is now northeastern Nuevo León, Cabeza de Vaca (1542, 48a, 50a; Oviedo y Valdés 1959, 4:307) mentioned that the Indians at one encampment gave the Spaniards ochre and bags of margarite (referred to as silver by Cabeza de Vaca), the latter identified as being used for face painting in a neighboring western group of Coahuila. In 1757 López de la Cámara Alta (1946, 116, 119) repeatedly referred to the blue color of tattooed Indians seen along the Rio Grande from its mouth upstream as far as Revilla. Powdered charcoal was widely used by American Indians to produce the blue color in tattooing.

Feathers

Although European observers referred to birds as being hunted by various Indian groups, little was noted about feathers and their uses by Indians. The only mention of feathers seems to have been that of León, who in 1686 encountered an unnamed Indian group in the Rio Grande delta area south of the river. He tried to entice these Indians to come closer and communicate with the Spanish party by leaving a piece of cloth and a knife near a tree. But only after the Spaniards had moved back from the tree would the Indians come forward. They took the Spanish gifts and left a bundle of feathers. Before leaving, the Indians waved some sort of feather banner (*bandera*) to signal the Spaniards to come to receive the Indian gift of feathers (León, Chapa, and Sánchez de Zamora 1961, 198; Reyes 1944, 171).

Weapons and Tools

Weapons

Without much question the weapon complex known as the bow and arrow was used by all Indian groups of the area, and it continued to be used by remnants of populations that survived into the nineteenth century. In 1747 Escandón (1946, 66) said that the bow and arrow was the only weapon used among the Indians he encountered in the Rio Grande delta area. In

1798 Conde de Sierra Gorda (1798, 1–5) noted that bows and arrows were still being used by Indian groups on both sides of the Rio Grande near the coast.

In 1886, while collecting a vocabulary from the Rio Grande Comecrudos still living at Las Prietas, Gatschet obtained words for bow, arrow, bow-string, and poison that was smeared on arrows. This is the only indication of the use of poisoned arrows anywhere in the area. It is not known whether poisoned arrows were used in hunting or in warfare, or in both (Swanton 1940, 59, 76, 90, 94, 98).

The only descriptive information on this weapon complex was recorded in 1738 by Ladrón de Guevara (1738, 64), and this pertained to Tana-quiapemes of the lower Río San Fernando and possibly also to other Indian groups then living there. The bow was described as having the length of its user, which suggests a minimal length of five feet. The arrows, which were carried in quivers, had shafts of reed (*carrizo*), foreshafts of heat-treated wood, and points made of flint or glass. Presumably the glass used came from bottles collected along the seashore. The points were said to be attached to foreshafts by tar. This tar was probably asphaltum that had washed ashore and was collected from the beach.

Of special interest is the report of spears being used, along with the bow and arrow, by only one population unit, the Negros of the Rio Grande delta, a group identified in 1757 by López de la Cámara Alta (1946, 117) as consisting of African blacks from a wrecked slave ship who had inter-married with local Indians. These Negros were said to have used the spear (undescribed) with great dexterity. It appears likely that this spear was of a style used by blacks somewhere along the coast of western Africa.

Cutting, Scraping, and Piercing Tools

Gatschet's Rio Grande Comecrudo vocabulary collected in 1886 refers to a scraping tool used to smooth a wooden stick, and there are words for knives used for various purposes, including the cutting and trimming of hides. It is indicated that the Comecrudos used a needle for tattoo-ing, which at that late date probably means the European metal needle (Swanton 1940, 64, 70, 76, 79, 85). In 1535, while among the Arbadaos some forty or fifty miles north of where the Rio Grande was crossed, Cabeza de Vaca (1542, 41b) was made to scrape animal hides, but he did not describe the tool used.

Pulverizing Tools

The only pulverizing tool recorded for the entire area was a fairly heavy wooden pole said by Cabeza de Vaca (1542, 46a–46b) to have been used for pulverizing mesquite bean pods by an unnamed group living near his crossing of the Rio Grande. The pestle had a diameter equivalent to that of a man's leg and was said to have a length of 1.5 *brazas* (about 5.7 ft.). The mortar was described as a hole in the soil, but this hole may have been in a local outcrop of bedrock. A similar tool is described by the chronicler Alonso de León (León, Chapa, and Sánchez de Zamora 1961, 20) for groups living in the Monterrey-Cadereyta-Cerralvo area during the first half of the seventeenth century.

Fire-making Devices

In 1738 the Tanaquiapemes and presumably other Indian groups of the lower Río San Fernando were said to be generating fire by use of a two-piece, wooden drill set. The rotating drill stick, probably having a blunt point at one end, was said to have a diameter of one *dedo* (about .7 in.). The drilling platform was a flat piece of wood one *cuarta* (about 8 in.) in length, two *dedos* in width, and one *dedo* in thickness (Ladrón de Guevara 1738, 65). Although not reported elsewhere, this device for starting fires was probably used by all the Indian groups covered in this study.

Log Rollers

Of considerable interest is the single record of log rollers being used to move a heavy object across flat terrain. Such rollers were used by the Río San Fernando Comecrudos to move a heavy boat salvaged from a French ship to an inland lake for use in fishing. The lack of documentary evidence makes it idle to speculate whether this device was of local independent origin or was something learned from Europeans (Escandón 1946, 57).

Containers

Pottery of native manufacture is not indicated by any European documents. Basketry was noted only in 1535 by Cabeza de Vaca (1542, 46a) when he visited Indians living near the Rio Grande. They were eating a mush of pulverized mesquite bean pods from a container said to be like a two-handled Spanish basket. Later, after crossing the Rio Grande, Cabeza de Vaca (1542, 49a) mentioned that Indian women carried water for the Spaniards. The containers were not described, but may have been made from hollowed-out prickly-pear pads, noted by Alonso de León (León, Chapa, and Sánchez de Zamora 1961, 21) as used for that purpose in northern Nuevo León during the first half of the seventeenth century. Cabeza de Vaca (1542, 48a) also noted small bags or pouches containing margarite while traversing an area somewhere west of the lower Río San Juan. These bags were probably made of animal skin.

Textiles

All cloth mentioned in documents is clearly identifiable as of European manufacture, and matting made of unidentified flexible splints is mentioned only as a covering for portable houses among the Arbadaos in 1535 (Cabeza de Vaca 1542, 41b) and among the Garzas and Malaguitas of Mier in 1757 (Tienda de Cuervo 1929, 415, 1930, 115).

Transportation and Communication

Canoes

Canoes, apparently of the dugout variety, were numerous among Indians of the Rio Grande delta area early in the sixteenth century, at least during the period 1519–1523, when Spaniards of the Garay expeditions were there (Herrera 1945, 3:272–273; Hoyo 1972, 1:67). The Garay documents merely indicate that canoes were used by Indians for transportation in warfare with Spaniards. Gatschet's Rio Grande Comecrudo vocabulary collected in 1886 contains a few words for boats, but these give no information on materials or uses (Swanton 1940, 76, 87).

Elsewhere boats were rarely mentioned in Spanish documents. The only boat noted for the lower Río San Fernando area is a ship's boat salvaged from a French vessel. This plank boat was rolled on logs to an inland lake for use in fishing by local Comecrudos (Escandón 1946, 34–35, 43, 57). Canoes were probably used by various Indian groups living along the Rio Grande upstream from Reynosa, but documents make no mention of them.

Roadways

A few documents pertaining to the Rio Grande delta indicate that some parts of it were originally forested and that other parts were covered by dense thickets. Across these heavily vegetated areas the local Indian groups had narrow paths that were kept cleared. In 1686, while traveling along the south bank of the Rio Grande, apparently just upstream from modern Reynosa, León noted one such path that was over one league, or about three miles, in length (León, Chapa, and Sánchez de Zamora 1961, 197–198; Reyes 1944, 168–169). These cleared paths or trails, which technically are primitive roadways, seem to indicate that the numerous Indian groups of the delta area were in frequent contact with each other. One of these paths was noted as late as 1777 by a Spanish land survey party north of the Rio Grande near the present boundary between Cameron and Hidalgo counties. The surveyors became lost in a dense thicket, and some of the Pauraques encamped nearby led them out along one of these trails (Copia Certificada 1790, 28; Davenport and Wells 1918–1919, 219). To the west Friar Solís (Kress and Hatcher 1931, 35) also made use of several narrow paths, apparently made by Indians, before reaching the banks of the Rio Grande twenty-six miles downstream from Laredo in 1767.

Smoke Signaling

The use of smoke signals for distant communication is recorded only for the Rio Grande delta, notable for its occupation by numerous Indian groups. In 1747 Escandón (1946, 61) stated that a leader of the Rio Grande Comecrudos used smoke signals to summon leaders of other Indian groups to come and see the Spaniards. One wonders if perhaps, during the period 1519–1523, when Garay attempted to colonize the lower Rio Grande, smoke signals may have sometimes been interpreted as indicating the locations of some of the forty Indian encampments reported.

Greeting Behavior

The Cuchendados, who lived some thirty miles north of the Rio Grande, were said to have stroked the faces and hands of Cabeza de Vaca (1542, 42b, 47a) and his companions with their hands and then stroked their own bodies. When Cabeza de Vaca (1542, 47a) had crossed the Rio Grande in 1535 and had entered an encampment of one hundred houses not far south of the river, apparently somewhere above its junction with the Río San Juan, he and his companions were welcomed by loud cries and vigorous slapping of hands against the thighs. This may have been a customary way of greeting important visitors.

Trade

No documents have been found that mention trade between Indian groups, but there are occasional references to trade between Spaniards and Indians. In 1738, when Ladrón de Guevara (1738, 64–65) was on the lower

Río San Fernando, the Tanaquiapemes and other unspecified Indians came to trade. The Indians brought deer hides and glass bottles (*limetas*) for which they received ribbon and tobacco. Presumably the bottles were wine bottles salvaged from shipwrecks or collected from beaches on the nearby Gulf coast. In 1772 at the salt lake known as Purificación, or La Sal del Rey (in northern Hidalgo County), three Spaniards of Reynosa were said to be on their way to trade with coastal groups. These villagers obtained hides, wax, and iron from the Indians. Also at this time, the Spaniards obtained several Indian children in exchange for livestock (horses, goats, sheep), various garments, food, tobacco, knives, and jewelry (Riperdá 1772, 392–438). Late in the eighteenth century, José de Evia (1968, 165) noted that Indians were still selling Indian children for horses and mules. Escandón (1751, 105) recorded not trade but gift exchanges with Comecrudos of the Río San Fernando. In 1747 he gave them biscuits, tobacco, knives, and various trinkets, and the Indians gave him fish. In 1750 he gave them clothing, tobacco, and a few horses, but there was no indication of what the Indians gave in return. Spaniards, for diplomatic purposes, frequently distributed gifts among Indians, but most of the accounts recording this do not mention reciprocal gifts from Indians.

Political Organization

It is difficult to discern the political structure of Indian groups in this region because documents refer only to Indian leaders with whom Spaniards dealt. These leaders were almost always men apparently chosen by Indian groups to deal with outsiders, Indian or European, in contact situations. The only woman leader recorded was the Zalayas Indian known as Margarita, who led the Garzas at Mier (Tienda de Cuervo 1929, 411). In each Indian group, there may have been one or more civil leaders who functioned in its routine internal affairs. Some indication of this appears in Gatschet's Rio Grande Comecrudo vocabulary, which contains words for at least two kinds of leaders, one of which is identified as a war leader (Swanton 1940, 76, 92). This seems to be supported also by Conde de Sierra Gorda's (1798, 1–5) statement that leaders of the Rio Grande delta groups had authority only in times of war.

Official Spanish documents that pertain to relations with Indian groups· often recorded the names of Indian group leaders. Each leader was identified as a *capitán*, a title that preceded the Indian leader's name. The recorded names of leaders were nearly always Spanish names, as Capitán

Santiago, Capitán Juan Isidro, or Capitán Antonio Francisco Cyprian. At least twenty-eight such names appear in documents whose dates range from 1686 to 1886, but most of them are in documents of the middle eighteenth century or after Escandón's colonization program began.

When several Indian groups were living together, or near each other in the same locality, one of the group leaders was sometimes recognized as the head leader of all the associated groups, and he was known to Spaniards as *capitán general*. It appears likely that in such cases the *capitán general* was the leader of the numerically dominant group. In the Rio Grande delta area, for example, Capitán Santiago of the Comecrudos was also the *capitán general* of some thirty local Indian groups. Such population estimates as were recorded seem to indicate that these Comecrudos had the largest population of any Indian group of the delta area (Escandón 1946, 61, 65, 67, 94). No documents mention how Indian leaders were chosen, and there is no reference to any sort of group council consisting of older, more experienced men. A few documents refer to situations in which actions taken by leaders were rejected by their people, but it is hard to interpret the recorded detail (see Riperdá 1772, 392–438; Ballí, Trejo, and Cano 1777, 1–28).

The limited information on group leadership does not show any notable differences between Indian groups anywhere in the area here under consideration. Occasional bits of biographical detail about Indian *capitanes* suggest that they were chosen because they knew the Spanish language, had some knowledge of Spanish ways, and had previously fought Spaniards. They were men considered best qualified for dealing with Europeans. In modern pioneer studies, Frederick H. Ruecking, Jr. (1954a, 1955a) attempted to group the Indians living along the lower Rio Grande and its vicinity into a single political unit referred to as Carrizo Cluster. He also assumed that all the groups of this area represented a single cultural and linguistic unit, but no historical evidence supports this association.

Warfare

Very little is known about warfare in Indian groups, and most of this is connected with the Rio Grande delta. It was recorded mainly in accounts of the earlier Spanish expeditions, especially those of Garay and León, all prior to the year 1688. These refer to conflict between Spaniards and Indians and mention the use of canoes and the bow and arrow in fighting; evasive action (campsites abandoned, all Indians taking refuge in nearby wooded areas); warriors following the enemy (Spaniards) at a safe distance; and intimidation (hostile gestures made from a safe position, accompanied by flute playing). Nothing is said about Indian war leaders.

Later documents confirm some of this information and indicate that it was also connected with warfare between Indian groups. As late as 1772, it was noted that one of the delta groups, the Mulatos, placed their encampments in open areas near the edge of woods, so that, in case of a surprise attack, they could quickly take cover (Ballí, Trejo, and Cano 1777, 1–28). In 1757 the Negros (African blacks) were said to have constantly been at war with their Indian neighbors (López de la Cámara Alta 1946, 116). The Negros had both the bow and arrow and the spear, but it is not known if they used the spear in warfare. León's mention of flute playing in connection with warfare is unique for the coastal area, but is recorded for an area much farther west, in Texas south of the Edwards Plateau (Campbell 1984, 8–9).

Farther up the Rio Grande, near the junction of the Río San Juan with the Rio Grande, León noted in 1686 that the Caurames were at war with an unidentified neighboring Indian group. He said that the Caurames had sent out scouts to spy on their enemy at night (León, Chapa, and Sánchez de Zamora 1961, 196–197).

Documents of the late eighteenth century occasionally refer to raids made by northern Indians, particularly Apache and Comanche, and mention that various Indian groups along the Rio Grande, from Reynosa to Revilla, offered to help the Spanish settlers in frontier defense, but there is little indication of whether or not they actually did so. They did, however, warn Spaniards of impending Apache or Comanche attacks, apparently obtaining advance information from other Indian groups of the area.

Religion and Curing

Ceremonies

In 1686, while in the Rio Grande delta area, León observed a recently abandoned ceremonial site, apparently somewhere east of present-day Matamoros. He recognized it only because of its concentration of human footprints, and he judged from the footprint patterns that some three hundred Indians had participated in the ceremony (León, Chapa, and Sánchez de Zamora 1961, 199; Reyes 1944, 172). León's observations should be of some theoretical interest to archaeologists because this evidence of group activity would not be recognized in routine archaeological survey and excavation. León would not have recognized the site if a heavy rainfall had obliterated the footprints.

Sometime between 1783 and 1796, Evia (1968, 165) visited an unnamed Indian group who lived near the mouth of the Rio Grande and who sang and danced every day during the few days the Spaniards were there. From the Rio Grande Comecrudos still living at Las Prietas in 1886, A. S. Gatschet obtained words for at least two ceremonial dances, one of which was identified as a peyote dance, and he also recorded the words of a dancing song about deer hunting. These informants said that the Comecrudos used to dance every day during the month of March (Swanton 1940, 75, 105–106). Gatschet also collected a word for dance in the Cotoname language, but his informants volunteered no additional information (Swanton 1940, 119).

Gatschet's Comecrudo vocabulary indicates that several musical instruments were associated with ceremonial dancing: a drum (undescribed); a gourd rattle containing *usachito* seeds; and tinkle bells (material unidentified, but said to contain small pieces of flint) that were attached to the legs of dancers just below the knee (Swanton 1940, 57, 75, 86–87, 96, 105–107). A gourd was seen in a Mulato ranchería in 1777, but its use was not identified (Ballí, Trejo, and Cano 1777, 1–28). In 1686 León (León, Chapa, and Sánchez de Zamora 1961, 199) mentioned another musical instrument, the flute, but this seems to have been used only in connection with warfare.

Farther up the Rio Grande, on both sides of the river, Cabeza de Vaca (1542, 47a, 49b) in 1535 witnessed considerable ceremonial behavior. At a ranchería on the Rio Grande, this included singing and dancing and use of a gourd rattle. The gourd rattle, which presumably had a wooden handle, contained pebbles and had holes bored through the gourd wall to release more sound. Indians on the Rio Grande told Cabeza de Vaca that the gourds came down the river during floods and were collected after the floodwaters had subsided. This gourd rattle was also used by shamans in curing rites for individuals. Gourd rattles were also observed by León (León, Chapa, and Sánchez de Zamora 1961, 24) among groups of the Monterrey-Cadereyta-Cerralvo area during the first half of the seventeenth century.

Shamans

European observations of curing specialists, or shamans, were rarely recorded. For the Rio Grande delta area, the only information comes from

Gatschet's linguistic work among the Comecrudos of the Reynosa area in 1886. Gatschet recorded the word for medicine man, or shaman. He was told the personal name (Kopte) of the last shaman who had functioned among them. It is clear from Gatschet's notes that one method used by Comecrudo shamans in treating disease was to suck blood from some part of the patient's body (Swanton 1940, 56, 74, 79, 84, 97).

Witchcraft

A document of 1777 refers to a case of witchcraft among Mulatos said to be living east of modern Reynosa. This involved an elderly woman who was said to be dying because she had been bewitched by another Indian woman (Ballí, Trejo, and Cano 1777, 1–28). In 1886 Gatschet obtained the word for "witch" from the surviving Comecrudos living at Las Prietas (Swanton 1940, 97).

Another apparent case of witchcraft is connected with the Malaguitas, who originally lived in the Cerralvo area of northern Nuevo León. In 1781 a Malaguita Indian man, then living at a place known as La Feria (in present Cameron County, Texas), had recently come from an unidentified Spanish mission, possibly one of the missions at San Antonio. He told of a man called Cotilla, not ethnically identified, who evidently had the powers of a witch, since he claimed that Spanish bullets could not penetrate his body. Cotilla had persuaded some of the Malaguitas to desert their mission (Ballí 1781, 1–3).

Cannibalism

There is only one record of cannibalism, and this refers to the Río San Fernando Comecrudos. In 1747 Escandón (1946, 34–35, 43) learned that a French ship had previously been wrecked on the nearby coast. These Comecrudos claimed that they had eaten the flesh of some of the surviving sailors they had killed.

Herbal Medicines

The use of plant materials for medicinal purposes was recorded only in documents of the nineteenth century. In 1828 Berlandier (1980, 1:246), a botanist, briefly referred to herbal medicine among the surviving Carrizos (Yemé group). He noted that various unspecified herbs were used for syphilis. Seeds of the *mauacate (Pithecellobium ebano)* were used as a purgative. Fevers were treated by drinking a tea made from *cenizilla* leaves (*Leucophyllum frutescens*), or by a concoction prepared by mixing tea from *cenizilla* and willow leaves with the sap of maguey (*aguamiel*).

In 1886 Gatschet recorded the word for a purgative used by the surviving Rio Grande Comecrudos (Swanton 1940, 89). This was probably prepared from one or more plants.

Miscellaneous Beliefs

In 1798 Conde de Sierra Gorda (1798, 1–5) noted that the surviving Indian groups still living on or near the Rio Grande delta east of Reynosa believed that storms could be stopped by beating the air. What the air was beaten with is not recorded. He also said that these Indians scattered ashes around encampments in order to prevent death from entering.

Games

Early documents say nothing about games and other pastimes among Indians, but Gatschet recorded a Rio Grande Comecrudo word for a wooden ball, which may indicate some native form of ball game (Swanton 1940, 76–77). In 1800 the missionaries at Camargo referred to several vices, including games (probably gambling games) that were depraving the Indians living near Camargo. The Indian groups specified were not from the Rio Grande delta but from the lower Río San Juan and Cerralvo areas. By 1800 various European card games were undoubtedly known to all surviving Indian populations.

Conclusions

It hardly seems necessary to point out that the descriptive information presented above is limited in scope and hence essentially impressionistic in character. For any particular Indian group, little can be said about its culture at any time during the 367-year period covered by documents. As there was considerable migration of displaced Indian groups from one area to another, it is not possible to identify certain cultural traits as characteristic of a particular area. In short, the recorded information on Indian cultures is too scant for fruitful analysis. Nevertheless, it is evident that more cultural information was recorded in documents than has previously been realized.

CHAPTER 8

Historical Demography

THE BASIC native population of northeastern Mexico consisted of numerous small groups known to Spaniards as Indians. The only exception to this is the case of the Negros of the Rio Grande delta, who appear to have been descendants of African blacks from a wrecked ship carrying slaves. These blacks had intermarried with local Indian groups. To the Spanish colonists of northeastern Mexico, all Indians looked very much alike, and documents rarely refer to minor variations in physique. But scattered here and there in the documents are bits of demographic information that are difficult to evaluate because of incompleteness and also because of the confusion concerning the names by which Indian groups were known. This information includes population figures, age groups, sex ratios, group intermarriages, and mortality connected with epidemics of diseases introduced by Europeans. Although demographers are usually not concerned with the physical characteristics of human populations, this chapter will briefly summarize what was recorded about Indian physique.

Physical Characteristics

In 1535, while traveling in the area east of Cerralvo, Alvar Núñez Cabeza de Vaca (1542, 48a–48b; Oviedo y Valdés 1959, 4:306–307) visited a temporary settlement of Indians who were notably different from all other Indians he had seen. Their skin color was much lighter, and over half of them had a clouded eye; some were blind. These observations probably refer to a remarkably high incidence of albinism. Although it cannot be proved, descendants of these Indians may have been a group in the same area later known to Spaniards as Blancos (see chap. 6).

One case of abnormal stature was recorded in 1752 at Mission San Agustín de Laredo of Camargo. This referred to a woman, identified as Tareguano, who was said to be a dwarf. As her body proportions were not described, it is not possible to determine what kind of dwarfism was involved, but she had learned to spin cotton and was known as an excellent worker (Organización de las Misiones 1946, 87–88). During a maritime reconnaissance of the Gulf coast late in the eighteenth century, José de Evia (1868, 161, 165) referred to the stature of an unnamed Indian group at the mouth of the Rio Grande. These Indians were said to be above average in stature. Early in the nineteenth century, Jean Louis Berlandier (1980, 1:244–245), a botanist, made observations at a settlement of Indians in northern Nuevo León known as Carrizos. These were probably the more westerly Carrizos who were sometimes referred to as Yemé. Berlandier noted that males were above average in stature and were generally beardless, although some had mustaches. Skin color was referred to as coppery, and he noted that almost all of them had very long upper lips (space between nose and mouth).

Two physical traits, skin color and head hair distribution, were altered by some Indian groups, and these alterations led to their being designated by Spanish descriptive names. Skin color was altered by tattooing, which appears to have been widely distributed in the general area. Probably more groups practiced tattooing than the documentary record indicates. The very fact that tattooing was practiced states something about skin color, for on a skin that is dark the tattooed patterns are not so visible. In Nuevo León removal of hair from portions of the scalp led to wide use of the Spanish name Pelones. Several groups whose native names were recorded were also said to have been known as Pelones. Apparently patterned removal of head hair was not so widely distributed as tattooing.

Size of Indian Population Units

Most of the population figures given for Indian groups are in documents written after 1747 and are mainly connected with Spanish missions. These figures are given in preceding subsections covering specific Indian groups. In Spanish mission records, population figures may refer to all the Indians in a mission at a specific date; they may refer to two or more Indian groups lumped together; or they may refer to a single named Indian group. As most of the Indian group names are of Spanish origin, the figures tell us nothing about remnants of former Indian groups who had merged and become known by a Spanish name. Furthermore, it is evident that missionaries usually gave population figures only for Indian groups represented in larger numbers. It seems obvious that figures derived from mission records say little about the size of Indian groups prior to displacement by Europeans.

Attempts were made to construct tables presenting population figures for sets of Indian groups, but the lack of uniformity and limited entries for most groups led to no significant conclusions. What mission records show best is decline in Indian populations. For the few Indian groups whose population was recorded more than once, the latest figure recorded is always smaller.

Population Density

It is possible to correlate the number of identified Indian groups in certain areas with the available population figures and say something about population density in three areas, namely, the Rio Grande delta, the lower Río San Fernando, and the Cerralvo area of northern Nuevo León.

All records seem to indicate that the Rio Grande delta was originally occupied by a large number of Indian groups who made use of its abundant food resources. The Francisco Garay documents of the period 1519–1523 refer to forty Indian settlements (Fernández de Navarrete 1955, 3:98). In 1747 José de Escandón (1946, 66) estimated that the sixteen Indian groups living on the delta south of the main river channel consisted of 2,500 families, which may be taken to indicate a population of some 7,500 individuals. As about the same number of Indian groups were living on the delta north of the main river channel, the total delta population may have been about 15,000. In 1757 Agustín López de la Cámara Alta (1946, 116) said that nine delta Indian groups had about 1,700 warriors, suggesting a total population of at least 5,000. As López de la Cámara Alta's estimates cover less than one-third of the Indian groups recorded by Escandón ten years earlier, his sample also suggests that the total Indian population of the delta in 1757 was about 15,000. Later population estimates indicate a striking decline in the delta Indian population, particularly after 1760, when Spanish ranches began to be established on delta lands. In 1772 the delta Indian population was given as 2,000; in 1793, as 800; and in 1798, as 656 (Estado de las Misiones 1946, 68, 69; Barragán 1793a, 39–42, 1793b, 344–345; Sierra Gorda 1798, 1–5). These figures included Indians who lived in the delta area between the coast and Reynosa Díaz.

The lower Río San Fernando area contained relatively few identified Indian groups. In 1747 the combined population of Comecrudos, Pamoranos, Pintos, Quedejeños, and Quinicuanes was estimated to consist of 300 families, one half of which were Comecrudos. Thus the total population of the area probably included no more than 1,000 Indian individuals (Escandón 1946, 34, 58, 93). Thereafter, the population figures, mainly derived from records connected with Mission Cabezón de la Sal, show a striking decline. By 1793 the lower Río San Fernando Indian population had declined to 353 or 88 families (Barragán 1793a, 39–42, 1793b, 344–345). This is approximately 35 percent of the population recorded for the year 1747.

So far as the record now stands, the Cerralvo area of northern Nuevo León was occupied by a much larger number of Indian groups than the Rio Grande delta. In the seventeenth century, Chapa (León, Chapa, and Sánchez de Zamora 1961, 190) recorded the native names of some seventy Indian groups said to be living within twenty-five to thirty miles of Cerralvo. This figure, however, probably includes remnants of Indian groups earlier displaced from areas near Monterrey and Cadereyta by Spanish colonists. In 1535 Cabeza de Vaca, while passing east of Cerralvo, visited four Indian encampments along a line of travel some eighty miles in length. The smallest camp had forty houses; the largest had one hundred houses, which suggest populations of 120 and 300, respectively. If we assume that the average camp had a population of 210, and further assume that there were seventy separate Indian groups in the area, we get a population of 14,700 in the Cerralvo area. As noted above, there probably were not as many as seventy Indian groups in that area in Cabeza de Vaca's time, and hence the figure of 14,700 is too high. This suggests that the Cerralvo area was not so densely populated as the Rio Grande delta.

Although these calculations are open to question, it seems very likely that the Rio Grande delta was the most densely populated area of northeastern Mexico and southern Texas. Areas both north and south of the delta were certainly less densely populated, and the nearest area of notable density is the Cerralvo area. It was from the Cerralvo area that so many Indian groups moved eastward down the Rio Grande to live at or near the Spanish settlements established by Escandón in the middle eighteenth century.

Factors in Indian Population Decline

There is no question about the decline of all former Indian populations of northeastern Mexico and vicinity. Although descendants of some Indian groups still live in the area today, they do not live together in social units bearing names that indicate Indian origin. Most Indian groups disappeared from the historical record by 1825, and only a few were still known in 1886, when A. S. Gatschet visited an Indian community near Reynosa.

Although in the area as a whole a number of factors involved in population decline can be recognized, it is difficult to find good documentation. Epidemics of diseases, particularly diseases introduced by Europeans, such as smallpox and measles, were an important factor in Indian population decline. Although documentation is limited, the mortality figures cited are impressive. In Nuevo León, during the seventeenth century, a number of Indian groups were almost wiped out by epidemics. Some epidemics were said to last for two or three years, passing from one Indian group to another (León, Chapa, and Sánchez de Zamora 1961, 93; Hoyo 1972, 2:412–414). In 1749 Escandón (1749a, 198, or 248) noted that an epidemic had reduced two Indian populations of Mission Divina Pastora de Santillana of Camargo from thirty-seven families to only fifteen families. In 1757 Tienda de Cuervo (1929, 348, 373) said that at Mission Cabezón de la Sal on the Río San Fernando sixty-nine Pintos and fifty-four Quinicuanes had died in a single epidemic. At Reynosa he noted that measles had reduced the number of Tejón women, leaving a sex ratio of seventeen males to seven or eight females. These cases all refer to early contacts with Europeans, and the mortality rates were probably higher than in later epidemics.

Additional factors that were involved in Indian population decline may be cited.

1. In early Nuevo León, the slave trade and punishment for rebellions led to removal of numerous Indians from that area (León, Chapa, and Sánchez de Zamora 1961, passim).

2. Numerous adult male Indians were probably killed during repeated Indian attacks on outlying Spanish settlements in eastern Nuevo León in the first half of the eighteenth century (Barbadillo y Victoria 1715; Lozada 1732; Fernández de Jáuregui Urrutia 1963, 12–23).

3. In the late eighteenth century, particularly along the lower Rio Grande, discouraged parents sometimes sold children to Spaniards to become servants and laborers. This was common enough at the time to warrant a viceregal investigation (Riperdá 1772; Cabello 1780a; Evia 1968, 165).

4. In any area there was always a slight loss in local Indian population because families or individuals went to distant Spanish missions, or to a distant hacienda or city to find employment.

5. Although difficult to prove, it seems likely that the last surviving individuals of some Indian groups may have become so discouraged about their future that children were no longer desired. ´

6. Late in the historic period, marriages between Indians and other castes were noted in entries made in registers of the parish church at Matamoros (Matamoros Registers MS). Children of these marriages were not regarded as Indian, and at least statistically signify population decline.

CHAPTER 9

Languages

SO FAR as is now known, the various languages once spoken by Indian groups of northeastern Mexico and southern Texas are extinct. All that is known about these languages comes from documents written by Europeans, and for the majority of Indian groups whose names are known, nothing whatever was recorded about their languages. This means that the total number of Indian languages and dialects spoken in the area will probably never be known. For the few languages that can be recognized, the vocabulary samples are usually small, sometimes consisting of only a few words, with or without indication of their meanings; and rarely is there a text sample to provide information on language structure. All these recorded samples are far from being truly representative of an entire language. Furthermore, there is little or no recorded information on how a particular language slowly changed through time, or how it was influenced by other languages spoken in the area. These severe limitations make it very difficult to classify languages and demonstrate genetic relationships.

For the lower Rio Grande area, only two recorded languages have been assigned formal names, Comecrudo and Cotoname. The last samples of both were recorded in 1886, shortly before they ceased to be spoken. It does not appear reasonable to assume that these were the only languages spoken by natives of the area, and it does not seem likely that remnants of various groups who migrated from other areas, especially Nuevo León, spoke either of these languages. One faint clue to the amount of linguistic diversity comes from Friar Vicente Santa María's (1930, 394) "Relación Histórica" of Nuevo Santander, written about 1790. Santa María counted up to thirty different languages spoken in the area now covered by the state of Tamaulipas. From some direct encounters and from several local informants, who were in frequent contact with the Indians, Santa María claimed that these languages differed in verbs, nouns, syntax, and dialects. Although areas occupied mainly by hunting and gathering populations are sometimes noted for linguistic diversity, as in California, Santa María was probably referring mainly to dialects, not to languages in the technical sense of modern linguists.

In addition to the Comecrudo and Cotoname languages of the lower Rio Grande, other languages have been recorded for rather widely scattered areas in northeastern Mexico and southern Texas. These include

Coahuilteco: Spoken by numerous bands of Indians who ranged over a large area between San Antonio, Texas, and Monclova, Coahuila (García 1760; Swanton 1940, 10–55; Troike 1959; Vergara 1965).

Solano: Spoken along both sides of the Rio Grande between Piedras Negras and Guerrero, northeastern Coahuila (Swanton 1940, 54–55).

Quinigua: Spoken along the mountain front of central and western Nuevo León, particularly in the Monterrey-Cadereyta-Cerralvo area (Hoyo 1960; Gursky 1964).

Carrizo Yemé: Spoken in the Cerralvo area of northern Nuevo León (Berlandier 1980, 1:246; Goddard 1979, 370–371).

Garza: Spoken in the Cerralvo area of northern Nuevo León (Berlandier 1980, 2:430–431; Goddard 1979, 370–371).

Maratino: Spoken in the Sierra Maratines area of southern Tamaulipas (Santa María 1930, 407–408; León 1901, 5–9; Swanton 1940, 122–124).

Naolan: Spoken near Tula in southwestern Tamaulipas (Weitlaner 1948, 219–220).

Aranama: Spoken along the lower Guadalupe River near the Texas coast (Swanton 1940, 124).

Karankawa: Spoken along the Gulf coast of Texas between Galveston and Rockport (Gatschet 1891, 73–98; Swanton 1940, 124–133).

Historical linguists have attempted to link these languages with Comecrudo and Cotoname. This matter will be reviewed later in the chapter.

Languages of the Lower Rio Grande Area

The earliest known language sample from the lower Rio Grande consists of two words recorded in 1686 during the expedition to the Gulf coast led by Alonso de León in search of La Salle's French settlement (León, Chapa, and Sánchez de Zamora 1961, 194–202; Reyes 1944, 159–180). León traveled from Cadereyta down the Río San Juan to its junction with the Rio Grande and then followed the Rio Grande to its mouth. He encountered Zacatiles and Caurames on the lower Río San Juan, and a Zacatiles leader known as Alonso served as a guide. Apparently this Zacatiles leader had not been down the Rio Grande from the site of Camargo, and León tried to obtain guides from Indian encampments along the Rio Grande. At one such encampment near the coast he managed to capture three Indian women, with whom apparently the Zacatiles could not communicate. According to León, the women pointed northward and uttered two words, *saguili* and *taguili,* which he thought might refer to places where the French had settled. The meaning of the two words remains unknown, and they have not been equated with words from any recorded Indian language of northeastern Mexico and Texas. The inability of the Zacatiles guide to serve as an interpreter indicates that, in 1686, at least one language spoken along the lower Río San Juan was different from one language spoken along the lower Rio Grande.

The best-known language of the lower Rio Grande is Comecrudo, for which A. S. Gatschet collected an extensive vocabulary at Las Prietas, near old Reynosa, in 1886. At that time only eight Indian individuals, all quite old, could still speak Comecrudo, and three of these served as Gatschet's informants (Gatschet 1891, 38; Swanton 1940, 5, 55). This large sample of the Comecrudo language makes it possible to identify other speech samples of the area as Comecrudo:

1. Three words from the language spoken by Tanaquiapemes, collected by Joseph Antonio Ladrón de Guevara (1738, 64).

2. A vocabulary of 148 words collected by Jean Louis Berlandier about the year 1829 from Indians he identified as Mulatos (Goddard 1979, 369–370).

3. A vocabulary of thirty-one entries obtained in 1861 by Adolph Uhde (1861, 184–186) from Indians at Reynosa then locally referred to as Carrizos.

In 1747 José de Escandón (1946, 34–35, 43, 56–58) made certain statements indicating that the Comecrudos of the lower Rio Grande did not speak the same language as the Comecrudos of the lower Río San Fernando. On the Río San Fernando near the coast, Escandón encountered Comecrudos, Pamoranos, Pintos, Quedejeños, and Quinicuanes. Among these groups Escandón could find no Indian who could tell him how far it was northward to the Rio Grande or who could even suggest a suitable route to follow. Six of these Indians (specific ethnic group affiliations not recorded) accompanied Escandón to the Rio Grande, where none was able to serve as an interpreter. As Escandón's main contact with the Rio Grande delta Indians was a local Comecrudo leader who evidently had authority over all other Indian groups of the area, it appears reasonable to interpret these circumstantial details as meaning that the Comecrudos of the Río San Fernando did not speak a language known to Comecrudos of the Rio Grande. A Spanish name, Comecrudo, had evidently been applied to two unrelated Indian groups.

Ten years afterward, in 1757, Agustín López de la Cámara Alta (1946, 116) made certain observations about Indians of the Rio Grande delta that seem to indicate that many of them spoke the same language. They were identified as Ayapaguemes, Catanamepaques, Comesecapemes, Gumesecapemes, Mayapemes, Pintos, Saulapaguemes, Tanaquiapemes, and Uscapemes. These, he said, spoke dialects of the same language. The differences he noted were mainly in certain sounds and words. It is possible that all of these groups spoke the Comecrudo language, since Ladrón de Guevara's three Tanaquiapemes words recorded in 1738 are now identifiable as Comecrudo. It would appear that Comecrudo was at least the dominant language spoken by Indian groups living on or near the Rio Grande delta. The evidence, however, is not good enough to support the statement that the thirty-one Indian groups listed for the delta area by Escandón in 1747 *all* spoke the Comecrudo language.

To summarize, it may be said that the following groups undoubtedly spoke Comecrudo: Uhde's Carrizos of Reynosa; the Comecrudos of the Rio Grande whose language was recorded by Gatschet; Berlandier's Mulatos of 1829; and Ladrón de Guevara's Tanaquiapemes of 1738. López de la Cámara Alta's comments on languages spoken in the delta area strongly suggest that the following groups also spoke Comecrudo: Ayapaguemes, Catanamepaques, Comesecapemes, Gumesecapemes, Mayapemes, Pintos of the Rio Grande, Saulapaguemes, and Uscapemes. These two lists are tied together by Gatschet's statement that, at Las Prietas, no Pintos or Tejones had survived in 1886, but his informants said that the two groups had spoken Comecrudo.

About the year 1829, Berlandier (1980, 1:248, 2:429) recorded 104 words that are now identified as representing the language known as Cotoname (Goddard 1979, 370). This vocabulary was obtained from an Eastern Carrizos group known as Yué. Berlandier regarded the language of the Carrizo Yué as different from that of the Western Carrizos known as Yemé. Over fifty years later, in 1886, when he was at Las Prietas, A. S.

Gatschet collected a vocabulary of 125 entries for the Cotoname. His informants were Emiterio and Santos Cavazos, and the former spoke both Cotoname and Comecrudo, which may have introduced some confusion into the linguistic record. The language now known as Cotoname is clearly recorded for only two Indian groups, the Cotonames and the Carrizos known as Yué.

For the sake of completeness, it may be noted that, in 1886, Gatschet's informants mentioned that the Tampacuas did not speak Comecrudo (Swanton 1940, 97). The language spoken by Tampacuas remains unknown, but we do know one language they did not speak.

Linguistic Classification

Manuel Orozco y Berra (1864, 1:290–309), the first scholar to categorize languages spoken in northeastern Mexico, wrote before the Comecrudo and Cotoname languages had been recognized. He referred to two sets of presumably related languages or dialects: one called Coahuilteco; the other, Tamaulipeco. While based to some extent on recorded language samples, particularly Coahuilteco, Orozco y Berra's scheme was essentially geographic. Coahuilteco was used for inland groups of western Nuevo León, Coahuila, and the northern part of Tamaulipas along the Rio Grande; and Tamaulipeco was used for coastal groups of almost all Tamaulipas (including some groups of adjacent eastern Nuevo León). He also referred to three isolated languages: that of the Hualahuises (Linares-Hualahuises areas of Nuevo León); that spoken by both Pisones and Janambres of southwestern Tamaulipas; and that of the Olives (extreme southern Tamaulipas). Apparently Orozco y Berra had seen no samples of the Tamaulipeco or the three isolated languages, and no samples have yet been found. Orozco y Berra's classification was often cited until more language samples became available for study (see Prieto 1949; Powell 1891; Thomas and Swanton 1911).

After recording the Comecrudo and Cotoname languages in 1886, A. S. Gatschet (1891, 36–39, 95–97) altered Orozco y Berra's scheme. Gatschet thought he detected relationships between the Comecrudo, Cotoname, and Coahuilteco languages, and this led him to use a new term, Pakawa, to symbolize the relationships. He also thought he detected relationships between his Pakawa and the languages spoken by Karankawan and Tonkawan Indian groups of the Texas area. Gatschet's term Pakawa was not accepted and soon dropped out of publications on American Indian languages.

In 1915, and again in 1940, John R. Swanton published the results of his analyses and comparisons of language samples then known from northeastern Mexico and southern Texas (Coahuilteco, Solano, Maratino, Comecrudo, Cotoname, Aranama, and Karankawa). In his 1915 publication, Swanton (1915, 17–40) viewed Coahuilteco, Comecrudo, and probably Karankawa as subdivisions of a Coahuiltecan language stock, and he saw a relationship between Cotoname and Tonkawa. He thought that all of these languages may have been remotely related to Atakapa, Aranama, Solano, and Maratino. In his 1940 publication, Swanton (1940, 144–145) was more cautious and modified his 1915 interpretations. With certain reservations, he recognized Coahuilteco, Comecrudo, and Cotoname as representing a linguistic family and then stated that these three languages may have been more remotely related to Solano, Maratino, and Karankawa.

Edward Sapir, who was especially interested in determining the remote relationships of all American Indian languages, accepted Swanton's 1915 interpretations and in a 1920 publication assigned Swanton's groups to a Hokan linguistic stock (Sapir 1920, 280–290). Later, in 1925, and again in 1949, Sapir recognized a Coahuiltecan family of languages that included Karankawa, Tonkawa, and Coahuilteco. His Coahuilteco included Comecrudo and Cotoname (Sapir 1925, 525–526, 1949, 173).

The interpretations of Swanton and Sapir, especially the latter, were accepted as reasonable for several decades, but eventually they began to be questioned because of discrepancies in the argument and especially because it came to be realized that the language samples involved were too small and too unrepresentative to demonstrate linguistic relationships. Ives Goddard (1979), in a recent reanalysis of the linguistic materials used by Swanton, states what now appears to be the prevailing view among linguists, namely, that it is not possible to demonstrate linguistic relationships on the basis of such limited information.

CHAPTER 10

Spanish Missions Nearest to the Rio Grande Delta

ONCE ESTABLISHED, Spanish missions became focal points of inter-action between Spaniards and specific Indian groups, and documents per-taining to missions constitute a major source of information on movements of Indian groups displaced by Spanish colonists of northeastern Mexico and adjacent areas. The interest here is in missions that were nearest to the Rio Grande delta. These were either on the lower Río San Fernando or along, or not far from, the south bank of the Rio Grande, extending from Reynosa upstream as far as Revilla (near present Guerrero, Tamaulipas). Documents connected with these missions help to distinguish between In-dian groups native to the Rio Grande delta and Indian groups displaced from various parts of colonial Nuevo León. Displacement was mainly northward to the Rio Grande and eastward to the Gulf coast of northern Tamaulipas.

Eight Spanish missions and their Indian populations will be discussed. Two of these were established in the seventeenth century about twenty-five miles south of the Rio Grande near present Agualeguas, Nuevo León: Santa Teresa de Alamillo and San Nicolás de Agualeguas. The remain-ing six missions were all established in the eighteenth century, in 1748 or shortly thereafter, during the extensive colonization of present-day Ta-maulipas by José de Escandón. One of these, Cabezón de la Sal, was near modern San Fernando on the lower Río San Fernando. The rest were dis-tributed along the Rio Grande: San Joaquín del Monte (Reynosa), Divina Pastora de Santillana and San Agustín de Laredo (both at Camargo), Purísima Concepción (Mier), and San Francisco Solano de Ampuero (Revilla). Table 4 associates specific Indian groups with each mission.

The five missions established along the Rio Grande and the single mis-sion on the lower San Fernando were among the last missions to be estab-

Table 4
Indian Groups at Missions Nearest to the Rio Grande Delta

Indian Groups

Aguatinejos 5	Mulatos 4, 6
Anda el Camino 4, 6	Narices 4
Blancos 1	Nazas 4
Borrados 6	Negros 4
Cacalotes of the Río San Juan 5	Paisanos 6
Carrizos of the lower Rio Grande 6	Pajaritos 6
Carrizos (?) 6, 8	Pames 4
Carvios 6	Pamoranos 3
Casas Chiquitas 4	Pauraques 6
Chinitos 8	Pelones 4
Comecrudos of the Rio Grande 4	Pintos of the Rio Grande 4
Comecrudos of the	Pintos of the Río San Fernando 3
Río San Fernando 3	Pistispiagueles 8
Como se Llaman 4, 6	Quedejeños 3
Cotonames 4, 6	Quinicuanes 3
Cueros Quemados 6, 7, 8	Saulapaguemes 4, 6
Garzas 2, 7, 8	Tampacuas 4
Guajolotes or Cacalotes of the	Tanaquiapemes 3
Rio Grande 4	Tareguanos 2, 6
Gualeguas 8	Tejones 4, 6
Guapes 6	Tortugas 5, 6
Malaguitas 4, 6, 7, 8	Venados 6
Malnombre 2, 6, 8	Zacatiles 4
Mayapemes 4, 6	Zalayas 2, 7

Key:
1. Santa Teresa de Alamillo (founded 1646).
2. San Nicolás de Agualeguas (1675).
3. Nuestra Señora del Rosario de Cabezón de la Sal of San Fernando (1749).
4. San Joaquín del Monte of Reynosa (1750).
5. Divina Pastora de Santillana (1749).
6. San Agustín de Laredo of Camargo (1749).
7. Purísima Concepción of Mier (1767).
8. San Francisco Solano de Ampuero of Revilla (1750).

lished in northeastern Mexico and Texas. Their buildings were constructed after the peak of the Spanish mission period had passed and were not architecturally impressive. Only Mission San Agustín de Laredo of Camargo had buildings of stone and mortar. These missions were all administered by Franciscan missionaries from Zacatecas.

Santa Teresa de Alamillo near Agualeguas

This mission, which had a life span of about thirty-two years, was the first Spanish mission established anywhere near the Rio Grande downstream from Laredo. It was designed to serve Indians of the Cerralvo area, especially the Axipayas, Blancos, and Mimioles (Hoyo 1972, 2:410). Its location was about seventeen miles north of Cerralvo, and it was abandoned in 1682, when its Indians were moved to another mission nearby, San Nicolás de Agualeguas.

San Nicolás de Agualeguas of Agualeguas

Mission San Nicolás was established near present Agualeguas, Nuevo León, in 1675, apparently for Indians of the Cerralvo area known as Malnombre. It was on Arroyo Agualeguas, a tributary of the Río Alamos, about twenty-five miles from the Rio Grande. In 1682, when Mission Santa Teresa de Alamillo, less than two miles away, was abandoned, the Indians then still living at Santa Teresa were transferred to San Nicolás (Barragán 1774, 1–3; González de Santianés 1783, 289–292; Cadena 1942, 19–23).

In 1715 Mission San Nicolás seems to have had Indians from at least four groups: Ayaguas, Calancheños, Garzas, and Malnombre (Causas Criminales 1782–1787, 152–153; Barragán 1774, 1–3). It is difficult to determine from the documents available whether Indians lived continuously at San Nicolás; the accounts seem to indicate that some of them visited the mission only for short periods now and then.

In 1770 or 1771, Friar Diego Vázquez, who had been at Mission San Nicolás for years, died, and the Indians all left the mission to subsist by hunting and gathering. Then, in 1773, the mission was legally declared a civil settlement. Indians who had been at the mission were persuaded to congregate at various other localities in northern Nuevo León (Vidal de Lorca 1775b, 252, 1778, 1–19).

All of the Indian groups mentioned above in connection with Mission San Nicolás de Agualeguas were native to the Cerralvo area, but only the

Garzas and Malnombre later lived at or near missions established along the south bank of the Rio Grande above Reynosa. Records of the Rio Grande missions, however, refer to two Indian groups who had formerly lived at Mission San Nicolás, the Zalayas and Tareguanos, both originally native to the Cerralvo area (Escandón 1751, 20; Tienda de Cuervo 1929, 411). Mission San Nicolás de Agualeguas may have received its name from the Gualeguas Indians, but no documents refer to Gualeguas as having entered this mission.

Cabezón de la Sal of San Fernando

The full name of this mission was Nuestra Señora del Rosario de Cabezón de la Sal, but in most documents it was referred to as Cabezón de la Sal. It was established in 1749 during José de Escandón's first colonization drive in what is now Tamaulipas. The first location was near a spring on land occupied by the Pinto Indians, not far from the junction of Arroyo Chorreras with the Río Conchas (Río San Fernando). This locality was about eight miles from the modern town of San Fernando (Yerro 1749, 286–287; Organización de las Misiones 1946, 29, 40, 50, 52, 63–65). Insufficient water and floods on the Río San Fernando forced the missionaries to move the mission several times to various localities along the Río San Fernando between Arroyo Chorreras and the Spanish village of San Fernando.

Approximately ninety families of Pamoranos, Pintos, Quedejeños, and Quinicuanes were reported to be living at the mission in 1750 (Escandón 1751, 104–105). Later some of the Comecrudos and Tanaquiapemes entered the mission, but in 1752 a flood destroyed the mission buildings, the cultivated fields, and the irrigation canal that had been dug by Indians. This forced all resident Indians to leave the mission to find food in the surrounding area. At this time the mission was reported to own ten yoke of oxen, 250 cows, more than 500 sheep and goats, two herds of brood mares, and an unspecified number of additional horses and mules (Organización de las Misiones 1946, 84–85, 90–92).

In 1753 Escandón found no missionary in residence at San Fernando. He gave 122 *fanegas* ("bushels") of corn to be distributed by the Pinto leader, Captain Marcos de Villanueva (Ladrón de Guevara 1753b, 166–167; Valcarcel 1754, 340–341). About three hundred Indians (fifty-six families) were said to have been at this mission. By 1757 Mission Cabezón de la Sal had been moved to a site less than a mile from the village of San Fernando (Tienda de Cuervo 1929, 347–362, 1930, 102; López de la Cámara Alta 1946, 111–112). This was the fourth time the mission had been moved during a period of less than ten years.

In 1770 the mission Indian population consisted mainly of Pintos (Gómez 1942, 63). Two years later, in 1772, Conde de Sierra Gorda gave the combined population of Pintos and Tanaquiapemes as one hundred. The mission was said to have sometimes had enough food for all the mission Indians, but at other times the Indians had to search for food in the woods. In 1774 the Pinto Indians asked to be moved to a place known as Mojarras (González de Santianés 1774, 1–2). A year later, in 1775, the mission was abandoned by its missionaries. Francisco de la Serna, who had been appointed secular protector of the mission, collected the mission property, including the livestock, and destroyed the mission buildings. The local Indians complained to the viceroy, but official investigations led to a decision that did not favor the Indians. Several Indian groups were reported to be living at San Fernando in 1788 (Vidal de Lorca 1788, table). All this led to a transfer of most of the Indians, in 1792, to Mission San Francisco de Helguera near present Santander Jiménez (Serie de Documentos 1783–1800, 7–43, 97–124; Puertollano 1793, 359; Sierra Gorda 1794, 356; Revillagigedo 1966, 85; González Salas 1979, 416–417). Documents apparently written before the removal indicate that 344 Pintos, Comecrudos, Tanaquiapemes, and Quedejeños were at San Fernando (Barragán 1793a, 39–42, 1793b, 344). These Indians eventually returned to the site of Mission Cabezón de la Sal, where others had probably remained. The former mission locality continued to be occupied by Indians through the remainder of the eighteenth century, and some Indians were still reported in the area as late as 1818. These remnants were probably served by the priest at the San Fernando church (Noticias de los Conventos 1790–1814, 1, 3, 13, 219, 221; Bedoya 1816, table; Numana 1817, table; Antillán 1818, table).

Except for the Pamoranos, who had originally lived in the Cerralvo area of Nuevo León, the Indian groups associated with Mission Cabezón de la Sal seem to have been native to an area along both sides of the Río San Fernando near the Gulf coast. The Pintos, Quedejeños, and Quinicuanes lived inland in the general vicinity of present San Fernando. The Comecrudos and Tanaquiapemes lived adjacent to the coast, but the latter also ranged farther north, some of them living in the Rio Grande delta area. The Pamoranos, clearly immigrants from another area, seem to have ranged the area that includes the Sierra Pamoranes, some fifty to sixty miles inland from the coast.

San Joaquín del Monte of Reynosa

In 1749 Escandón established Reynosa at a site, near the present town of Reynosa Díaz, about thirteen miles up the Rio Grande from the modern city of Reynosa. Shortly afterward Indians began congregating for a mission, and in 1750, 312 Indians were identified as Comecrudos, Narices, Nazas, and Pintos and were said to be living on mission lands about one mile up the Rio Grande from the village of Reynosa (Yerro 1749, 283–284; Escandón 1751, 48–50, 52; Valcarcel 1756, 106). Mission San Joaquín del Monte got off to a slow start. A report of 1752 (Organización de las Misiones 1946, 86–87) noted that there was not enough food for some 300 Indians and that floods on the Rio Grande had hindered construction of buildings. At that time the mission had only two structures described as *jacales* (walls of brush and mud, roof thatched).

In 1753 Escandón revisited Reynosa and noted the presence of the same Indian groups cited above, and he also mentioned that Pintos and Zacatiles were about to enter the mission. According to him, there were at least 300 Indians in the vicinity of Reynosa, and the mission might have to be abandoned because not enough food could be produced for the Indians (Ladrón de Guevara 1753c, 325–328). When Tienda de Cuervo visited Camargo in 1757, he found that the mission had been moved to a new site about two miles from Reynosa at a locality known as El Desierto, where fields were being prepared for cultivation. The mission had 350 sheep, 80 cows, 15 mules, and 10 horses. The missionary and the Indians were at odds with each other because the former had baptized fifty-one children and only three adults (Tienda de Cuervo 1929, 372–373, 376–377, 381, 1930, 108; López de la Cámara Alta 1946, 116–117).

It was not until 1767 that Mission San Joaquín finally received full title to more than one hundred square miles of land west of Reynosa. Near this tract was a marsh known as Ciénega de Pajaritos that the Indians had been using as a source of wild plant products, especially fruits (Reynosa Grants 1767, 23–25, 28–29). In 1770 Lino Nepomuceno Gómez (1942, 61) reported a total mission population of 222 and said that the Indians of Mission San Joaquín were still having to go to the woods for much of their food. In 1772 Conde de Sierra Gorda named Pintos and Tejones as the main Indian groups represented at the mission, but said that Comecrudos had lived there at various times. He gave the total Indian population as 275 and noted that the Indians grew corn and other vegetables on the floodplain of the Rio Grande (Estado de las Misiones 1946, 68–69).

In 1785 municipal officials of Reynosa reported that Comecrudos, Pintos, and Tejones were living at the mission at least part of each year, but that most of their time was spent in searching for food on nearby ranches and unoccupied woodlands. They said that the mission had no church and that the Indians were served by the parish church of Reynosa. The mission's flock of three hundred sheep was being rented to a Spaniard, and the mission had only seventeen cows. The Indians were cultivating small plots of corn, squash, cantaloupes, and watermelons on the Rio Grande floodplain, but their crops were quickly consumed (Ballí and Hinojosa 1785, 1–3). A later document of 1788 refers to the presence of Comecrudos, Tejones, and Cacalotes at the mission (Vidal de Lorca 1788, table). These and other Indian groups continued to be mentioned in documents during the period of 1790–1814 (Noticias de los Conventos 1790–1814, 1, 3, 5, 130, 135–136, 152, 219, 221). In 1802 the town of Reynosa was moved from its old site at Reynosa Díaz to its present location, mainly because of floods in the Rio Grande valley. The Indians, however, remained at the old location but used the new church at Reynosa. In 1809 the Indians asked for a missionary and a Spanish protector, but nothing seems to have been done about their request (Ballí 1809, 1–5).

Early in the present century, Herbert E. Bolton (1965, 449) inspected the now missing registers of San Joaquín del Monte, which cover the period 1790–1816, and found the names of numerous Indian groups not mentioned in early mission documents. This indicates that small numbers of many Indian groups had entered the mission after 1772. Although the evidence is difficult to digest, it appears that the Indian groups associated with Mission San Joaquín del Monte during its entire existence came from various areas (see Table 4). Of the groups first recorded at the mission, the Comecrudos, Pintos, and Tejones seem to have come from the Reynosa area and the Rio Grande delta to the east; the Narices, Nazas, Pelones, and Zacatiles were refugees from eastern Nuevo León. Later groups came mainly from the delta area and its margins near the Gulf coast. Some were recorded by native names, such as Malaguitas, Mayapemes, Saulapaguemes, and Tampacuas; others by Spanish names, such as Anda el Camino, Casas Chiquitas, Como se Llaman, Mulatos, and Negros, all apparently remnants of various groups with native names that had been recorded by the first Spaniards to visit the delta area in 1747 and shortly afterward. Other groups of Mission San Joaquín, such as Carrizos and Cotonames, had come to the Reynosa mission from areas farther up the Rio Grande. The Pames were probably captives brought from Sierra Gorda. In general, the Indians represented at Mission San Joaquín del Monte seem to have come mainly from areas along the Rio Grande.

Divina Pastora de Santillana of Camargo

This mission, which existed only during the years 1749–1750, was at a locality called El Tepextle, the site of modern Camargo, on the south bank of the Rio Grande. It was established for three immigrant groups from Nuevo León: Aguatinejos, Cacalotes, and Tortugas, all of whom were referred to as Pelones by Spaniards of that time. These Indians had been helpful to Escandón during his expeditions of 1747 and 1749. It is said that when they learned that they would have to share the mission locality with Spanish settlers, they abandoned the mission and returned to their homelands on the upper Río San Juan in Nuevo León. At that time the three Indian groups were said to have a combined population of less than two hundred. Mission Divina Pastora followed its deserting Indians and was reestablished for them in the Pilón valley near modern Montemorelos (Velasco 1715–1753, 285–338; Escandón 1749a, 195–199, or 245–250, 1749b, 441, 1749c, 190–194; Bueno de la Borbolla 1749, 206–210; Ladrón de Guevara 1969, 69–70).

San Agustín de Laredo of Camargo

In 1749 Escandón established the village of Camargo on the south bank of the Rio Grande near its junction with the Río San Juan, but he did not immediately assign lands for a mission. Two friars were left at Camargo to organize and build the mission, which was eventually placed on lands at the junction of the two rivers. The first structure seems to have been an *enramada* ("brush arbor") (Yerro 1749, 283–284). Families from six Indian groups congregated at the mission site: Cueros Quemados, Guajolotes, Paisanos, Pajaritos, Tareguanos, and Venados. Juan Antonio Viruela, a leader of the Tareguanos, the most numerous group, was elected governor of the *congrega* (Escandón 1751, 19–22). A total of 359 Indians was recorded at the mission in 1752, and these included Indians from the six groups named above, the seventh being identified as Tejones. At this time the mission was said to have 10 yoke of oxen, 100 cows, 270 sheep, 6 goats, 32 horses, and 12 mules (Organización de las Misiones 1946, 87–88).

By 1757 Mission San Agustín had been moved to the south side of Camargo. The Indian groups were essentially the same as recorded earlier, and the total number was given as 243. By this time the Indians were living in adobe brick houses with thatched roofs that were clustered around the missionary's dwelling, which was built of stone and mortar. A permanent church was under construction. On the nearby mission lands were fields in which corn, beans, squash, watermelons, and cantaloupes were grown. Some of the Indians had their own fields for growing corn and squash. The mission also had at least four hundred horses. It was recorded that the Indians, with missionary approval, at times went out into the surrounding area to hunt deer and gather wild fruits (Tienda de Cuervo 1929, 398–402, 1930, 111).

Again in 1770 the mission was said to be flourishing, with 246 Indians, among whom were noted Cueros Quemados, Pajaritos, Tareguanos, Tejones, and Venados, indicating that the mission Indian population had changed very little. Some of the Indians had become stonecutters, masons, and carpenters. The Indians continued tilling their own fields, which were on the floodplain of the Rio Grande and subject to destruction by floods (Estado de las Misiones 1946, 68–69).

It is evident that the principal Indian groups identified with Mission San Agustín de Laredo up to the year 1770 were Cueros Quemados, Guajolotes (cf. Cacalotes), Paisanos, Pajaritos, Tareguanos, Tejones, and Venados. It may be noted that, except for the Tareguanos, all these groups have names of Spanish origin (their native names remain unknown). The Tejones can be linked with the Rio Grande below Camargo, but the remaining six groups can be linked with an area along the south side of the Rio Grande between Camargo and Mier, particularly the area lying between the Río San Juan and the Río Alamos. In 1735 Fernández de Jáuregui Urrutia (1963, 22) listed the names of fourteen Indian groups that had been attacking Spanish settlements of the Cerralvo area of northeastern Nuevo León (Cerralvo is fifty miles or less from both Camargo and Mier). On this list are the names of the same six Indian groups noted above. It appears likely that these eighteenth-century groups with Spanish names represent accretions of remnant Indian groups whose native names were recorded for the Cerralvo area during the seventeenth century (see León, Chapa, and Sánchez de Zamora 1961, 190).

After 1770 individuals and families from other Indian groups, apparently in small numbers, entered Mission San Agustín de Laredo. This is indicated by the mission registers that were examined early in the present century by Bolton (1965, 450–451). The groups identified for this later period (see Table 4) can be traced to various areas: the Rio Grande val-

ley below Reynosa (Anda el Camino, Como se Llaman, Mayapemes, Mulatos, Pauraques, and Saulapaguemes); northwest and northeast of the Rio
Grande immediately above Camargo (Carrizos, Cotonames, and Malaguitas); from parts of eastern Nuevo León (Borrados, Malnombre, and
Tortugas); and from unknown localities (Carvios and Guapes).

Various documents refer to Indian groups associated with the Camargo
mission up to the year 1818. Some of these refer to the Indians as working
for the Spaniards of Camargo; some were said to be growing corn in their
own fields; and others supported themselves mainly by hunting, fishing,
and food gathering (Vidal de Lorca 1788, table; Noticias de los Conventos
1790–1814, 1, 3, 5, 13, 219, 221, 237, 239; Bedoya 1816, table; Numana
1817, table; Antillán 1818, table; Barragán 1793a, 39–42, 1793b, 344–
345; Nava 1816–1823). Undoubtedly some of these Indians maintained
their ethnic identity until later in the nineteenth century.

Purísima Concepción of Mier

Mier was established in 1753, but its mission, Purísima Concepción,
seems to have existed in name only. The records say nothing about mission structures having been erected. It is said that, in 1753, about 132
Malagueros (Malaguitas) and Garzas had congregated at Mier (Valcarcel
1756, 108). Later, in 1757, Garzas, Malaguitas, and Zalayas were reported
as living at Mier (Tienda de Cuervo 1929, 411–414, 1930, 115; López de
la Cámara Alta 1946, 122). Apparently the Indians, as well as the local
Spaniards, were served by a missionary from Camargo, some twenty-five
miles farther down the Rio Grande. It was not until 1767 that a friar arrived to administer to Mier's Spaniards and Indians. In 1770 Gómez
(1942, 60) reported that about 101 Garza Indians at Mier wanted to have
a mission built for them. They were living at Mier, but each day they had
to go out into the countryside for food. In 1772 Conde de Sierra Gorda
noted that no mission had been built at Mier, and that about 85 Garzas and
Malahuecos (Malaguitas) were in constant contact with Spaniards of Mier.
These Indians sometimes cultivated small fields on the floodplain of the
Rio Grande, where they were subject to destruction by floods (Estado de
las Misiones 1946, 69). The Garzas were recorded as still living in the
vicinity of Mier during the period 1790–1818, supporting themselves by
hunting and gathering (Noticias de los Conventos 1790–1814, 1, 3, 5,
13, 131, 219, 221, 237, 239; Bedoya 1816, table; Numana 1817, table;
Antillán 1818, table).

The only Indian groups consistently linked with the missionary work at

Mier prior to 1790 were Garzas, Malaguitas, and Zalayas, all of whom seem to have been native to an area north of Cerralvo along the lower courses of the Río Alamos and the Río Sabinas. After 1790, and as late as 1818, brief missionary reports allude to other Indian groups heard of in the area surrounding Mier, but none of these seem to have had any contact with missionaries at Mier. The names included Aguichacas, Anda el Camino, Chinitos, Cotonames, Cueros Quemados, and Pajaritos (Noticias de los Conventos 1790–1814, passim; Bedoya 1816; Numana 1817; Antillán 1818). In late times there was evidently considerable mobility among the surviving Indian groups of the lower Rio Grande. Two of these groups, Aguichacas and Anda el Camino, were from the Rio Grande delta area.

San Francisco Solano de Ampuero of Revilla

The establishment of this mission apparently had been planned together with that of the village of Revilla in 1750 (Escandón 1751, 133–136), but its first missionary, Friar Buenaventura Rivera, did not arrive until 1751. In 1752 José de Silva found him at Revilla, but the mission had not yet been established. The nearest Indian groups, Carrizos and Garzas, were said to be living about eighteen miles from the village (Organización de las Misiones 1946, 88–89). A year later, in 1753, Escandón finally assigned land to the mission (Ladrón de Guevara 1753a, 229–235; Valcarcel 1754, 341).

Friar Miguel de Santa María de los Dolores took charge of the mission about 1754, but three years later, in 1757, he claimed that no Indians had been settled there. At times he managed to attract small numbers of Malnombre and Cueros Quemados, but they left as soon as they had consumed the mission's food supply (Tienda de Cuervo 1929, 423–427, 430–432, 1930, 119). During his visit of 1757, Agustín López de la Cámara Alta (1946, 125) found that all Indians were far from this mission.

In 1770 Gómez (1942, 20) found the mission led by Friar Juan Manuel de la Parra. At that time only twenty-five Indians were noted, mainly Garzas, Gualagueños (Gualeguas), and Malahuecos (Malaguitas), who frequently left the mission. Conde de Sierra Gorda, in 1772, noted that there was no formal congregation of Indians at Revilla. The Indians had come for short periods and then left. Some forty families of Malnombre and Cueros Quemados had once been there, along with a few Carrizos. These Indians at times had cultivated small fields on the floodplain of the Rio Grande (Estado de las Misiones 1946, 69–70, 73). Later, in 1788, Melchor Vidal de Lorca (1788, table) indicated that some Cacalotes were living in the vicinity but not in a formal settlement. In 1790 a routine missionary report mentioned that an Indian group called Chinitos was living at the village of Revilla. These otherwise unidentified Chinitos, who supported themselves by hunting, were the last Indians to be reported in the vicinity of Revilla (Noticias de los Conventos 1790–1814, 1). It is evident that Mission San Francisco Solano de Ampuero was not a successful mission, probably because of its location in an area with limited natural resources and because it never received much support from the viceregal government.

At least seven Indian groups were clearly associated with the Revilla mission: Carrizos (probably the Yemé), Chinitos, Cueros Quemados, Garzas, Gualeguas, Malaguitas, and Malnombre. These are all groups that were from an area that extended from the Revilla section of the Rio Grande southward to the Sierra de Picachos near Cerralvo. Some of these, particularly the Cueros Quemados, also ranged across the Rio Grande into the adjacent part of what is now Texas. At various times documents refer to other Indian groups seen or heard of in the region surrounding Revilla, but none of these can be connected with the Revilla mission.

Other Missions Entered

Many Indian groups associated with the Spanish missions described above were also represented, usually in small numbers, at more distant missions of Coahuila, Nuevo León, Tamaulipas, and Texas. In Table 5 these more distant missions are listed, their locations and foundation dates indicated, and for each mission the appropriate Indian group names are given. Tables 4 and 5 make it clear that a single Indian population rarely entered just one mission, for a few families or stray individuals found their way to various widely distributed missions. The ultimate ramifications of European displacement of Indian groups were evidently very complex and, for lack of recorded evidence, difficult to explain.

Conclusions

It seems reasonably clear that most of these missions were established in localities where Spanish settlements were being established, or were soon to be established, and where there were numerous Indian groups who had been, or might become, troublesome. As all projected Spanish missions were to be based on irrigation agriculture, a mission had to be suitably located for diversion of water into irrigation canals. It was primarily for

Table 5   Indian Groups from the Rio Grande Delta and Adjacent Areas at Other Missions

Indian Groups

Anda el Camino 14	Pamoranos 1
Borrados 4, 5, 11, 12, 13, 14	Pasnacanes 7
Cacalotes of the Río San Juan 4	Pauraques 13
Cacalotes (?) 6	Pelones 4
Carrizos of the upper	Piguiques 7, 11, 12, 15
Rio Grande 3, 6, 8	Pintos of the Rio Grande 10
Carrizos (?) 13	Pintos of the
Casas Chiquitas 14	Río San Fernando 1, 18
Comecrudos of the	Quinicuanes 1
Río San Fernando 18	Quedejeños 1, 17, 18
Guajolotes or Cacalotes of the	Saulapaguemes 14
Rio Grande 13	Tampacuas 8
Guajolotes of Sierra de	Tanaquiapemes 14, 18
San Carlos 5	Tortugas 4
Malaguitas 2, 8, 9, 11, 12, 13, 16	
Manos de Perro 11, 15	
Mayapemes 14	
Mulatos 14	
Nazas 4	
Pajaritos 6	

this reason that missions were placed near the major perennial streams of the area.

All of these missions were less than 150 miles from the Gulf coast. The four Rio Grande missions were more or less evenly distributed along the river at intervals of 20 to 30 miles. No missions were established anywhere on the delta of the Rio Grande. Mission San Joaquín del Monte of Reynosa, however, was at the apex of the triangular delta area, some 85 miles from the Gulf shoreline. Most of the delta Indian groups who entered missions went to the mission at Reynosa. Few delta Indians entered missions farther up the Rio Grande.

Mission San Agustín de Laredo of Camargo, where the Río San Juan enters the Rio Grande, and the missions at Mier and Revilla were entered by local Indians from both sides of the Rio Grande, but they were also entered by other Indians who lived farther to the south of the Rio Grande,

Table 5   (continued)

Key:

Nuevo León Missions
 1. San Cristóbal de Hualahuises (founded 1644).
 2. Guadalupe de las Salinas (1636).
 3. Nuestra Señora de los Dolores de la Punta de Lampazos (1698).
 4. Nuestra Señora de la Purificación (1715).
 5. Nuestra Señora de la Concepción (1715).

Coahuila Missions
 6. San Miguel de Aguayo of Monclova (1675).
 7. San Francisco de Vizarrón (1737).
 8. San Juan Bautista (1700).
 9. San Bernardo (1702).

Texas Missions
10. San Antonio de Valero (1718).
11. Purísima Concepción de Acuña (1731).
12. San Juan Capistrano (1731).
13. San Francisco de la Espada (1731).
14. San José y San Miguel de Aguayo (1720).
15. Nuestra Señora de la Bahía del Espíritu Santo (1749).
16. Nuestra Señora del Refugio (1795).

Nuevo Santander (Tamaulipas) Missions
17. Purísima Concepción de Infiesto of Soto la Marina (1750).
18. San Juan Nepomuceno de Helguera of Palmitos (1749).

especially between the Río San Juan and the Río Sabinas farther west, the area in which the early Spanish settlement of Cerralvo had been established. Almost all of the missions along the Rio Grande were also entered by at least a few Indian groups who originally lived on the upper tributaries of the Río San Juan in Nuevo León. It is quite clear that the missions of Camargo, Mier, and Revilla received more Indians who had been displaced from various parts of Nuevo León. Mission Cabezón de la Sal on the lower Río San Fernando was entered mainly by Indians native to the area, but at least one group, the Pamoranos, had formerly lived in the Cerralvo area.

Analyses of mission-related documents reveal certain critical limitations. When Indians from a particular ethnic group are reported to be living at a mission, it is usually not possible to determine whether additional Indians from the same ethnic unit were still living elsewhere under native conditions. Hence, population figures recorded at missions must be used with caution. Another limitation is that most documents do not identify all Indian groups represented at a given mission. They merely name the Indian groups represented by a considerable number of individuals. If the baptismal, marriage, and burial registers of all missions had survived, the list of Indian groups represented at missions would be lengthened. These registers usually indicate the ethnic affiliation of Indian individuals who were baptized, married, and buried at the mission. The value of mission registers is demonstrated by Bolton's (1965, 449–451) published lists of Indian groups whose names he saw in the registers (now lost) of the missions at Reynosa and Camargo.

These missions, especially those established in 1749, or shortly thereafter, did not last very long. Some, such as those at Mier and Revilla, were never fully organized or in continuous operation. Most missions were located too near the river channels and consequently suffered during massive floods; some missions had to be moved one or more times. Missions were never able to produce enough food by irrigation agriculture to feed the resident Indians, who often left the mission to find food by hunting and gathering. When the missions were in operation, all surviving Indian groups appear to have steadily declined in numbers, and there was no new reservoir of recently displaced Indians from which missionaries could obtain recruits. Furthermore, the missions of northern Tamaulipas were established at a time when the older missions of Coahuila and Texas had few local Indians to recruit and were trying to recruit Indians from the coast north of the Rio Grande. They managed to enlist only a few Indians from the Rio Grande delta and immediate vicinity. Actually, the missions of northern Nuevo Santander had ceased to exist even before the viceregal government ordered all missions secularized (shortly after 1790). It is clear, however, that small remnants of various Indian groups continued to live in mission areas until well into the nineteenth century, after which their ethnic identities were lost.

Summary and Conclusions

THE MAIN differences between this study and previous studies of the historic Indian populations of northeastern Mexico and southern Texas may be listed as follows:

1. This study is based upon a much larger number of primary documents.

2. Attention is focused on establishing the clearest ethnic identity possible for each Indian group of a specific area, the delta of the Rio Grande, and areas adjacent to it.

3. The confusion in Indian group names is squarely faced, and an attempt is made to explain why European colonists from Spain tended to ignore native group names and replace them with names of Spanish origin.

4. In the delta and adjoining areas, a special effort is made to distinguish between Indian groups native to those areas and groups that had migrated from other areas after being displaced by European colonists. This is achieved, so far as the records permit, by tracing the names of Indian groups through successively later documents and noting changes in location.

5. Special attention is also given to environmental variations and differences in population density.

6. As other studies have tended to overgeneralize from very limited data on languages and cultures, these generalizations have been critically examined and tested by new information not previously utilized.

7. As earlier studies have not been greatly concerned with Indian groups connected with Spanish missions, brief histories of certain missions are presented, and all Indian groups known to have been at each mission have been tabulated.

The Rio Grande delta area and vicinity was one of the last areas in northeastern Mexico to be colonized by Europeans. This colonization began in 1747, and most of the information recorded about named Indian groups dates after that year. In broad perspective, what is now known indicates that the delta, because of its terrestrial and marine resources, was occupied by a rather large number of Indian groups who lived by hunting, fishing, and food collecting. The names of at least forty-nine Indian groups have been recorded, and most of these appear to have been native to the area. Relatively few Indian groups displaced from other areas seem to have actually lived in the delta area, but numerous refugee groups from northeastern Nuevo León moved down the Rio Grande and lived near the delta, particularly in the Reynosa and Camargo areas.

The areas both north and south of the Rio Grande delta were poorer in natural resources and seem to have been only intermittently occupied by Indian groups. The nearest concentrations of Indian populations were at considerable distances north and south of the delta, near Baffin and Corpus Christi bays to the north and on the lower Río San Fernando to the south. In neither of these areas was there a concentration of Indian groups comparable to that of the Rio Grande delta. Relatively few refugee groups from Nuevo León seem to have reached these areas.

The main problem connected with establishing ethnic identities for Indian groups in these areas is linking native names with descriptive names applied by Spaniards. This has led to much confusion because documents rarely equate native names with Spanish names. This is further complicated by the fact that some Spanish names were applied to two or more Indian groups in widely separated areas, and there is no indication that these identically named groups were linguistically and culturally related. Circumstantial evidence seems to indicate that Spaniards were not able to master hundreds of names of native origin, derived from different Indian languages, and for practical purposes coined names for sets of displaced Indian groups that had assembled in various localities. Unless additional documents can be found that correlate more native names with Spanish names, it will not be possible to sort out the various Indian populations of northeastern Mexico.

It is now evident that the documentary record is too incomplete for recognition of discrete languages and cultures in the area. Linguists consider it likely that numerous languages were spoken in northeastern Mexico and southern Texas and agree that the recorded vocabularies are too small for demonstrating relationships between any two languages. Only two languages, Comecrudo and Cotoname, can be linked with the Rio Grande delta area. These were formerly considered to be related to the language known as Coahuilteco, but this interpretation seems to have been abandoned.

The scattered references to cultural behavior, derived from documents written over a period of several hundred years, cannot be sorted out and associated with very many Indian groups. At best they are impressionistic, and it is not realistic to suppose that all groups shared these cultural traits. As new documents come to light, more references to culture will undoubtedly be found.

References

Abbreviations used:

AGI   Archivo General de Indias. Seville.

AGN   Archivo General de la Nación. Mexico City.

AHT   *Archivo de la Historia de Tamaulipas.* Compilado y editado por Gabriel Saldívar. Mexico City.

AMR   Archivo Municipal de Reynosa. Reynosa.

BAT   Bexar Archives Translations. Barker Texas History Center. University of Texas at Austin.

BLAC   Benson Latin American Collection. University of Texas at Austin.

BTHC   Barker Texas History Center. University of Texas at Austin.

DEHCT   Documents for the Early History of Coahuila and Texas and the Approaches Thereto, 1600–1843. Documents from Biblioteca Pública del Estado de Jalisco, selected, copied, and calendared by C. E. Castañeda. Transcription. Barker Texas History Center. University of Texas at Austin.

NA   Nacogdoches Archives. Transcription. Barker Texas History Center. University of Texas at Austin.

PITESM   *Publicaciones del Instituto Tecnológico y de Estudios Superiores de Monterrey.* Monterrey.

PTCHS   *Preliminary Studies of the Texas Catholic Historical Society.* Austin.

QTSHA   *See SHQ.*

SA   Salce Arredondo Collection. Benson Latin American Collection. University of Texas at Austin.

SFGA   San Francisco el Grande Archives. Transcription. Barker Texas History Center. University of Texas at Austin.

SHQ   *Southwestern Historical Quarterly* (formerly *Quarterly of the Texas State Historical Association*). Austin.

SIBAE   *Smithsonian Institution, Bureau of American Ethnology, Bulletin.*
         Washington, D.C.

Almaráz, Félix D., Jr., translator and editor
  1980   *Inventory of the Rio Grande Missions: 1772, San Juan Bautista and San*
         Bernardo. Archaeology and History of the San Juan Bautista Mission Area,
         Coahuila and Texas, Report no. 2. San Antonio: Center for Archaeological
         Research, University of Texas at San Antonio.
Altamira, Marqués de
  1750   [Sobre las poblaciones hechas por Escandón.] AGN, Provincias Internas 172
         (BTHC, 2Q211, 513:460–467).
Alvarez Barreiro, Francisco
  1729   Plano Corographico de los dos Reynos el Nuevo de Extremadura ō Coaguila
         y el Nuevo de León . . . Situadas entre los 23 y 31 de Latitud Boreal y entre
         los 269 y 274 Longitud . . . (BTHC, Map Collection, JPB 42, 1729).
  1730   Descripz.^{on} de las Provincias internas de esta N.^{a} Esp.^{a} q sirve p.^{a} la mas
         clara intelig.^{a} de los Planos o Mapas, que la acompañan . . . (incomplete).
         AGI, Audiencia de México, Dunn Transcript 1723–1729 (BTHC, 2Q146,
         81:108–118).
Antillán, Miguel
  1818   Estado abreviado de las Misiones de esta Provincia de N.S.P.S. Francisco de
         las Zacatecas. AGN, Misiones 11, 1 L. (BLAC, Microfilm).
Arnold, J. Barto, and Robert Weddle
  1978   *The Nautical Archeology of Padre Island: The Spanish Shipwrecks of 1554.*
         New York: Academic Press.
Ballí [Vallí], José Miguel
  1809   Copia de representación que me ha hecho el Yndio Jph Miguel Valli Gober-
         nador de las Naciones de los Pintos, Tejones, y Comecrudos, en solicitud de
         que se les de misionero y Protector o defensor. AGN, Misiones 11, 5 L.
         (BLAC, Microfilm).
Ballí, Juan Antonio
  1781   [Sobre unos Indios Malaguitas que fueron detenidos en Reynosa.] AGN,
         Provincias Internas 146, 3 L. (BLAC, Microfilm).
Ballí [Bayi], Juan Antonio, and Juan José de Hinojosa [Ynojosa]
  1785   Orden del Señor Lasaga para que se remita los Padrones de los Indios.
         AMR, Carpeta de Indios, 3 L.
Ballí, Juan Antonio, Joseph de Trejo, and Antonio Margil Cano
  1777   De Joseph Abito Cantu, Apolinario Moya, y Lucas Sosa Vesinos de esta
         Jur.^{n} por la acusacion de haver extrahido un Yndito de poder de sus Padres
         Yndios de la Nacion de los Mulatos: hayase Yncurso tambien un Yndio
         Christiano reducido a esta Mission llamado Jph Miguel. AMR, 28 L.
Barbadillo y Victoria, Francisco de
  1715   Consulta que hace el Señor Alcalde de Corte Don Francisco Barbadillo Vic-
         toria a su Exc.^{a}. AGN, Historia 30 (BTHC, 2Q178, 352:63–70).
Barragán, Francisco Nepomuceno de
  1770a [Visita hecha por Fray Francisco Nepomuceno de Barragán.] AGN, Provin-
         cias Internas 119, 3 L. (BLAC, Microfilm).

1770b [Correspondencia del R. P. Visitador de la Provincia de Zacatecas.] AGN, Provincias Internas 119 (BTHC, 2Q209, 502:129–132).

1774 Consulta del R^do P. Fr. Fran^co Nepomuceno Barragán comisario de las Misiones de la provincia del Nuevo Reino de León [dirigida] a su Governador Dn. Melchor Vidal Lorca. AGN, Provincias Internas 143, 3 L. (BLAC, Microfilm).

1793a [Visita al Nuevo Santander cuya información esta dirigida al Sr. Don Andrés de Llanos Valdés.] AGN, Provincias Internas 40:39–42 (BLAC, Microfilm).

1793b Ynforme que por el oficio de 23 de Septiembre de . . . corriente año 93 me manda V. E. que le de de las Misiones que esta santa Provincia sirve con la individualidad que el citado oficio expresa. AGN, Provincias Internas 5:344–353 (BLAC, Microfilm).

Barrio Junco y Espriella, Pedro de
1979 *Visita General del Nuevo Reino de León.* Dirección General de Investigaciones Humanísticas, Actas no. 10, Serie: Documentos X. Monterrey: Universidad Autónoma de Nuevo León.

Barrios y Jáuregui, Jacinto de
1760–1762 Testimonio de los Autos de visita de esta provincia de San Francisco de Coahuila, Nueva Extremadura, hecha por Don Jacinto de Barrios y Jáuregui. Saltillo Archives (BTHC, 2Q313, 2:153–239).

Bedoya, Antonio
1816 Estado abreviado de las misiones de las Provincias de N.S.P.S. Francisco de los Zacatecas. AGN, Misiones 11, 1 L. (BLAC, Microfilm).

Benson, Nettie Lee, translator and editor
1950 *Report that Dr. Miguel Ramos de Arizpe . . . Presents to the August Congress on the Natural, Political, and Civil Conditions of the Provinces of Coahuila, Nuevo León, Nuevo Santander, and Texas. . . .* Austin: University of Texas Press.

Berlandier, Jean Louis
1969 *The Indians of Texas in 1830.* Washington, D.C.: Smithsonian Institution Press.

1980 *Journey to Mexico during the Years 1826 to 1834.* Translated by Sheila M. Ohlendorf. 2 vols. Austin: Texas State Historical Association and Center for Studies in Texas History, University of Texas.

Blair, W. Frank
1950 The Biotic Province of Texas. *Texas Journal of Science* 2(1):93–117.

Bolton, Herbert E.
1916 *Spanish Exploration in the Southwest, 1542–1706.* New York: Charles Scribner's Sons.

1965 *Guide to Materials for the History of the United States in the Principal Archives of Mexico.* New York: Kraus Reprint.

1970 *Texas in the Middle Eighteenth Century: Studies in Spanish Colonial History and Administration.* Austin: University of Texas Press.

Branda, Eldon Stephen, editor
1976 *The Handbook of Texas: A Supplement.* Vol. 3. Austin: Texas State Historical Association.

Brown, L. F., et al.

1980 *Environmental Geologic Atlas of the Texas Coastal Zone: Brownsville-Harlingen Area.* Austin: Bureau of Economic Geology, University of Texas.

Bueno de la Borbolla, Vicente

1749 [Informe del gobernador sobre el paraje del Tepextle.] AGN, Provincias Internas 173 (BTHC, 2Q211, 514:206–210, or 257–260).

Cabello, Domingo

1780a Expediente. Cabello submits his reports concerning activities of some citizens of Nuevo Santander who buy and sell Indians. BAT (BTHC, 2C40, 96:33–39).

1780b Letter 241, Cabello to de Croix. BAT (BTHC, 2C40, 98:78–79).

1784 Strength report and daily record of occurrences at San Antonio de Béxar Presidio, for March 1784. BAT (BTHC, 2C52, 125:16–24).

Cabeza de Vaca, Alvar Núñez

1542 La Relación que dio Alvar Núñez Cabeza de Vaca de lo acaefcido en las Indias in la armada donde yva por governador Panphilo de Narbaez. . . . BTHC, Photostat.

Cadena, Protasio P.

1942 *Reseña Histórica, Social, Económica y Geográfica del Municipio de Agualeguas.* Agualeguas, N.L.: N.p.

Campbell, T. N.

1979 *Ethnohistoric Notes on Indian Groups Associated with Three Spanish Missions at Guerrero, Coahuila.* Archaeology and History of the San Juan Bautista Mission Area, Coahuila and Texas, Report no. 3. San Antonio: Center for Archaeological Research, University of Texas at San Antonio.

1983 Coahuiltecans and Their Neighbors. In *Handbook of North American Indians.* Edited by William C. Sturtevant. 10:343–358.

1984 The Cacaxtle Indians of Northeastern Mexico and Southern Texas. *La Tierra, Journal of the Southern Texas Archaeological Association* 2(1):4–20.

Campbell, T. N., and T. J. Campbell

1981 *Historic Indian Groups of the Choke Canyon Reservoir and Surrounding Area, Southern Texas.* Choke Canyon Series 1. San Antonio: Center for Archaeological Research, University of Texas at San Antonio.

1985 *Indian Groups Associated with Spanish Missions of the San Antonio Missions National Park.* Special Report 16. San Antonio: Center for Archaeological Research, University of Texas at San Antonio.

Cantú, Nicolás

1771 [Correspondencia del teniente de Reynosa.] AGN, Provincias Internas 119 (BTHC, 2Q209, 502:128).

Carr, John T., Jr.

1967 *The Climate and Physiography of Texas.* Report 53. Austin: Texas Water Development Board.

Carta de Climas

1970 *Carta de Climas: Matamoros 14 R-VIII y Reynosa 14 R-VI.* Comisión de Estudios del Territorio Nacional y Planeación, Secretaría de la Presidencia. Mexico City: Instituto de Geografía, Universidad Nacional Autónoma de México.

Cartografía de Ultramar
  1953   *Cartografía de Ultramar: Carpeta II Estados Unidos y Canadá Relaciones de Ultramar; Tiponomía de los Mapas que la Integran.* Madrid: Servicios Geográficos e Históricos del Ejército.
Causas Criminales
  1782–1787   Causas Criminales seguidas contra vagos y sospechosos de complicidad con los Indios Barbaros. AGN, Provincias Internas 144, cuadernos 1, 2, 3, 4 (BLAC, Microfilm).
Cavazos Garza, Israel
  1963   El Licenciado Francisco de Barbadillo Vitoria, Pacificador y fundador de pueblos. *Humanitas* (Universidad de Nuevo León) 4:375–390.
  1964   *Cedulario Autobiográfico de Pobladores y Conquistadores de Nuevo León.* Monterrey: Biblioteca de Nuevo León 2, Centro de Estudios Humanísticos de la Universidad de Nuevo León.
  1966   Catálogo y Síntesis de los Protocolos del Archivo Municipal de Monterrey, 1599–1700. *Serie: Historia 4. PITESM.*
  1973   *Catálogo y Síntesis de los Protocolos del Archivo Municipal de Monterrey, 1700–1725.* Monterrey: Centro de Estudios Humanísticos de la Universidad Autónoma de Nuevo León.
Cervantes de Salazar, Francisco
  1971   *Crónica de la Nueva España.* Biblioteca de Autores Españoles. Vol. 2. Madrid: Ediciones Atlas.
Concepción Marriage Register
  MS   Libro de Casamientos de esta Misión de la Purísima Concepción Pueblo de Acuña, 1733–1789. San Fernando Archives, San Antonio (Texas Catholic Archives, Austin, Microfilm).
Cook, T. D.
  1958   Rio Grande Delta. In *Sedimentology of South Texas.* Houston: Gulf Coast Association of Geological Societies. 52–53.
Coopwood, Bethel
  1899–1900   The Route of Cabeza de Vaca, in Four Parts. *QTSHA* 3(2):108–140, 3(3):177–208, 3(4):229–264, 4(1):1–32.
Copia Certificada
  1790   Copia Certificada del Testimonio de las Tierras de Llano Grande y la Feria Denunciadas y Adjudicada a Don José de Hinojosa y Doña Rosa María Hinojosa de Ballí. Camargo Archives (BTHC, 3E136, Titles to Llano Grande, 10–55).
Copia de las Actas
  1753   Copia de las actas del Cabildo de San Cristóbal de Hualahuises relativas a los habitantes de las misiones, incluyendo a los indígenas de varias naciones, Noviembre 29 Diciembre de 1753 (incomplete, no signature). SA 53:1–24. BLAC.
Correa, Thomas
  1768   [Correspondencia del general misionero en este pueblo de la Purísima Concepción.] AGN, Misiones 13:140–141 (BLAC, Microfilm).
Cortés Alonso, Vicenta
  1954   *Noticias Sobre las Tribus de las Costas de Tejas Durante el Siglo XVIII.*

Madrid: Tirada Aparte de Trabajos y Conferencias del Seminario de Estudios Americanistas de la Universidad de Madrid. Reprinted in *Trabajos y Conferencias* 4: 133–140.

Cruillas Registers
MS   Libros de Bautismos no. 1 (1767 al 1786) y no. 3 (1804 al 1821), and Libro de Matrimonios no. 1. At Parroquia de San Fernando, Tamaulipas.

Dabbs, J. Autrey
1940   The Texas Missions in 1785. *PTCHS* 3(6): 1–24.

Davenport, Harbert, and Joseph K. Wells
1918–1919   The First Europeans in Texas, 1528–1536. *SHQ* 22(2): 111–142, 22(3): 205–259.

Dávila Padilla, Agustín
1955   *Historia de la Fundación y Discurso de la Provincia de Santiago de México.* Mexico City: Editorial Academia Literaria.

Díaz de Bustamante, Joseph Ramón
1791   El cap.^{n} de la 3ª Comp^a da parte del inconveniente por no poder aiar aora el Rio . . . AGN, Provincias Internas 55: 79–81 (BLAC, Microfilm).
1792   El capitan de Laredo ha pasado aviso a las Justicias del Norte para que esten en precausión, esta preparando los 30 hombres de esta compañia, 10 vecinos, y 5 Carrizos. AGN, Provincias Internas 55: 150–151 (BLAC, Microfilm).

Díaz del Castillo, Bernal
1955   *Historia Verdadera de la Conquista de la Nueva España.* 2 vols. Mexico City: Editorial Porrúa.

Dolores, Mariano Francisco de los, et al.
1762   Informe rendido por los ministros de las Misiones de el Rio de San Antonio a Fr. Francisco Xavier Ortiz. AGN, Historia 28 (BTHC, 2Q177, 347: 162–183), or SFGA, vol. 27, leg. 99, no. 9 (BTHC, 2Q256, 835: 38–76).

Dunn, William Edward
1911   Apache Relations in Texas, 1718–1750. *QTSHA* 14(3): 198–274.

Eguilaz de Prado, Isabel
1965   *Los Indios del Nordeste de Méjico en el Siglo XVIII.* Publicaciones del Seminario de Antropología Americana 7. Seville: Universidad de Sevilla.

Escandón, José de
1749a   Copia de dos Cartas, escritas a el Governador, de el Nuevo Reyno de León, sobre la fundación, de una Mission, en el Paraje de el Tepestle. AGN, Provincias Internas 173 (BTHC, 2Q211, 514: 195–199, or 245–250).
1749b   [Logros de pacificación en el Nuevo Santander.] AGN, Provincias Internas 173 (BTHC, 2Q211, 514: 418–452).
1749c   [Informe sobre la misión en el Paraje del Tepextle.] AGN, Provincias Internas 173 (BTHC, 2Q211, 514: 190–194, or 240–244).
1749d   [Estado que al presente tiene la Colonia del Nuevo Santander.] AGN, Provincias Internas 173 (BTHC, 2Q211, 514: 481–490).
1750   [Correspondencia desde Reynosa.] AGN, Provincias Internas 172 (BTHC, 2Q211, 513: 449–460).
1751   Quaderno de las 18 Poblaz.^{nes} fechas por el General Dn Jph de Escandón, y numero de familias q.^{e} en cada una de ellas se hallan avecindadas. AGN, Provincias Internas 180 (BTHC, 2Q213, 520: 1–373).

1753   [Testimonio del Estado de las 20 Nuevas Poblaciones de la Colonia del Seno
       Mexicano.] AGN, Provincias Internas 172 (BTHC, 2Q211, 513:330–337).
1946   Reconocimiento de la Costa del Seno Mexicano. Vol. 2. *AHT.*

Espinosa, Isidro Félix de
1708   Relación de las Misiones de Coahuila. AGI, Audiencia de México (BTHC,
       2Q146, 77:29–43).
1746   *Chrónica Apostólica y Seráphica de todos los Colegios de Propaganda Fide
       de esta Nueva-España, Parte Primera.* Mexico City: Viuda de d. J. B.
       de Hogal.

Estado de las Misiones
1946   Estado de las Misiones entre 1753 y 1790. Vol. 4. *AHT.*

Evia, José de
1968   *José de Evia y sus Reconocimientos del Golfo de México, 1783–1796.*
       Edited by Jack D. L. Holmes. Madrid: Ediciones José Porrú Turanzas.

Fernández de Jáuregui Urrutia, Joseph Antonio
1963   Descripción del Nuevo Reino de León (1735–1740). Serie: Historia 1.
       PITESM.

Fernández de Navarrete, Martín
1955   *Colección de los Viajes y Descubrimientos que Hicieron por Mar los Es-
       pañoles Desde Fines del Siglo XV.* Biblioteca de Autores Españoles. Vol. 3.
       Madrid: Ediciones Atlas.

Fernández de Oviedo. *See* Oviedo y Valdés.

Fundación de Presidios
1741   Fundación de Presidios, Villas y Misiones. SA 36:1–65. BLAC.

Gallo, José Nepomuceno
1792   [Sobre la necesidad de una misión para los Tanaquiapemes entre la Amargosa
       y la Tijera.] AGN, Provincias Internas 40:7–12 (BLAC, Microfilm).

García, Bartholomé
1760   *Manual para Administrar los Santos Sacramentos de Penitencia, Eucha-
       ristía, Extrema-Unción, y Matrimonio . . .* Mexico City: Imprenta de los
       Herederos de Doña Maria Rivera.

García, José Joaquín [Joseph Joachín]
1766   Ynforme Privado que expone al Sor. Don Joseph de Glabes . . . El Padre
       Predicador Apostolico Fray Joseph Joachin Garzia . . . en que demuestra
       evidentemente, por experiencia ocular el engaño o dolo, conque procedió
       dho Jph Escandón. AGI, (BTHC, 2Q147, 86:116–170).

Garza, Francisco
1750   [Dos cartas sobre el pedimento para mudarsc los Indios Pelones al Valle del
       Pilón.] AGN, Provincias Internas 173 (BTHC, 2Q211, 514:218–219,
       222–230, or 268–269, 272–280).

Garza Falcón, Clemente
1737   Tanto de la fundación de Bizarrón en 5 de Abril de 1737. DEHCT (BTHC,
       2Q261, 13:383–390), or SFGA (BTHC, 2Q248, 3:26–33).

Gatschet, Albert S.
1891   *The Karankawa Indians, the Coastal People of Texas.* Archaeological and
       Ethnological Papers of the Peabody Museum, Harvard University. Vol. 1,
       no. 2. New York: Kraus Reprint.

Giraldo de Terreros, Alonso
  1734   List of inhabitants of San Bernardo. AGI, Audiencia de México (BTHC, 2Q147, 84:20–24).
Goddard, Ives
  1979   The Languages of South Texas and the Lower Rio Grande. In *The Languages of Native America: Historical and Comparative Assessment.* Edited by Lyle Campbell and Marianne Mithun. Austin: University of Texas Press. 355–389.
Gómez, Lino Nepomuceno
  1942   *Visita a la Colonia del Nuevo Santander, hecha por el Licenciado Don Lino Nepomuceno Gómez, el año de 1770.* Introducción de Enrique A. Cervantes. Mexico City: Contribución de la Secretaría de Agricultura y Fomento al V Congreso Mexicano de Historia.
Gonzáles, J. H.
  1790   [Carta expedida el 14 de Abril por la Justicia de Laredo.] AGN, Provincias Internas 159 (BTHC, 2Q210, 508:42–45).
González, José Eleuterio
  1975   *Colección de Noticias y Documentos para la Historia del Estado de Nuevo León.* Monterrey: Universidad de Nuevo León.
González, Pascual
  n.d.   [Quejas que dan los Indios Cadimas, Cometunas, Narices, y Nazas sobre las hostilidades y perjuicios de los gobernantes.] AGN, Provincias Internas 173 (BTHC, 2Q211, 514:349–363).
González de Santianés, Vicente
  1773   Relación de las Misiones que se Establecieron en la Colonia del Nuevo Santander. AGN, Provincias Internas 174 (BTHC, 2Q212, 515:365–383).
  1774   Testimonio del expediente formado sobre que se traslade (los Indios Pintos) al arroyo de Mojarras y que se exponga para las providencias que se le prevengan. AGN, Provincias Internas 113, 2 L. (BLAC, Microfilm).
  1783   [Copia de la carta dirigida al Excelentísimo Señor Gobernador de Nuevo León.] AGN, Provincias Internas 26:289–292 (BLAC, Microfilm).
González Salas, Carlos
  1977   Dos Cronistas Franciscanos del Nuevo Santander: Simón del Hierro y Vicente de Santa María. *Humanitas* 18:427–437.
  1979   Las Misiones Pachuqueñas en Nuevo Santander (1791–1827). *Humanitas* 20:415–443.
Guadalupe, Joseph de
  1754   Querella de San Juan Capistrano por los agravios y Daños que le causa Vizarrón. Archivo del Colegio de Santa Cruz de Querétaro, KN 15, Leg. 4 (BTHC, 2Q237, 768:172–183).
Guerra Cabasos, Ig.°
  1831   Libro donde consta los Indigenas que por nó tener oficio ó modo de vivir conocido seles bá dando amos a quien trabajen en cumplimiento de las Leyes y nota de 5 de Marzo P°P.° del Exmo Sõr. Gobernador de este Estado. AMR, 7 L.

Guimbardo, Ignacio F.
1768   [Sobre la guerra civil de los Indios del Pueblo de Concepción y Purificación.] AGN, Misiones 13:139 (BLAC, Microfilm).

Gursky, Karl-Heinz
1964   The Linguistic Position of the Quinigua Indians. *International Journal of American Linguistics* (Baltimore) 30(4):325–327.

Herrera, Antonio de
1945   *Historia General de los Hechos de los Castellanos, en las Islas, y Tierra-Firme de el Mar Occeano.* Vols. 3, 4, and 5. Asunción, Paraguay: Editorial Guarania.

Hodge, Frederick Webb
1971   *Handbook of American Indians North of Mexico.* (*SIBAE* 30, 2 vols.) New York: Rowman and Littlefield.

Hoyo, Eugenio del
1960   Vocablos de la Lengua Quinigua de los Indios Borrados del Noreste de México. *Humanitas* 1(1):489–515.
1963   Indice del Ramo de Causas Criminales del Archivo Municipal de Monterrey (1621–1834). Serie: Historia 2. *PITESM.*
1972   Historia del Nuevo Reino de León (1577–1723). 2 vols. Serie: Historia 13. *PITESM.*

Huisar, Pedro
1796   Padron de todos los Yndividuos Yndios de esta Mission de Sn Jose de Aguallo, inclusos los Parv.^{os} y su Juez Local. NA, vol. 8 (BTHC, 2Q249, 176:161–165).
1797   Padron que manifiesta el num^o de Yndividuos Yndios, q^e avitan esta Miss^n de Sr S^n Jph de Aguallo inclusos los Parvulos, Febrero 6 de 1797. NA, vol. 9 (BTHC, 2Q294, 177:72–76).
1798   Padron de los Yndios de la Mission de Sor. San Jose de Aguallo inclusos los Parbolitos. NA, vol. 9 (BTHC, 2Q294, 177:80–84).
1799   Padron de los Yndios de la Micion de Sr S^n Jose de Aguallo ynclusos los parbulos, Enero 6 de 1799. NA, vol. 9 (BTHC, 2Q294, 177:186–189).

Jiménez Moreno, Wigberto
1943   Tribus e Idiomas del Norte de México. In *El Norte de México y el Sur de Estados Unidos. Tercera Reunión de Mesa Redonda sobre Problemas Antropológicos de México y Centro América.* Mexico City: Sociedad Mexicana de Antropología. 121–133.

Johnson, Leroy, Jr.
1983   Review of *Historic Indian Groups of the Choke Canyon Reservoir and Surrounding Area, Southern Texas,* by T. N. Campbell and T. J. Campbell. *Bulletin of the Texas Archeological Society* 54:345–355.

Johnston, Marshall Conring
1955   Vegetation of the Eolian Plain and Associated Coastal Features of Southern Texas. Ph.D. diss., University of Texas at Austin.

Kinnaird, Lawrence
1967   *The Frontiers of New Spain: Nicolás de Lafora's Description, 1766–1767.* New York: Arno Press.

Kress, Margaret Kinney, and Mattie Austin Hatcher
  1931   Diary of a Visit of Inspection of the Texas Missions made by Fray Gaspar José de Solís in the Year 1767–1768. *SHQ* 35(1):28–76.

Krieger, Alex D.
  1955   Un Nuevo Estudio de la Ruta Seguida por Cabeza de Vaca a Través de Norte América. Ph.D. diss., Universidad Nacional Autónoma de México.
  1961   The Travels of Alvar Núñez Cabeza de Vaca in Texas and Mexico, 1534–1536. In *Homenaje a Pablo Martínez del Río en el XXV Aniversario de Los Orígenes Americanos*. Mexico City: Instituto Nacional de Antropología e Historia. 459–474.

Kutac, Edward A.
  1982   *Texas Birds: Where They Are and How to Find Them.* Houston: Lone Star Books.

Lacomba, Claudio
  1788   Sobre los Yndios de todos estados y clases que se compone la Nación de los Carrizos. AGN, Provincias Internas 53:400–401 (BLAC, Microfilm).

Ladrón de Guevara, [Joseph] Antonio
  1738   Notiz.ˢ q a sacado Antº Ladron de Guevara Vezº y Notario ppbᶜᵒ del Nuevo R.ⁿᵒ de Leon parte de Nueva España Arreglandose a la Esperiencia q. de los yndios Barbaros sus Costumbres y demas le asiste En Diversas Entradas q hizo a sus Tierras. AGI, Audiencia de México (BTHC, 2Q147, 85:49–65).
  1753a   Testim.º De las Vltimas diligencias, practicadas en la Visita de la Villa de Revilla por el señor General Don Joseph de Escandón. AGN, Provincias Internas 172 (BTHC, 2Q211, 513:215–235).
  1753b   Testim.º De las Vltimas diligencias, practicadas en la Visita de la Villa de S.ⁿ Fernando, por el Señor General D.ⁿ Joseph de Escandón. AGN, Provincias Internas 172 (BTHC, 2Q211, 513:149–168).
  1753c   Testim.º De las Vltimas dilig.ˢ practicadas en la Visita de la Villa de Reynosa, por el Señor General D.ⁿ Joseph de Escandón. AGN, Provincias Internas 172 (BTHC, 2Q211, 513:308–329).
  1969   Noticias de los Poblados de que se Compone el Nuevo Reino de León, Provincia de Coahuila, Nueva-Extremadura, y la de Texas (1739). Serie: Historia 10. *PITESM.*

Lampazos Baptism Register
  MS   Baptism records (1700–1727) in Archivo de la Parroquia de San Juan Bautista en Lampazos Estado de Nuevo León (Genealogical Society of Utah, Microfilm 605568).

Laredo Registers
  MS   Bautismos Libros 1 and 2, Entierros Libros 1, 2, and 3, and Casamientos Libro 1 (1789–1858). Archivo de la Iglesia de San Agustín de Laredo, Texas (Texas Catholic Archives, Photostats, Austin).

Lasaga, Diego de
  1783   El Gov.ᵒʳ del Nuevo Santander da parte a V.E. de que los Indios de la Micion de S.ⁿ Fernando de Nacion Pintos mataron un Baquero en la Villa de Burgos. AGN, Provincias Internas 64, pt. 2 (BTHC, 2Q205, 481:268).

1786 Expediente que sobre hostilidades y aumento de tropas en la Colonia del Nuevo Santander promovió desde el año 1781 hasta el corriente de 86 el Governador actual de aquella Provincia D.ⁿ Diego de Lasaga, Extracto del Expediente. AGN, Provincias Internas 64 (BTHC, 2Q205, 481 : 330–355).

León, Alonso de, Juan Bautista Chapa, and el Gral. Fernando Sánchez de Zamora

1961 *Historia de Nuevo León, con Noticias sobre Coahuila, Tamaulipas, Texas, y Nuevo México.* Estudio Preliminar y Notas de Israel Cavazos Garza. Biblioteca de Nuevo León 1. Monterrey: Centro de Estudios Humanísticos, Universidad de Nuevo León.

León, Nicolás

1901 *Familias Lingüísticas de México.* Mexico City: Imprenta del Gobierno Federal en el Arzobispado.

Llano Grande Grant

1879 Llano Grande Grant. Spanish Archives, San Patricio 723, General Land Office. Austin.

Lohse, E. A.

1958 Mouth of the Rio Grande. In *Sedimentology of South Texas.* Houston: Gulf Coast Association of Geological Societies. 55–57.

López, Jh Franc.ᶜᵒ

1793 Misión de San Juan Capistrano Dependiente de la Villa de Sn. Sˢ Fernando Padron de las Almas que Existian en 31 de Diziembre 1793. NA, vols. 8 or 9 (BTHC, 2Q294, 176:135–137, or 177:124–126).

López de Gómara, Francisco

1954 *Historia General de las Indias.* Obras Maestras. 2 vols. Barcelona: Editorial Iberia.

López de la Cámara Alta, Agustín

1758 Mapa General Ychnographico de la Nueva Colonia de Santander ó Tausaulipas . . . Library of Congress, Map Library (State of Tamaulipas, Santander Colony, 24 Town plans inset, 1 inch = 8,228 varas del Rey. Photostat B.M. add. MS, 17,657). Original map in the British Museum.

1946 Descripción General de la Nueva Colonia de Santander. Vol. 5. *AHT.* See also AGN, Historia 53:128–129 (BLAC, Microfilm) or (BTHC 2Q179, 358:146).

Lozada, Juan

1732 Pazes de los Indios del Nuevo Reyno de León. AGN, Historia 30 (BTHC, 2Q178, 352:80–102).

Luviaur, Thomas de

1773 [Los méritos de Andrés Goycochea.] AGN, Misiones 13:163–167 (BLAC, Microfilm).

MacManus, F. E.

1885 *La Sal del Rey, or the King's Salt.* . . . Brownsville, Texas: Maltby, Jr., Printer.

Martínez Pacheco, Rafael

1788a Copy of a letter from Martínez Pacheco to Vgalde reporting the shooting of José Antonio Baquera by a Borrado Indian. San Antonio de Béjar, September 29, 1788. BAT (BTHC, 2C68, 156:74–75).

1788b Log of operations for the presidio of San Antonio de Béxar for the month of
        September, 1788, by Martínez Pacheco. Royal Presidio of San Antonio de
        Béxar. September 30, 1788. BAT (BTHC, 2C68, 156:81−84).
Martínez Piñera, Francisco
  1781 Collera de Yndios que se hallan reos en el Quartel de esta Villa [Santa Maria
        de Aguayo]. AGN, Provincias Internas 146, 2 L. (BLAC, Microfilm).
Mártir de Anglería, Pedro
  1944 *Décadas del Nuevo Mundo.* Colección de Fuentes para la Historia de Amé-
        rica. Buenos Aires: Editorial Bajel.
Matamoros Archives
  MS   In BTHC.
Matamoros Registers
  MS   Libros de Bautismos no. 1 (1800−1809) and no. 2 (1810−1826); Libro de
        Entierros no. 2 (1812−1831); Libros de Casamientos no. 1 (1810−1816)
        and no. 2 (1816−?). Nuestra Señora del Refugio de los Esteros, Parish
        Church. Matamoros.
Mier Grants
  1767 Copy and Translations of Visita General Granting, Mier. Starr County Por-
        tions, 1767. Spanish Archives, General Land Office, Austin.
Muñoz, Manuel
  1790 Parte que en la fha de 8 de Abril le paso el Justicia de Laredo, el que dice que
        el 7 a las quatro de la tarde fue attacada por mas de 200 Enemigos. AGN,
        Provincias Internas 159 (BTHC, 2Q210, 508:39−41).
Naranjo, Leopoldo
  1934 *Lampazos: Sus Hombres, su Tiempo, sus Obras.* Monterrey: Talleres J.
        Cantú Leal.
Nava, Juan María
  1816−1823 Libro 1° donde Consta las Partidas de Baptismos de Adultos, Par-
        bulos, Casamientos y Entierros de los Yndios de la Nacion Carrizo, Catequi-
        zada, por el R. P. Fr. Juan María Nava de la Orden N.S.P.S. Fran^co Como
        Cura MinTro. de esta Villa de Srā Stā Anna de Camargo en el año de 1816.
        Camargo Archives (BTHC, 3E129).
Noticias de los Conventos
  1790−1814 Noticias de los conventos, custodias, y misiones de las provincias de
        Veracruz, San Luis Potosí, Colonia del Nuevo Santander, Nuevo Reino
        de León, San Pedro y San Pablo de Michoacán, y Tampico de la orden de
        San Francisco de los Zacatecas 1790−1814. W. B. Stephen's Collection,
        no. 1394, 243 L., BLAC.
Numana, Patricio
  1817 Estado abreviados de las Misiones de esta Provincias de N.S.P.S. Francisco
        de los Zacatecas. AGN, Misiones 11, 1 L. (BLAC, Microfilm).
Núñez Cabeza de Vaca, Alvar. *See* Cabeza de Vaca, Alvar Núñez.
Ocaranza, Fernando
  1955 Fundación de Nuevas Misiones Franciscanas en el Año de 1803. *Americas*
        11(3):449−472.

Oliva, Joseph Antonio, and Diego Ortíz de Posada
1756Documentos relativos a la restitución de los Indios a la misión de San Juan Capistrano por la de San Franco. Bizzarón. SFGA (BTHC, 2Q251, 11:2–22).

Organización de las Misiones
1946Organización de las Misiones, 1749–1752. Vol. 3. *AHT.*

Orozco y Berra, Manuel
1864*Geografía de las Lenguas y Carta Etnográfica de México.* Mexico City: Imprenta de J. M. Andrade y F. Escalante.

Ortíz Parrilla, Diego
1767Autos y Diligencias Fechas por el Coronel D. Diego Ortíz Parrilla, Sobre las Circunstancias de la Isla de las Malaguitas, que Comunmente Han Llamado Isla Blanca. AGN, Historia 396 (BTHC, 2Q188, 397:1–42).

Oviedo y Valdés, Gonzalo Fernández de
1959*Historia General y Natural de las Indias.* Bibloteca de Autores Españoles. Vol. 4. Madrid: Ediciones Atlas.

Paredes, Conde de
1686Remite una copia de la carta que le escrivio el Gou^{or} del nuevo Reyno de leon en que se refiere noticias que auia dado un Indio de auer gente de Heuropa en la Vahia del Espiritu s^{to} . . . AGI (BTHC, 2Q144, 68:77–82).

Pedrajo, José Manuel
1793Padron de las Almas, q.^{e} tiene la Miccion de Sor. San Jose, en 31 de diciembre de 1793 con exprecion, de nombres, Calidad, Pays, oficio, Y edad, que cada una Persona tiene. NA, vol. 8 (BTHC, 2Q294, 176:116–123, or 127–134).

Pérez-Maldonado, Carlos
1947*Documentos Históricos de Nuevo León.* Monterrey: Impresora del Norte.

Peterson, Roger Tory
1963*A Field Guide to the Birds of Texas and Adjacent States.* Boston: Houghton Mifflin.

Peterson, Roger Tory, and Edward L. Chalif
1973*A Field Guide to Mexican Birds.* Boston: Houghton Mifflin.

Powell, J. W.
1891*Indian Linguistic Families of America North of Mexico.* Annual Report 7. Washington, D.C.: Bureau of American Ethnology.

Prieto, Alejandro
1949*Historia, Geografía y Estadística del Estado de Tamaulipas.* Mexico City: Manuel Porrúa.

Puertollano, Ysidro de
1793[Informe de las 11 misiones que tiene el apostólico Colegio de Pachuca.] AGN, Provincias Internas 5:354–359 (BLAC, Microfilm).

Quintanilla, José Lorenzo
1780[Diligencias sobre las muertes hechas por los Indios Mesquites y Mulatos, y examinación de diez testigos sobre esta materia.] AGN, Provincias Internas 146, 17 L. (BLAC, Microfilm).

Ramón, Diego
1707 Diario de la jornada que executo el Sargento m.^{r} Diego Ramón. . . . AGN, Provincias Internas 28 (BTHC, 2Q203, 466:53−71).

Razón de los Utencilios
1753? Razón de los utencilios que tiene este Pueblo y Miss^{on} de S^n Christóval de los Gualahuizes, Padrón de feligrezez e Yndios de Nueva Convercion [No signature]. SA 55, 4 L. BLAC.

Refugio Registers
MS Libro 2 de Bautismos y Libro 2 de Entierros Hechos en la Misión de Nuestra Sra. del Refugio de la Bahía desde el año 1807. BTHC (Original at parish church, Matamoros).

Revillagigedo, Conde de
1792 Sobre la necesidad de establecer misión entre los parages nombrados Tixera y la Amargosa para la reducción de la nación de Yndios nombrados los Tana-quiapemes. AGN, Provincias Internas 40:28−29 (BLAC, Microfilm).
1966 *Informe sobre las Misiones, 1793, e Instrucción Reservada al Marqués Branciforte, 1794.* Mexico City: Editorial Jus.

Reyes, Candelario
1944 *Apuntes para la Historia de Tamaulipas en los Siglos XVI y XVII.* Mexico City: Talleres Graficos Laguna.

Reynosa Grants
1767 Copy and Translations of Charter Visita Granting: Reynosa, Hidalgo, and Cameron Counties Portions, 1767. Spanish Archives, General Land Office, Austin (a second copy at Texas Catholic Archives, Austin).

Riperdá, Barón de
1772 Sobre la quexa que dió el Barón de Riperdá de que los vecinos de la Colonia del Nuevo Santander quitaban a los Indios sus hijos para venderlos por esclavos. AGN, Historia 84 (BTHC, 2Q184, 374:392−438).

Rivas, Manuel
1688 Diario del Cap.^{n} Mnl Rivas. AGI (BTHC, 2Q144, 69:7−17).

Rivera y Villalón, Pedro
1945 *Diario y Derrotero de lo Caminado, Visto Obcervado en el Discurso de Visita General de Precidios situados en las Provincias Ynternas de Nueva España.* Edited by Guillermo Porras. Mexico City: Libreria Porruá Hermanos.

Rubí, Marqués de
1768 Digttamen, que de orden Exmo. Señor Marqués de Croix, Virrey de este Reyno expone el Mariscal de Campo Marqués de Rubí. AGI, Audencia de Guadalajara, Dunn Transcripts (BTHC, 2Q140, 46:7−62).

Ruecking, Frederick H., Jr.
1953 The Economic System of the Coahuiltecan Indians of Southern Texas and Northeastern Mexico. *Texas Journal of Science* 5(4):480−497.
1954a Bands and Band-clusters of the Coahuiltecan Indians. *Student Papers in Anthropology* 1(2):1−24. Austin: Department of Anthropology, University of Texas.
1954b Ceremonies of the Coahuiltecan Indians of Southern Texas and Northeastern Mexico. *Texas Journal of Science* 6(5):330−339.

1955a The Coahuiltecan Indians of Southern Texas and Northeastern Mexico. M.A. thesis, University of Texas at Austin.

1955b The Social Organization of the Coahuiltecan Indians of Southern Texas and Northeastern Mexico. *Texas Journal of Science* 7(4):357–388.

Sal del Rey, La

MS   La Sal del Rey: Real Salina de la Purificación. Spanish Archives, San Patricio 738, General Land Office, Austin.

Saldívar, Gabriel

1943   *Los Indios de Tamaulipas.* Publicación no. 70. Mexico City: Instituto Panamericano de Geografía e Historia.

San Fernando Registers

MS   Libro de Bautismos no. 4 (1810–1829) y Libro de Entierros (176?–177?) de la Villa de San Fernando de las Presas. En la Parroquia de San Fernando, Tamaulipas.

San José Registers

MS   Libros de Bautismos (1777–1823), Casamientos (1778–1822), y Entierros (1771–1830) Pertenecientes a la Misión de San José y San Miguel de Aguayo. San Fernando Archives, San Antonio (Texas Catholic Archives, Austin, Microfilm).

Santamaria, Francisco J.

1978   *Diccionario de Mejicanismos.* Mexico City: Editorial Porrúa.

Santa María, Vicente

1930   Relación Histórica de la Colonia del Nuevo Santander y Costa del Seno Mexicano. *Publicaciones del Archivo General de la Nación XV* 2:351–481.

Santander Registers

MS   Libro en que se asientan los Parbulos que se Baptisan en esta Villa de los Cinco Señores del Nuevo Santander, 1749–1818. Santander (Genealogical Society of Utah, Microfilm 6403810).

Sapir, Edward

1920   The Hokan and Coahuiltecan Languages. *International Journal of American Linguistics* 1(4):280–290.

1925   The Hokan Affinity of Subtiaba in Nicaragua. *American Anthropologist* 27(3):402–435, 27(4):491–527.

1949   Central and North American Languages. In *Selected Writings of Edward Sapir in Language, Culture, and Personality.* Edited by David G. Mandelbaum. Berkeley and Los Angeles: University of California Press. 169–178.

Serie de Documentos

1783–1800   Serie de Documentos en los que se Describe los Hechos por los Cuales la Nueva Mision de Helguera de Palmitos Fue Fundada para los Indios de San Fernando por el Colegio de Pachuca. AGN, Provincias Internas 229:7–124 (BLAC, Microfilm).

Sevillano de Paredes, Miguel

1727   Visita de las Misiones del Rio Grande del Norte por Fr. Miguel Sevillano de Paredes en 15 de Octubre de 1727. AGN, Historia 29 (BTHC, 2Q178, 348:35–68).

Sierra Gorda, Conde de

1773   El Conde de Sierra Gorda expone su dictamen aserca de la Nueva Mision de que consultan el Gov^{or} de Nuevo R.° de León y el Comisionado de aquellas misiones, se ponga en el Paraje, nombrado el Valle Viejo en virtud de las Sup^{or} de orden de V.E. AGN, Provincias Internas 143, 15 L. (BLAC, Microfilm).

1780a Consulta del Governador de la Colonia sobre las ventajas que ha logrado con los Yndios Barbaros. AGN, Provincias Internas 147, 12 L. (BLAC, Microfilm).

1780b Correspondencia del Conde de Sierra Gorda al Exmo Señor Virrey Dn Martin Mayorga. AGN, Provincias Internas 123:361–363 (BLAC, Microfilm).

1790a [Correspondencia del Conde de Sierra Gorda en su marcha para Laredo.] AGN, Provincias Internas 159 (BTHC, 2Q210, 508:81).

1790b [Correspondencia del Conde de Sierra Gorda en Laredo.] AGN, Provincias Internas 159 (BTHC, 2Q210, 508:83–84).

1791 Sobre los Bárbaros, Información que Mandó el Capitán de la Villa de Camargo José Antonio de Garza Falcón. AGN, Provincias Internas 55:292–294 (BLAC, Microfilm).

1794 [Dos cartas sobre los méritos hechos por el Conde de Sierra Gorda.] AGN, Provincias Internas 122:353–359 (BLAC, Microfilm).

1798 El Gobernador del Nuevo Santander da el Estado de Naciones de Yndios informando sus Circunstancias. AGN, Misiones 16, 5 L. (BLAC, Microfilm).

Swanton, John R.
1915 Linguistic Position of the Tribes of Southern Texas and Northeastern Mexico. *American Anthropologist* 17(1):17–40.

1940 Linguistic Material from the Tribes of Southern Texas and Northeastern Mexico. Bulletin 127. *SIBAE*.

Tato y López, Julián Antonio
1797 Correspondencia dirigida al Gobernador Político y Militar de esta Provincia del Nuevo Reyno de León. AGN, Provincias Internas 193:428–430 (BLAC, Microfilm).

Thomas, Cyrus, and John R. Swanton
1911 Indian Languages of Mexico and Central America and Their Geographical Distribution. Bulletin 44. *SIBAE*.

Tienda de Cuervo, José
1929 Inspección de la Provincia Efectuada por el Capitán de Dragones Don José Tienda de Cuervo. In *Estado General de las Fundaciones Hechas por D. José de Escandón, en la Colonia del Nuevo Santander Costa del Seno Mexicano*. Vol. 1. Publicación 14. Mexico City: Archivo General de la Nación. See also AGI (2Q148, 89:83–85).

1930 Informe del Reconocimiento e Inspección de la Nueva Colonia del Seno Mexicano. In *Estado General de las Fundaciones Hechas por D. José de Escandón, en la Colonia del Nuevo Santander Costa del Seno Mexicano*. Vol. 2. Publicación 15. Mexico City: Archivo General de la Nación.

Translación de Reinosa
1956 Translación de la Villa de Reinosa a la Loma de San Antonio, 1802. *Boletín del Archivo General de la Nación* 27(3):427–494.

Troike, Rudolph C.
1959 A Descriptive Phonology and Morphology of Coahuilteco. Ph.D. diss., University of Texas at Austin.
1961 Researches in Coahuiltecan Ethnography. *Bulletin of the Texas Archeological Society* 30 (for 1959): 301–309.
1962 Notes on Coahuiltecan Ethnography. *Bulletin of the Texas Archeological Society* 32 (for 1961): 57–63.

Trowbridge, A. C.
1923 A Geologic Reconnaissance in the Gulf Coastal Plain of Texas, Near the Rio Grande. In *Shorter Contributions to General Geology, 1922.* Edited by David White. Professional Papers 131. Washington, D.C.: United States Geological Survey: 85–107.

Tunnell, Curtis D., and W. W. Newcomb, Jr.
1969 A Lipan Apache Mission: San Lorenzo de la Cruz, 1762–1771. *Texas Memorial Museum, Bulletin 14.*

Uhde, Adolph
1861 *Die Länder am untern Rio Bravo del Norte.* Heidelberg: J. C. B. Mohr.

Valcarcel, Domingo
1754 Autos en los que da quenta a V. Ex.ª con testimonio el Coronel Don Jph de Escandon del estado de las veinte nuevas Poblaciones de la colonia del Seno Mexicano. AGN, Provincias Internas 172 (BTHC, 2Q211, 513:330–348).
1756 [Testimonio del estado de la Colonia.] AGN, Provincias Internas 172 (BTHC, 2Q211, 513:27–124).

Valero Registers
MS Libros de Bautismos (1703–1782), Casamientos (1703–1783), y Entierros (1709–1825) Pertenecientes a la Misión de San Antonio de Valero. San Fernando Archives, San Antonio (Texas Catholic Archives, Austin, Microfilm).

Valverde, Acisclos, and Luis Antonio Menchaca
1767 Memorial Del R. P. Presid.ᵗᵉ al cap.ⁿ del Presidio de S.ⁿ Antonio para q.ᵉ se haga la diligencia juridica q.ᵉ va inserta a fin de averiguar a q.ᵉ mission pertenecen vnos indios q.ᵉ los minros de la Mission de Nᵒ S. P. S. Fran.ᶜᵒ de la Espada recogieron: Año de 1767. AGN (BTHC, 2Q188, 397:277–280).

Vedoia, Licenciado
1749 Sobre la Antecedente Consulta de Escandon y sus Propuestas P.ª la Pacificaz.ᵒⁿ y Poblaz.ᵒⁿ de dha Costa del Seno Mexicano a q.ᵉ en todo se difiere. AGI (BTHC, 2Q148, 89:147–188).

Velasco, Carlos
1715–1753 [Documentos que mandó sacar el gobernador de Nuevo León, Carlos de Velasco a pedimento de los Indios.] AGN, Provincias Internas 173 (BTHC, 2Q211, 514:285–338).

Vergara, Gabriel de
1965 El Cuadernillo de la Lengua de los Indios Pajalates [1732] por Fray Gabriel del Vergara y el Confesionario de Indios en Lengua Coahuilteca. Edición de Eugenio del Hoyo. Perfil Biográfico de Fray Gabriel de Vergara por Lino Gómez Canedo. Serie: Historia 3. *PITESM.*

Vidal de Lorca, Melchor

1774a Testimonio de la Solicitud de los Yndios Pintos de la Mision de Cabezon de la Sal de que se Transladen al Arroyo de Mojarras. AGN, Provincias Internas 108:228 (BLAC, Microfilm).

1774b Sobre el Testimonio que trata de la solicitud de los Yndios Pintos de Cabezon de la Sal que intentan transladarse al arroyo de las Mojarras. AGN, Provincias Internas 108:233–234 (BLAC, Microfilm).

1775a [Sobre la reducción de Indios vagos de Nuevo León a sus domicilios.] AGN, Provincias Internas 108:248–251 (BLAC, Microfilm).

1775b Relación de los Yndios Vagos que andavan en la Provincia del Nuevo Reyno de León, que se han recoxido por su Governador en la Visita. AGN, Provincias Internas 108:252 (BLAC, Microfilm).

1778 Relación de la Visita, que executo en la Provincia del Nuevo Reino de León su Governador el Coronel de Ynfantería de los R.ˢ Exerc.ˢ Don Melchor Vidal de Lorca, y Villena. AGN, Provincias Internas 117, 19 L. (BLAC, Microfilm).

1788 Plano o Extracto General que Demuestra el Estado de las Misiones de Yndios, assi Cristianos como Gentiles; Con exprecion de sus Naciones, y Formalidades de Ellas. AGN, Provincias Internas 50:33 (BLAC, Microfilm).

Villarreal A., Carlos

1969 *Monografía Geográfica e Histórica de Cadereyta Jiménez, Nuevo León.* Monterrey: Gráfica Popular.

Villaseñor E., Roberto

1967 El Coronel Dⁿ José Escandón y la Conquista del Nuevo Santander. *Boletín del Archivo General de la Nación* 8 (3–4):1159–1210.

Webb, Walter Prescott, editor-in-chief

1952 *The Handbook of Texas.* 2 vols. Austin: Texas State Historical Association.

Weddle, Robert S.

1973 *Wilderness Manhunt: The Spanish Search for La Salle.* Austin: University of Texas Press.

Weitlaner, Roberto J.

1948 Un Idioma Desconocido del Norte de México. *Congrés International des Américanistes, Actes* 28:205–227.

West, Robert C.

1964 Surface Configuration and Associated Geology of Middle America. In *Natural Environment and Early Cultures. Handbook of Middle American Indians.* Edited by Robert Wauchope. Austin: University of Texas Press. 1:33–83.

Wheat, Carl I.

1957 The Spanish Entrada to the Louisiana Purchase, 1540–1804. In *Mapping the Transmississippi West, 1540–1861.* Vol. 1. San Francisco: Institute of Historical Cartography.

Wilcox, Seb. S.

1946 The Spanish Archives of Laredo. *SHQ* 49(3):341–360.

Winfrey, Dorman H., and James M. Day

1966 *The Indian Papers of Texas and the Southwest, 1825–1916.* Vols. 1–3. Austin: Pemberton Press.

Ximénes, Diego
  1762   Relación del Estado de las Misiones de la Precidencia del Rio Grande del Norte, pertenecientes al Colegio de la Santa Cruz de Queretaro. AGN, Historia 29 (BTHC, 2Q178, 348:108–115, or 349:104–111).
Yerro, Fray Simon del
  1749   Diario que hizo el P.ᵉ Fray Simon del Yerro en el Seno Mexicano año de 1749. AGN, Historia 29 (BTHC, 2Q178, 29:270–302).
Zorrilla, Juan Fidel
  1949   *El Poder Colonial en Nuevo Santander*. Biblioteca Mexicana 52. Mexico City: Manuel Porrúa.

Index